Pluck

-Z

ALSO BY DONNA MORRISSEY

PLUCK

A Memoir of a Newfoundland Childhood
and the Raucous, Terrible, Amazing
Journey to Becoming a Novelist

DONNA MORRISSEY

VIKING

VIKING

an imprint of Penguin Canada, a division of Penguin Random House Canada Limited

Canada • USA • UK • Ireland • Australia • New Zealand • India • South Africa • China

First published 2021

www.penguinrandomhouse.ca

LIBRARY AND ARCHIVES CANADA CATALOGUING IN PUBLICATION

Title: Pluck : a memoir of a Newfoundland childhood and the raucous, terrible, amazing journey to becoming a novelist / Donna Morrissey.
Other titles: Memoir of a Newfoundland childhood and the raucous, terrible, amazing journey to becoming a novelist
Names: Morrissey, Donna, 1956- author.
Identifiers: Canadiana (print) 20210092270 | Canadiana (ebook) 20210092580 | ISBN 9780735239197 (softcover) | ISBN 9780735239203 (EPUB)
Subjects: LCSH: Morrissey, Donna, 1956- | CSH: Novelists, Canadian (English)—Biography. | LCSH: Anxiety disorders—Patients—Canada—Biography. | LCSH: Brothers—Death—Psychological aspects. | LCGFT: Autobiographies.
Classification: LCC PS8576.O74164 Z46 2021 | DDC C813/.54—dc23

All photos courtesy of the author.

Book design by Lisa Jager
Cover design by Lisa Jager
Cover images: (house) © Luke Stackpoole / UnSplash; (hook) valdis torms / Shutterstock

Printed in Canada

10 9 8 7 6 5 4 3 2 1

Penguin
Random House
VIKING CANADA

For Rick,
Now you know . . .

Some of you say, "Joy is greater than sorrow," and others say,
"Nay, sorrow is the greater."
But I say unto you, they are inseparable.
Together they come, and when one sits alone with you at your board,
remember that the other is asleep upon your bed.

KAHLIL GIBRAN, THE PROPHET

PLUCK

METAMORPHOSIS

PROLOGUE

IF YOU WERE A BIRD FLYING over the most easterly fringe of
Canada you'd see a great island broiling out of the Atlantic, its
granite shores rollicking with fishing boats and flakes and fishermen. A sweep of coloured houses face the wind, smoke whirling
from their chimneys, youngsters scrabbling after sheep and hens
and grandmothers scrabbling after youngsters, hiding now within
swaths of sheets billowing around them from the clotheslines.

Swoop inland and you'd see the quilted greens and browns
of its forests, sequined with ponds and rioting rivers and water-
falls. Should you glide up the forty-mile inlet of White Bay on
the northwest side of the island, with its steep wooded hills
shouldering the sky, you might hover over a strip of beach with
two tiny outports at either end. They're a five-minute walk apart
and about ten houses each, separated by a point of land jutting
into the sea. Upper Beaches and Lower Beaches. That's where I
was born on January 13, 1956. Upper Beaches. Or, to those on the
Lower Beaches, *up on the point*. Likewise, we referred to them as
down below.

Not much came to us before the late sixties. Televisions, telephones, cars, roads, none of that. Most visitors were fogbound

fishers, the odd aunt or uncle, the occasional young man or woman coming ashore to go courting. Yet lots came to us in different ways: songs, dances, jannying. Yarns spun on the spot and growing with each teller of the tale. No doubt things have opened up since I was a girl. Still, such an environment, culture, and circumstance spawned a uniqueness of character that resides in most of us who grew up there. I never tire of talking about it.

It was during an adult education course, after I'd graduated university in my thirty-eighth year, that I started writing. I'd met an older woman named Elly who enraptured my mind with stories of skeleton women trapped in bad marriages who ended up walking the floors of frozen oceans, trying to get out; stories of how we see ourselves not as swans but as ugly ducklings, of how we eat the poison apple of sleep rather than invite spiritual awakening. It was in the midst of one of those tales when she turned to me and said, "You're dragging your own bag of bones, dear. Go find your voice and write your own myth."

I bought an alarm clock. Every morning I got up at six, and before going to work I'd sit with the homeless in a downtown café, writing, writing, writing. I wrote about the pigeons hobbling around on the icy sidewalk beneath my window, the sun rising over the southern hillside, the peonies in my grandmother's garden, the irks and ills of my siblings, of my mother, my father, my grandparents, until my pen took on a life of its own and my father became a boy called Luke, my mother a girl called Claire, my brother Glenn a cat called Pirate. I myself would carry many names.

I write words spoken by my mother. I write words spoken by aunts and uncles. I write about what I've seen, heard, and, well, made up. Thus far it has fed into six novels situated in Newfoundland culture, some of those novels undergoing up to seven translations. When I asked my Japanese editor why her publisher had been attracted to *Kit's Law*, the story of a girl growing up in a rural Newfoundland outport, she answered, "It is a story of faith, the elderly, and family love. It is what our Japanese culture was built upon, and we struggle now to keep it."

It matters not our differences, then, because we all eat from the one basket of life with its fruits of joy, kindness, goodness, and patience. We all speak the universal language of love, laughter, fear, and grief evoked by this tremendous and terrible journey through life. And of the fruits in the basket it's joy I covet the most, as it allows me to see the beauty in a frost-etched window and hear the singing of broken glass being swept by my mother's broom. And joy is fed by love. It's fed by gratification and blessedness and it is the seventh heaven. It was the memory of joy that kept me going during my trials of physical and spiritual impoverishment. It was the memory of joy that sustained me through the dark hole I fell into during my forties, joy that held me throughout the hellish battle for sanity in a world suddenly turned on its head. And yet it was during those moments when joy was blanketed by fear, grief, contempt, guilt, shame, and so many other ills that I was kicked, bruised and hurting, into consciousness—which is, I believe, where God lives.

For our truly conscious moments happen when something—big or small—awakens us to a deeper way of seeing things, dredging us up from innocence into awareness. Looking back, I see those moments (some of them lasting for days, months, perhaps years) as lampposts pinpointing my journey through the dark corridors of my past. This memoir follows a trajectory through some of the more significant of these, leading up to the death of my mother and the publication of my first novel, one that her courage helped me create during her final days. For each moment recounted here there are thousands more not written. And whenever my personal story becomes lost in my mother's story, it is because she carried me in hers.

IMAGINATION

FEAR

IT CAME WITHOUT BEING BECKONED. It came within a flash. It touched cold against my skin, and before I could grasp what it was it seeded itself inside the moist dark marrow of my bones.

I was eight. It was warm and sunny, the ocean lapping along the shore. I was heading for home, proud of the six-foot slab I'd just pulled from the sea for firewood. It was smelly and water-sogged heavy. When I reached the first house, Aunt Rose's place, she was leaning on her fence, staring down the road. Something was wrong. My aunts were hovering on the road in front of my house. The aunts never hovered in a huddle on the road. They were always inside, doing things. They came out only when a youngster cried too hard or they needed a bit of kindling from the porch to flame a fire. They'd scoot to another's house for a cup of tea or to borrow a bit of pork fat or butter. They'd team up with buckets and rags and clean the school or Aunt Rene's or Grandmother's house if those women were feeling too poorly to do it themselves. They never huddled and hovered in a group on the road.

Aunt Rose lifted the latch of her gate and stepped outside. She hadn't been outside her gate in sixty years. She caught sight of me and her wrinkly mouth trembled. "Your little brother is dead, my love, your little brother is dead. Sin, sin, just startin' to walk and now he's dead."

I didn't know what *dead* was. I'd seen a chicken in Grandmother's henhouse once that was stiff and dirty and cold to the touch, and Grandmother had said it was dead. But Baby Paul wasn't a chicken. And he was in hospital because he had a cough. I didn't know what *hospital* was, either.

My father bounded out of our house and jumped into his truck, firing up the engine. I dropped the slab. My mother came running too, her sweater half on, Aunt Beat holding the truck door open for her. My mother was barely inside before it jolted forward. I held out my arms, running. The brakes squealed as Dad rolled down his window, his voice catching on a wet cough as he yelled, "Go home, go on home now."

They roared off in a flurry of dust from the dry gravel road, the aunts wringing their hands and staring after them. Aunt Marg whimpered, "My, oh my, she got to go through this agin, now."

I looked at Aunt Marg. I didn't understand her words but I felt something bad in them. My sister Wanda was beside me now, and her hand found mine. Our brother Ford was struggling in Aunt Beat's arms, flailing his little fists after the truck, crying *Baby Ball, Baby Ball*. It always made everyone laugh when he said *Baby Ball* for Baby Paul. No one was laughing in that moment.

Aunt Beat ushered us inside our house and made us molassey bread and put us to bed when it got dark. Mom and Dad still weren't home. Come morning the aunts were drifting and whispering through the house like a searching wind. Grandmother gave me and Wanda and Ford big warm hugs and helped us dress and fed us hot oatmeal sweetened with dates and bade us to be quiet. The aunts had told us Paul was dead but not what dead was and when Wanda asked they said, "The angels took him, my love, the angels took him away, he's an angel too now."

Their voices were sad. It didn't fit with the pretty smiling angels in our mother's Bible.

Mother came downstairs. She was wearing a black dress. She sat quietly in her rocking chair and this time she didn't mind that Wanda and I stood on the rockers on either side of her. Her sadness was deeper than the aunts' and I knew not to ask her what dead was. I only knew it was wrong.

There was a soft knock on the back door. Mother took hold of our hands. She held them tight as the door opened and one of our uncles entered. He was carrying an oblong white box at his side and it had a thick white strap that was looped around his shoulder. My mother dropped my and Wanda's hands and raised hers to her face and started crying.

Our uncle walked past us; the aunts stood back with bowed heads. The only sounds were their sniffles. My mother rose. Wanda and I stepped off the rockers and held hands. Mother followed our uncle into the living room where no one ever went and whose door was always closed. It was always cool in there, even in the summertime. It was much cooler this morning with the curtains drawn. I was surprised to see Father lying on the sofa that was never used. His face was burrowed into the cushions and I thought he was sleeping. It felt wrong; he never slept in this room. His shoulders were heaving and he was making little whimpers as though he were fretting inside his dreams.

Our uncle laid the white box atop a table and slowly removed its cover. There was a smell I didn't know, but I thought of soap. I stretched up on my toes to see inside. Baby Paul lay there. His face was still, so very, very still. So still it struck away all memory of him ever having puckered and laughed. His little lips looked blue and frozen. My mother sobbed harder. She touched her hand to his forehead and held it there. Aunt Claire's face broke into crinkles as she started to sob and I thought she was mocking my mother, so I kicked her leg. She bent down and smothered her face against my shoulder, then led Wanda and me to the door.

I didn't want to go. I kept looking behind me, seeing my father still lying on the sofa with his back to everyone, his face deeply buried in the cushions. Aunt Claire took us to her house and fed us canned peaches in little orange glass bowls. Bedtime, she took us back home and the other aunts were still there and Mother sat in her rocker, her face in her hands, and Father was gone.

The aunts washed us, dressed us in our pyjamas, and walked us quickly through the living room where Baby Paul still lay in the white box. The smell of soap was strong. They hurried us upstairs and put us to bed. Mother came and kissed us and tucked us in. I was afraid to put my arms around her neck, as I always did, and squeeze her tight. Everything was wrong.

I woke up before Wanda. I listened for the kitchen sounds that greeted every morning like birdsong. I heard silence. It spoke a language I didn't know. I got out of bed and peeked into Mother's room, but neither she nor Father was there. I crept down the stairs and into the living room. The white box was on the table, the cover was off. Baby Paul was still and silent as stone. The little bump of his nose was the only curve on his tiny white face. I crept closer. The smell of soap from yesterday became stronger. I lifted my hand as my mother had done. I touched it to his forehead and leapt back with a cry of fright. His skin was cold, as cold as sea ice. I knew then what death was. It was that stillness inside Baby Paul. And it was cold. Death killed Baby Paul. Just like it done Grandmother's chicken.

Perhaps, if not for that sudden realization that Baby Paul would never leave this box and crawl about the floor again, or gurgle spit down his chin and flail his arms and wet his diapers, and perhaps if the door hadn't opened at that moment and my grandmother hadn't come swooping through, taking my hand and leading me to the kitchen for a little rocking and some bread and tea, perhaps I might've felt it when that sliver of fear entered me. Perhaps I would have spoken of it to my mother. As it was, I quickly lost myself inside Grandmother's chatter and that of my aunts milling about, making oatmeal for everybody and frying bacon. And those times throughout the day when I was alone and thought back to that flash of knowing with Baby Paul, and that touch of fright that had accompanied it, I stole away from it, tucked it away like a horrid secret, as though I were the only one who knew that death killed Baby Paul.

BROKEN MOMENTS

MY FATHER FOUND HIS OWN WAY around Baby Paul's death. It extended a path he'd already forged from the death of two previous babies who had lived but a few short hours. My father had deepened early into being a man, but until the passing of that first infant he'd never been touched by death.

He was born and raised on this strip of beach with four siblings; they grew up tough and barefoot in the summers. They'd have toast and tea for breakfast, but around lunchtime, Father told me, he'd traipse over to his better-off cousin's house and hang around the yard, hoping to be called in for a bite of bread. He never was. He'd often chase down a goat belonging to an elder up the shore, pumping milk from its teats into his mouth—for laughs, he'd say if he got caught. But he knew his hunger. Suppers they ate well: fish and spuds or rabbit and spuds or moose and spuds or seal and spuds. Sometimes, just spuds. He never went to bed hungry. School was a one-room structure that housed all grades from one to six. Nobody bothered past grade six. He quit, too, leaving behind the one mystery that intrigued him but that no one could explain, not even his teacher—his name. Enerchius.

"Where? Where did you get that name, Mudder?" he grew up

demanding, for he was never able to spell it the same way twice. "From the Bible," she kept telling him. He'd skimmed through it several times, trying to find his name. Besides, his mother could hardly read. *A mountain*, he came up with one day. *She copied it letter for letter from a map or some friggin' thing.* "She called me after a mountain in Egypt. And you too," he said to his brother Elikum. "Bet you a gawd-damn she called you after the northeast face or something."

He was called Nerky as a baby, his brother Likey. Then, as they grew older, Nerk and Like. His other three siblings were more commonly named: Les, Gord, and Beat (Beatrice).

He took up smoking when he was nine, doctor's orders, to cure the wheezing in his lungs. He left school when he was twelve, crawling out his bedroom window on the sly one morning; taking his axe, he followed his father five miles up through the woods and into deep country. By the time his father caught sight of him, they were too far from home for him to go back alone. He became a logger that day. Except for that one summer when he fished for six weeks to pay off his suit, on hold at the merchant's, for his upcoming confirmation at the Anglican church on the Rooms, two miles up the shore. The price of the suit was thirty-two quintals of dried fish. All summer he rowed off from shore in his father's punt, twice a day, mornings and evenings, jigging cod. By evening's end, after he'd pulled his last cod aboard for that day and bled it, his arms were leaden with fatigue. He'd then row ashore, his shoulders groaning and a grin on his face. He loved it, he said, fishing and logging. Times, he said, when he'd stand up in the boat as it was coasting towards shore, its belly full of fish, then drop to one knee and salute in gratitude the few houses and the wooded hills making up the Beaches. God's supper, he'd say of the fish. God's blood, he'd say of the water buoying his boat to shore.

All this my father told me one hot sunny day when we were stuck in traffic in Halifax. When I got home I copied his words straight into a story I'd just started writing about a fisherman called Sylvanus Now, inspired by my father and the broken hearts of the fishermen during the loss of the Newfoundland fishery. Many times throughout the writing of this memoir I've searched through my works of fiction for the truth I borrowed from an extreme moment of sorrow or joy in actual life, like my father's pride when rowing ashore with a boatload of fish. Naturally I rewrote those scenes with different words, but I've often caught myself slipping back into the words I'd already written, as though they're so emotionally engraved on my heart that there can be no other way of conveying the stories they tell.

>—▷

My father would wear his suit again and with greater pride, he told me, the day he married my mother. He never told me about Baby Paul. He never told me about poor little Milton, his first-born, who lived for four hours. Or poor little Elsie, born a year after Milton and living for just two hours, her tiny body too crippled to cope outside our mother's. He never told me about how he ran from his babies and his grief. And from my mother and her grief. It was my mother who told me those things.

Her name was Claudine Adele Ford. She came from Jackson's Arm, another isolated outport thirty miles out the bay from the Beaches: a four-hour ride by motorboat, five hours by dogsled when the bay froze over. Her father was quiet, spending long hours in the evenings staring out the window. When he was sixteen he'd lied about his age and left the calm of his vegetable garden and logging trails and sailed to England. From there he was sent into the blood-soaked trenches of World War I. There'd been nothing to prepare him for the hell into which he descended. Those times, then, after his return, when he'd sit before a darkened window, his gaunt eyes staring back at him as the flankers from his pipe burned an arc onto the floor around his chair, my mother and her siblings would often be hushed by their own mother. *He thinks about the war*, she would whisper.

My mother was dark-haired and dark-eyed. She was wiry and readying for work as a missionary before she was ten. She made orphan dolls out of sticks and scant bits of cloth, and once she even cut a fat ringlet off her cousin's hair to glue onto one of them. It was her mother's idea that she become a missionary. Her mother used to work in the post office and knew much of the larger world; she'd often talk to her about people going hungry elsewhere, about how lucky they were to have so much. Each summer the whole outport would gather to box up wild meat they'd canned themselves, jars of preserves, cloth and knitted goods. Then, my mother's favourite part, they'd form a circle and hold hands and say a prayer to bless the food before sending it through the post to the needy. It made her feel good, she said, to know she was helping others. That's when her mother connected her through letters with a cousin on her father's side who'd moved to the United States years before and had become a missionary.

My mother studied hard and made top grades in school. She'd sneak into the church on weekdays when nobody was about and sit up front in a pew, swinging her legs and crossing herself before the sweet Jesus hanging on a cross above the altar, asking him to make her a missionary like her cousin. She was seventeen and had just graduated from grade eleven—the highest senior grade in Newfoundland—when she excitedly said yes to a job teaching at the Beaches. She was, she believed, one step closer to fulfilling her dream.

Instead she met Nerk. Blond and blue-eyed and more handsome than was fair. He was wearing his suit that Sunday he came to invite her for a walk. It fit tightly across his shoulders and was a bit short in the sleeves, and peeking beneath his sharply creased pants were the toes of his rubber boots. He was shy. Too shy for dating and romance stuff, so he proposed six weeks after they met to get around "all that," he said to her. When the bay froze over that January he harnessed his own dog, borrowed one from his brother and two from his uncle, and bundled my mother onto a dogsled to make the five-hour trek over ice to her home in Jackson's Arm. He was going to ask her father for her hand in marriage. Once there he clung to the gatepost, too shy to follow her inside the house. She called him foolish. His ears burned. It started to snow. She called out to her father and together they plied his fingers from around the gatepost and prodded him inside the house, his neck and ears had the rosy glow of a hand-cupped flame.

They were married on a cold rainy day in September. The easterly winds gusted at her veil as her dreams of being a missionary scattered like confetti around her feet. She became pregnant, then afraid. She was into her ninth month before asking her sister-in-law Aunt Beat, a mother of two, "How do babies come out?"

"You silly thing, where'd you think they comes out?"

"My belly button, I think."

"Nay, maid, you silly thing. From down there."

Down there? She had no notion, but knew enough to steer the talk towards something else. "Perhaps I should go to the hospital," she said.

"Up to you, maid. Everybody goes to Aunt Suze's up Hampden. What's you afraid?"

"I was just thinking."

"Go to the hospital if you like."

She shook her head. It was too far, too costly. And she'd never been in a hospital. She took her chances and lost, and grieved deeply.

She took her chances again with poor little Elsie the following year and lost again and her grief grew deeper. Her third pregnancy and her fear of losing another was great. She would take no more chances. She planned a trip to the hospital by train. She packed her bag during the last week of her eighth month—so's to be ready, she said. And jinxed herself, she later believed. For she went into labour two weeks early. A hellish wind was stirring up the sea and whipping at her face with slob snow as Father helped her into the open boat to motor the three miles up the bay to Hampden where the midwife was. It was Friday the thirteenth and my grandmother was not without her superstitions; the aunts, too, joined in with her fretting.

"Nay, nay, maid, it's too dirty on the water," Aunt Beat pleaded as my mother bundled herself inside the boat. "Stay home, stay home, we'll see your baby born."

"No, no, I've lost two, I'll not risk another one," she cried. "Go on, Nerk. Get us going."

He hunched over the four-horsepower motor in his thirty-foot boat, hove on the flywheel, and *put-put-putted* them through the growing swells. He stood with his back to the wind, water soaking his face as he stared grimly ahead. His brother Les sat at the stern with the steering rod. My mother stifled her cries with blankets as her contractions grew harder, but my father heard her. He saw the pain twisting her face. And he looked to the heavens, calling on this awful God as would make a birthing woman suffer so. The winds grew stronger, whitecaps fringing the breaking waves. Her whimpers grew louder, her body writhing beneath the blankets. He almost plunged himself overboard as they neared the slowly approaching shoreline. Her mouth was a thin white line, her eyes stark with fright. A few youngsters were hanging around the shore, curious as to who'd be on the water in weather like this. "Get the midwife!" he roared, flailing his arms at them. "Go get the gawd-damn midwife!"

He cut the motor a minute before she ran aground and he was over the side, up to his knees in the frigid waters. Within minutes half a dozen men were running down the beach. They helped haul the boat ashore and he lifted her over the side and his brother helped carry her, still bundled in the blankets. They made it to Effie Osmond's, the first house off the beach, and the midwife was quickly at the door and I was born screaming with life.

"There now," said Effie, whose second name I bear. "Friday the thirteenth, and what's that they says now about it being unlucky?"

A few days later her house burned down. Grandmother wagged her finger but Mother was heartened; my sister Wanda and brothers Ford and Paul would be birthed by the same midwife.

And perhaps Mother might've forgiven herself for the loss of her first two babies if Paul hadn't caught a fever when he was nine months old. When it lasted for over two days, she became frightened and took him on the two-hour train ride to the hospital. He contracted diphtheria there, which killed him. Grief weakened her, distorted her thinking with avenging thoughts: *This is my punishment for failing my first two babies.*

She wanted to share that thought with my father, but it was his way to run from those things he couldn't keep from hurting her. And it became hers to brood in silence, to blame herself for the death of her three babies. Three more healthy pregnancies followed poor little Paul: Glenn and Tommy, both born in a hospital, and the youngest, Karen, birthed by a midwife. And then we were six: three boys and three girls. My mother buried her fears as our footsteps sounded loudly across her floors. But she could never bury the silence of those absent ones.

Those were the things my mother told me as she lay on her hospital bed the morning after her first mastectomy during her fifty-ninth year. She'd had a dream, she half whispered, her mouth crushed against her pillow, of standing on a seashore and seeing her three babies beneath the waves, staring up at her. Blaming her. When she'd opened her eyes onto the barren hospital walls she was flooded with a grief that was always there, she whispered, and when she'd looked down at her shorn breast she was besieged by the thought, *This is my punishment.*

She told me more, much more about those times. But it is from my own bag of bones that I construct the bulk of her story, and mine. As with my mother, I too fell into the darkness of illogical thought. Tragedy has a way of tripping us up. It sharpens our senses, rendering us more vulnerable in times of illness and unease. It casts shadows and cripples our minds in ways unbeknownst even to ourselves. Till one day, as with my mother on her pillow that morning, the moment comes when our crippled truths bare themselves.

>—▷

A pall fell over our household during the days that followed our baby brother's burying. Mother's sister, our prettiest Aunt Shirley with her curly blond hair and doll-blue eyes and wafting scent of flowers, came up from Jackson's Arm and spent long days with her. I snuck behind them as Mother led her upstairs to her bedroom and pulled out the bottom drawer of her dresser where Baby Paul's clothes were still folded. When Mother hurried downstairs, Aunt Shirley knelt before the drawer. She picked up one of Baby Paul's garments, shook it out, brought it to her mouth, and kissed it. Then she refolded it into a box she'd carried upstairs with her. She did that with each little piece of clothing till the drawer was empty and the box filled.

When Aunt Shirley left to go back to Jackson's Arm, taking the box with her, the house felt emptier. Ford toddled about, hollering for *Baby Ball, Baby Ball*. Our father, who always took us to church on Sundays while Mother cooked dinner, stayed home instead. It made Mother sadder, and she argued with him.

Her knees started swelling with arthritis, hurting so bad that our father had to carry her up the stairs at bedtime. He began taking us to church again just to make her feel better. But he wouldn't go inside with us anymore. He'd sit in the truck and wait. Then, when the service was over and we were driving home, he'd warn us to *never* tell Mother. We never did. She served up our hot dinner of spuds and cabbage and all the other vegetables steaming in the pot, always wearing her Sunday dress, asking us questions as we ate about what the minister had preached. When Dad said nothing Wanda and I would fill in the silence with newsy bits about Florry Brett singing the hymns to the high heavens and no one able to match her draggy, off-key nasal twang. And Sally Gale wore nothing more than a green feathery feather on her head for a hat, and Uncle Charley Osmond clocked two more boys in the head with his hymnbook for giggling and whispering.

Mother would tut and click her tongue over our stories, piling more potatoes onto our plates as we tried to finish everything because it pleased her to watch us eat. She took longer with washing us at bedtime and teaching us our prayers and was always rocking Ford and singing to him. She fussed over Father and fussed over us, making sure we took our cold medicine. And once, when she fussed too long over mending one of Father's mitts as he stood waiting for it, sweating beneath his heavy clothes, he snapped at her with impatience: "Lovie, lovie, what's taking so long, I got to go." And she snapped right back: "What difference do a minute make when I might never see you agin?"

"Will we see Baby Paul agin?" Wanda asked after Father left.

"He's with the angels," said Mother.

"How do you know?"

"Because God made us. And when we die, we go back to Heaven where God made us."

"How come we can't see God?"

"God lives in Heaven too."

But Wanda persisted. "If we put every house on the Beaches on top of each other, and all the stages on top of the houses, can we reach Heaven?"

I huffed with impatience. "God, m'dear, nobody can reach Heaven."

"Paul did."

"You got to be dead first."

"That's why we says our prayers," said Mother, cutting short the argument. "So we all goes to Heaven someday."

I went outside then, where there was nary a cloud in the wide sunny sky. I climbed the hill, lay on my back on the rock overlooking the houses, and stared hard up into the blue. It looked so soft, so near. It felt as if my hand would go right through if I touched it. A sudden feeling of affection for God washed over me. *Please give me a sign that you're up there*, I prayed ardently. *Show me your hand, that's all, God—just reach down your hand and show it to me, I won't tell, I promise I won't tell, I prooomiiise!*

God doesn't bargain. No matter how hard I prayed and stared at that sky, I saw nothing but blue. Looking back, I wonder now if that was how Michelangelo first imagined the finger of God before he extended it towards Adam's.

When a miracle did happen later that week, I had forgotten about the hand of God.

We were finishing our supper when Ford dozed off in his high chair. Just like that, his head drooped onto his shoulder, a crust of bread like a brown moustache across his face. Mother cried out, "Well, the blessed Lord!" and Wanda and I spurted out laughing and Dad laughed and Fordie blinked himself awake, the crust falling from his mouth. And Mother laughed. For the first time since Baby Paul was taken, we all laughed.

»——▷

The wintry winds were especially fierce for those of us living at the bottom of White Bay. The easterlies barrelled straight down the forty-mile inlet and blasted our little beach with ice and snow; as the old fellows would say, it was so damn cold it froze the ocean a mile deep. Our fathers and uncles, during those days before oil stoves, drove their horses and sleds across the ice and brought back firewood from the other side of the bay, and our mothers axed ice from the wells, and we young ones shovelled out the doorplaces and chicken coops and outhouses while the elders knitted extra socks and mitts for the men working in the woods. Some springs were equally fierce with the ocean busting through the ice and crashing and roaring up over the beach, swallowing the road and licking its chops at our doors and dampening the bared butts of those hunkering over the hole in their outhouses built over the beach. Sometimes it felt like God's mercy alone that kept the sheds, stages, and outhouses clinging to their foundations.

One wickedly wild night in March, perhaps a year now after Baby Paul's death, I woke up to Father lugging Wanda and me downstairs along with all our bedding. Mother came behind, bringing Ford and our new squalling baby, Glenn. There were no lamps lit, just flashes of orange flickering across the walls and ceiling from the cracks in the stovetops. Perhaps once or twice a year we'd get a storm so cold our parents would bundle us next to the stove and Wanda and I would romp and giggle beneath our blankets. This night, though, our parents hushed us to be quiet.

I pushed up on my elbow and watched as they sat at the table as they always did. I noted their boots standing nearby, their coats and caps on the back of their chairs. The house shuddered beneath a gale of wind, the windowpanes rattling, wind whistling down the chimney, smoke puffing through the stovetops. A loud roar sounded from the ocean. Mother pulled back from the window, her hand to her throat, and Father half rose as flicks of white foam struck against the glass.

Wanda scrabbled to her feet with delight, wanting to watch through the window too, but Father ordered her back beneath the blankets. Mother was wringing her hands in worry. "Oh my, Nerk," she whispered. Father replied, "It's calming, it's starting to calm," but she was shaking her head. She came over and lay down beside the baby who was on the other side of Wanda, next to Ford. His face was a little whitish wafer in the dim light. It was when Mother touched the back of her hand to his forehead that I felt fear shifting its chilled head inside my spine. She went back to the table, but I kept staring at that little wafer face, so still in sleep. I wanted to lean closer and touch his forehead too, but I was afraid. That he might be cold, that he might smell of soap. That death might be inside my new brother.

AWAY

MY FATHER HAD A DOG that went wild. Trixie just bolted up through the wooded hillside one day and never returned—except on cold stormy nights, when she'd sit on the clifftop behind our house and howl with the northerly winds. Dad would often stand below, whistling for her. "Come on home, girl," he'd call out. "Come on home." But Trixie would just look down at him and howl, eventually vanishing back into the woods.

"Where does she go?" I asked.

"Away, she goes away," said Grandmother. "Mind you steers clear them woods. She'll drag you away too."

Away. Where the girl with the white hair and skin, and eyes the pale blue of a jackrabbit's, came from for a visit once. Away. Out the bay where the sea met the sky and the eye could not follow. She came from Away in a motorboat with her mother and father to visit one of our aunts. All of us youngsters, eyes brown as cocoa, stood at the water's edge, staring at her whiteness. I stood too close, sniffed too hard. She backed away then went off with Wanda and a few other younger cousins. She was from La Scie, I heard one of the aunts say. I heard it as *the last Sea*. I kept standing there, looking out the bay towards where *the last sea* was, where girls are white to the roots of their hair and have jackrabbit eyes.

I ran over to where Mother was putting a bucket of bleached water out on our front steps to soak the mop in.

"Where is *the last sea?*"

"Out around the bay," she said.

"But I can't see it."

"It's too far away."

"I want to go to Away," I told her.

She laughed. "There's no place called *Away*. Any place from here is *away*. Then, when you're there, this place becomes *away*."

I snuck up through the woods on the sly, hiding from Grandmother, pretending I was Trixie. Dropping on all fours, I trotted to the clifftop and flopped onto my belly, looking out over the Beaches and seeing what Trixie saw. I saw nine houses arcing out from the bottom of the hillside; circling back in, they sheltered a big patch of grassy land behind them. The patch was covered with pathways leading to everyone's back door as well as Nan's henhouse and Uncle Frank's woodhouse and Uncle Les's barn and Uncle Jer's well and Uncle Like's spud cellar. I saw clotheslines criss-crossing the space above the patch; on wash days, their pulleys screamed like wounded horses. I saw the hillside covered with more pathways that everyone took to go hunting, trapping, logging, berry picking, hiding, playing, cutting bonfire boughs. I saw Grandmother plodding across the patch and I looked beyond the houses to the ocean in front of them. I looked up to the bottom of the bay where Hampden was, sixty or seventy houses. A big place. I'd been there a few times, in a boat. But it was the other direction that drew me, where the sea and sky vanished into each other, leaving no seam for my eye to see through. Away. I sat up on my haunches, looking towards Away. I gnawed the riddle of Mother's words: *Away becomes the place you just left.* I pawed the ground with frustration and flopped back down on my belly, unable to untangle the twisted thought.

>—>

I was ten when Away came to the Beaches. It started with our first woman teacher. She had soft dark hair and wore lipstick and nice dresses. We girls fought to hang our coats next to hers on the school porch. School was the same as when Father had gone there: six grades in the one room that smelled of chalk, a potbelly stove throwing off heat and smoke near the back, a bucket of coal next to it. Our new teacher's name was Miss Marina Tucker, a foreign name to us on the Beaches; it sounded like music on our tongues. She brought us new ways of doing things in school and taught us different songs, ones like "Dashing Through the Snow" and "Froggie Went a-Courtin'."

She invited everyone to the school just before Christmas and called it a "concert." A concert was us singing. We stood proudly near the Christmas tree she'd helped us decorate with bulbs we each brought from our houses. All the parents came, the men too, wearing their church clothes, and sat watching as we stood before the tree, belting out the new songs. They laughed and shook their heads over the foolishness of a frog courting a mouse and clapped as we finished each song. I never felt so proud.

But that was nothing compared to what she brought to us next.

It was a wet drizzly spring morning. Miss Tucker answered a knock on the school door and came back inside with a big cardboard box that she laid on her desk. She didn't say a word, just opened the box, smiling. She began taking out books and holding them up for us to see their shiny, colourful covers with their crazy lettering and funny titles. *The Cat in the Hat. Bartholomew and the Oobleck.*

At recess she passed them around to whoever wanted to stay inside and read. I stayed inside. I stared at the blue cover with the cat in the red-striped hat and stretched-out neck. I opened the pages to Thing One and Thing Two flying kites through a house and bumping pictures off walls and the four corners of the Beaches melted into Away. A fish fell into a teapot and a mother's new dress went sailing around the house on kite string and things got crazier and crazier.

I didn't go outside at recess for the rest of the school year. I begged my mother for books. There weren't any. You had to send *away* for them. You had to know *where* to send *away* for them. "Make your own book," she said one day after coming home from Hampden to find me searching through her parcels, praying for books.

"How can I? I don't know how."

"You got imagination, use that."

Imagination. I didn't know what that was. Then I saw my first picture show.

It was a nasty night—no stars or moonlight to light the dark, the easterlies blowing a gale and blasting sounders hard upon the shore. Darryl and his sister Ruby went door to door to every house

Down Below and then raced through the pitch-black stretch up to us on the Point. Their father had bought a generator, they said, and would be having "shows" once a week. I didn't know what a show was. "It's like a radio," said Mother, nodding towards our big battery-operated one that looked like a cabinet with knobs, "only it has moving pictures." Darryl held up a coloured poster of a masked man on a rearing white horse, the words THE LONE RANGER scrawled beneath. I didn't know who or what the lone ranger was, but the second Darryl and Ruby left, Wanda and I were clawing at the door like dogs needing to piss.

"No! No gawd-damn way," said Father. "Dirty night like this, not fit to be walking Down Below, and we got no money." He went and hunkered in his armchair by the radio, giving us sulky looks and listening to the news through the static.

I looked at Mother, screwing up my mouth. Father never liked anything. He never went to parties or card games or dressed up in old clothes and went jannying at Christmastime. When his best buddy Dougie got married and everyone was at his wedding at the schoolhouse, twenty feet down the road, Dad put on his good shirt and jacket and sat at our kitchen table. After the wedding supper and the cake cutting, Dougie brought up a piece to Dad and had a glass of beer with him. Mother called him foolish and went to all the parties and picnics. But she was as stuffy as Father when it came to us youngsters. We were the first to be hauled in at night and the last to be let out in the mornings. We were not allowed to row off from shore in our boat like the rest of our cousins or climb too far up the hills or wander out of sight up the road or down the road. *Something can happen*, she always said. *Something can happen.*

It's because she lost her babies, our aunts said.

Before the door had fully closed behind Ruby and Darryl and the poster, I was before Mother, my eyes beseeching her. Perhaps she remembered something of her own desires when she was younger, of wanting to travel to Africa and other places. She touched my face and gave the smallest of nods.

Wanda was still whining at the door. I gave her "the look" and we both threw cautious glances at Father hunching over the radio as we crept away. Mother snuck us a dime each and shushed us out the back door with our coats and boots in our hands. We dressed hurriedly on the back step, and then, lickety-split, we were racing down the road. It was fiercely dark and windy, a rough sea washing the shoreline. A bunch of cousins were huddling near the last house down, waiting to see who else was coming before chancing it through the dark stretch.

Holding hands, we strung out across the road and raced past the black walls of the rotting fish shack that was haunted by an old crone with a creaky lantern. We passed the brook hissing down the slimy rock face where Grandmother said the devil hid. We made it to the first house Down Below, then, letting go of each other's hands and without a word spoken, we leapt over the break-water onto the beach to escape being rocked by the brothers, Rob and Joey, who lay in wait with their stockpile of sharp, skiddy rocks, yearning for some youngster from up on the Point to venture into sight.

The rocks didn't come. The brothers must have gone to the show. We slowed to a walk, then scurried past the home of Aunt Fanny—a stooped old woman who'd fly out her door with her broom, jabbing at any of us youngsters from the Point trying to pass her house—and we were clear.

Winded, we crowded into Uncle Art and Aunt Gladys's house. I sat with the other youngsters on a long plank laid across four wood stumps. Behind us were the adults on a row of chairs; behind them were the elders on a daybed stretching across the back wall. Aunt Gladys sat by the stove, rocking a baby. The room was a-charm with excited talk. There was a sheet hanging from the ceiling, covering the kitchen sink and a window. I wondered at that, but my attention was caught on a square black box with knobs sitting atop a stool. *A show was like a radio but with pictures*, Mother had said.

Soon the lamp was blown out. A soft clacking hum sounded and then a funnel of light shot across the room, sending the white sheet before us into a blaze of light. I cried out, as did others, and clutched Wanda's hand to my right and my cousin Selma's to my left. Music thundered and a masked man atop a white horse reared up, the horse neighing shriller than a dozen rusted pulleys on a frosted morning. I stared at the moving pictures that followed, interrupted only by Aunt Gladys talking low to the elders, explaining the plot, by Uncle Art's back when he shuffled behind the sheet to get something from the sink, making the Lone Ranger wobble across his shoulder blades, and when the show shuddered to a stop, the film slipping off the wheel and piling onto the floor because Darryl, who was supposed to be watching it, was flirting with the girls instead, and it took Uncle Art, soundly bawling out Darryl, ten or fifteen minutes to reel the tape back on and get it all working again.

When the show was over and the lamp was lit, we crowded outdoors, our blood running hot, then galloped up the road, smacking our thighs and neighing like horses. Fast as we were, we didn't outgallop the brothers Rob and Joey, who'd sat beside us as comrades minutes earlier but had now taken up arms by their stockpile of rocks. We ran to the beach; Wanda took a hit between her shoulders and our cousin Garry got one in the head. We whipped back a barrage of our own rocks and made it to the dark stretch without blood being spilled. Grabbing hands, we booted past the devil's hissing brook and the haunted fish shack and came into sight of the first house. Then we saw something that made us stop. Wanda and I screamed. A tongue of fire was leaping from our chimney, licking orange into the night sky. We all started running and screaming.

Mom got to her feet when I raced in, yelling, "The chimney's on fire, the chimney's on fire!" Father shot up from where he was sleeping by the radio and was out the door before his eyes opened. Mother ran for the stairs as outside the aunts and uncles came running with buckets of water. Aunt Beat and Aunt Marg busted in through our door and raced upstairs to where Mother was hauling the boys out of bed. I ran outside to where Father was up on the roof, dousing a bucket of water down the chimney, his brothers quick behind him with more water while others skimmed up the ladder, buckets slopping over. Then Dad shouted, "She's out, she's out, b'ys, she's out!"

There were great sighs of relief on the ground when everyone put down their buckets and wiped their brows and shook out their wet clothes from where the water had slopped over. We youngsters got our heads patted for saving the house from burning down. Finally we were all ushered inside. Dad prowled the floors, muttering and fisting his hand. "The gawd-damn green wood—that's what done it, the gawd-damned green wood."

"What's green wood?" I asked, prowling along beside him, still pumped with excitement.

He stopped and stared at me and Wanda, seeing us for the first time, and as though we were suddenly the cause of the fire he roared, "Where was ye? What were ye doing out so gawd-damned late?"

Wanda stepped forward with the haughtiest of looks. "We were at the show," she said boldly. "The Lonnnnne Ranger," she ended with a flourish.

"*The Lone Ranger*," Father mocked. "Another gawd-damn thing to tarnish your minds."

"He kept your ass from being tarnished this evening," said Mother. Wanda and I looked at her, agog. Then the two of us ran upstairs giggling, Mother behind us.

>>——▷

I took to the hills by myself after the night of the show. Its fantastical images lingered with me for days. Unlike the pictures reading conjured, these were so concrete, so tangible, that they felt true. More than just seeing it, I could've reached out and touched that swinging door leading into the saloon. I could have smelled the cigarette smoke and whisky. And the horses were so vivid I could almost imagine what it would be like to ride one, to feel it galloping beneath me, buckskins slapping around my legs. And when the smart fellow's girl cried at the end, I cried too. Her tears were as actual as my own. I couldn't figure it. God, angels, I got. But this was different.

Mother saw how feverish I'd become since the show. "Perhaps your father was right on that one," she said.

"It felt so *reeal*."

"My, Donna, it's real people, but they're *acting*. They're imag-
ining stories and playing them out. Like ye crowd when you're
acting out games."

A trickle of light lit through the dark. Pretend. They were all
pretending. *Acting*. It was real and it wasn't. *Imagination*. A light
bloomed. I got it!

I started stealing farther and farther away from the houses
by myself. I took to sitting on stumps, sucking on smokes I'd stolen from Father's pack, and *acting* like a grownup: *Yes, maidy, that
gawd-damn dirty old water, that smotherin' jeezly easterly wind,
them gawd-damn youngsters, come here, you bleedin' little blood-of-a-
bitch, come here, I wipes your nose, give Mommy a kiss.* Same games
we'd always played, but this time I was doing it with knowing.

To get away from my sister and our cousins I began hiding
out by the brook running down the rock face across from the fish
shack. It wasn't scary during the day. I'd lie back with the sun
warming my face, daydreaming about cowboys and horses buck-
ing with the wind. Crouched by the stream, I'd dig tiny tributaries
running away from it, flattening out wagon trails running alongside the "river," building lonesome homesteads with clutters of
pebbles, making corrals out of sticks. With more sticks I'd make
people and imagine their stories. One stickwoman wore a pink
frilly gown as she waited patiently in the saloon for the Lone
Ranger. Outside, a horse rescued another woman from an avalanche, nipping onto her dress with his big white teeth and dragging her to safety, breaking his leg in the process. There were dogs
and bad guys and babies and always horses saving drowning
people and kittens from overflowing rivers. Once, when I was

immersed in the game, Wanda and a posse of cousins sprang out at me. Reddening with embarrassment, I stamped everything back into mud and fled up through the woods, raining a fistful of rocks at them. Then I turned tail, swung onto a path, and galloped like fury, swatting my butt and yodelling *Hi-ho Silver, awaaaaaay!*

FLEDGLINGS AND FEATHERS

DAD'S SISTER AUNT BEAT WAS standing in her doorway sweeping when she beckoned me to her stoop one windy winter morning. I was launching myself off the roof of Grandmother's chicken coop and landing in waist-deep snow with Wanda and some others, gasping for breath amid the drifts. I'd just turned eleven and was breathing through a green woolly scarf wrapped around my face that I'd gotten for a birthday present.

"You're a big girl now," Aunt Beat said as I stood looking up at her. "You needs to help your mother with the baby. She got arthritis in her knees. Hard for her now, getting up and down."

"I always helps with the baby," I said, but Aunt Beat was after giving the floor its final sweep and closing her door.

Grandmother was hunched down beneath a swath of shawls and scarves in front of her chicken coop, tossing in soaked bread from a bowl. "Crawl in, crawl in and get the eggs," she coaxed me. I dropped to my knees and crawled into the dark cobwebbed coop, holding my nose against the smell of hens' shit.

"It's her heart," Grandmother was muttering when I backed out with the three eggs. "It's them old needles the doctor's sticking in her knees. Got her heart made bad now. Rather she have arthritis than be dead."

A chill burned through my chest. I dropped the eggs in Grandmother's lap and grabbed hold of Wanda. "We got to help with the baby—Mom got a bad heart," I said.

"I always helps Mom, you never helps."

I pushed her down and ran for home. Mother was scrubbing something burned off the stovetop with a soapy rag, scolding Ford and Glenn for making our dog Bullet bark. I looked at her heart. My first memory was standing on a bed in a strange dark room, pissy pyjama pants clinging cold to my legs, when the door opened and a crack of yellow light fell in. My mother stood in the light, and when she bent down and scooped me up I felt the warmth of her against my cold self. I wanted to feel the warmth of her now. Instead I went to the crib where our new baby, Tommy, lay kicking and fretting. I lifted him up without being told and sat rocking him. When Wanda came in, kicking off her snow-covered boots and coat, she stood too, for a moment, staring at where our mother's heart was. Then she went and got the broom and started sweeping.

Despite her limping around with swollen knees, our mother never acted sick. Plus, she wanted to do more than just housework—which is why she talked Dad into turning the living room that was never used into a store. One day he came home from Corner Brook, sixty miles west, with boxes of groceries stacked in the back of his truck. That became my first real job, wiping off shelves in the store and stamping prices on the cans. My pay was handfuls of candies stolen from the little boxes lining the bottom shelf, candies like I'd never seen: chewy pinks dusted with sugar, minty greens, chocolatey-nutty gooeys, syrupy rock-hard jaw-breakers. It was the best job ever, but I wanted higher pay. I wanted a bike.

Darryl Osmond from Down Below had a shiny green two-wheeler that I drooled over like I had a mouth full of taffy every time he sped by, dinging the bell on his handlebars.

"No," said Father. "No money. Stop asking for gawd-damn bikes."

"Not bikes, *bike*. It's only *one*. It's only me that wants a bike," I was forever yelling after him, but he never listened. He called me "Wanda" half the time, and called Wanda "Donna." If Wanda got caught stealing candy, he'd punish us both. If I got sent to bed for mouthing back, Wanda got sent to bed as well. Whining to Mother usually helped, but she held out against the bike too. No money.

Then, one day, there was a bike. I was inside the house watching through the window as a quick rain shower dried up outside and Dad pulled up in his truck—he'd driven the forty miles to Jackson's Arm that morning. In the back of the truck was a two-wheeler. Its blue enamel gleamed in the freshly washed sun. My heart pounded like a caught bird's and I released a shriek: "I got a bike, Dad got me a bike!"

"Who got a bike?" Mother called. Fear quivered through me in the ten seconds it took to turn from the window, jam my feet back into my sneakers, and bolt through the door. Had I really seen a bike?

I had. Droplets of rain glinted off its shining handlebars lodged on top of the truck's spare tire. I leapt off the steps and yanked open the tailgate. The truck sputtered into silence as Father shut off its motor. I grasped the handlebars, the rubber grips warm and wet against my palms, and tugged the bike across the tailgate. Another hefty tug and it clattered beside me, its spokes cool against my legs, a tantalizing smell of grease coming from its chain.

Dad opened the truck door, rusted hinges whining. When I faced him with smiles he paused, looking at me strangely. Then the passenger door opened and Wanda poked out her head. My sister. We'd stopped holding hands months and months before. For lots of reasons, but none I could ever think of whenever Mom pulled us apart, asking why in God's name we were intent on killing each other.

Wanda. I'd forgotten she'd gone to Jackson's Arm with Dad that morning.

She toppled out of the truck. She toppled everywhere these days. Ten years old and the only thing growing was her hair—big fat ringlets down her back. Every other part of her was short and puddly—like she was still *five*. Like she had no bones, Mother used to say of her when she was a baby. Pick her up and she'd flop over like a floppy toy. She was toppling towards me right now, her face cross as a cat's when cornered by a dog. "That's my bike, not yours, my dear," she said.

I sneered. She stood scarcely taller than the bike itself. She was so chubby she couldn't sit on a straight-back chair without toppling over. And her stupid ringlets tangled with the slightest breeze. I, on the other hand, was tall and skinny; my arms were wiry and long, made for a bike. Besides, Wanda had never wanted a bike. *I* wanted a bike. I'd *always* wanted a bike. I turned to Father as Wanda's words refused to register. He wasn't looking at me, he wasn't even noticing, he was sauntering up the steps to the door, singing the one line of a silly old song he was always singing over and over. *Doooown by the riverrrrr . . .*

"Dad! She said it's *her* bike," I yelled after him.

"Ye share it," he called back, and the door closed.

I gaped in disbelief. Share? Me and Wanda? We shared *nothing*. Hives would break out if our skin so much as touched.

Wanda yanked the bike from my grasp. I kept staring after Father's back. My heart pounded hot blood to my face as I shook with rage and screamed, "*It's not fair!*"

I kicked at the bike and missed, grazing Wanda's ankle. She dropped to one knee, wailing. I bolted past her and into the house.

Father was yelling at Mother in the kitchen and she was yelling back. "It's Donna, Nerk. It's *Donna* who's always asking for a bike."

"They can share it," he shouted. "They can share the gawd-damn thing. It don't matter who owns it, they *both* owns it."

"It matters to *Donna*."

"Gawd-dammit it, lovie, some girl was selling her bike for twenty dollars and I had it in my pocket, and I bought it cuz they're always wanting a bike—"

"*Donna's* always wanting a bike."

"Gawd-dammit, lovie!" He took off his cap and slapped it on the table, catching me standing there staring at him. His eyes darkened. He opened his mouth to speak but no words came. I kept staring into his eyes—there was something stirring in them, almost as though he were pleading with me. It roused something sickening in my heart. I did not know then what I was seeing. I did not know it was the end of the month and that the end of the month was always a lean time before the next paycheque came in.

I did not know that Baby Paul died during that last week of lean-
ness when there was no money and that the welfare officer had
refused Father a loan of thirty dollars for gas to get to the hospital.
I did not know that Father punched the welfare officer in the face
and held nothing but humiliation and helplessness in his pockets
as he walked back out to the truck where Mother was waiting and
weeping; or that his humiliation turned to humility when the new
Czechoslovakian doctor stepped out of his office and gave him
the thirty dollars. I did not know then that Father believed if he'd
gotten to the hospital sooner, he might've saved Baby Paul. I did
not know that my childish desire was a greater poverty for him
to bear than his empty pockets. That the wounding of a heart can
lead to a wounding of pride, and when, as my father's eyes pleaded
with me and he pulled out his emptied pockets, it was himself he
was holding accountable. For he was seeing me for the first time,
in this broken moment, as separate from the brood. And he was
believing he had not fed me sufficiently, and he was feeling himself again a failure as a father.

I knew none of these things in that moment. I knew only that
horrid pleading look on Father's face and that I had caused him
to look that way. "Ye's can share it!" he shouted at me in a twisted
voice and walked out of the kitchen.

I dashed for the door, my face burning. The bike was lying on
its side on the gravel. Wanda had already walked away, abandon-
ing it. I tore off running down the beach but my father's hurt
chased me—and something more. When I was scarcely four years
old and standing on the road in a pothole, water inching up the
sides of my rubber boots, he'd yelled, *Don't get your feet wet!* He
was crouching nearby, chiselling oakum into the seams of his

boat. I stuck out my tongue at him, took another step, and water ran cold inside my rubbers. When he roared again, throwing down his chisel, I ran, arms and legs pumping. I ran so hard my teeth jiggled. I got to the school and threw myself onto the ground; I'd started scrabbling underneath it when his hands clamped down on my ankles. I screamed. He lifted me up, threw me over his shoulder, and started laughing, running with me hanging, head first, down his back, bouncing up and down. I pounded his back with my fists and shouted at him to put me down. It wasn't in my realm of thinking that his hands could loosen accidentally and I might fall. But that day running down the beach, I felt Father's hands loosen. I had pushed my beak through the shell and learned that this thing containing me could be broken.

The rocks rolled beneath my feet as I tried to run faster, but I couldn't get up speed. I could no longer race like the wind, with all things blending into a blur. In becoming separate from the family fold before my father's eyes, I had become separate unto myself as well.

Another rain cloud shook itself; heavy drops splattered against my neck and shoulders. Mother called. I turned back, trudging home. When I kicked off my wet sneakers inside the house, one of them fell near Father's boots. I noticed their worn soles, the dried mud stuck to their sides. I picked one up and brushed off the mud. I picked up the other and brushed it off, too. Then I lined them up neatly next to my sneakers and felt comforted.

DESIRE, RAGE, AND ROCK 'N' ROLL

I WAS TWELVE. Electricity had come to the Beaches. Every window in every house was lit up. Every doorway had a hundred-watt bulb throwing halos of light into the night. Television and telephones quickly followed. Everything and everyone was in a state of change. Change—an inheritance given to us the day we're born, one that challenges our every step along the way. But Grandmother never budged. She continued in her old ways: nailing horseshoes over her door to ward off evil spirits, blanketing her windows against lighting to prevent being blinded, throwing salt over her shoulder to avoid bad luck.

"Nerrrrk! Nerrrrk!" she called out from her stoop one night during a heavy rain. "There's goin' to be a flood. Nerrrk! Nerrrrrrrrrk!"

Father wrenched his head up from his pillow and scraped up his window and bawled out into the night, "Go in the house, Mudder; for gawd's sake, go in the house."

"Goin' to be a flood, Nerk, mark my words, there's goin' to be a flood."

"Then go get in the gawd-damn boat."

"Mark my words!"

He laughed. "Mudder, Mudder, you got me drove."

I lay awake, feeling bad for Grandmother, for she believed in her fears. I, too, was filled with fear and excitement that night. In the morning we'd be bused from the Beaches to the high school in Hampden. And Father, to help Mother more because of her arthritis growing worse, had quit his job working in the woods for ten days in, four days off, and had taken the job of school bus driver. He'd bought a light blue bus that sat up to ten people. He'd even made a plywood sign, painting it lemon yellow with the words SCHOOL BUS in big black letters, and attached it to the top.

Morning came too early. We climbed aboard the new-smelling bus with its purple padded seats and chatted nervously, clutching our new book bags and paper-bagged lunches. But as we neared Hampden High School, we fell silent. It looked so big. It had four different classrooms, we'd been told, with four different teachers. About a hundred students were standing in front of its doors. I'd never seen so many people before. And not one of them, I noticed, was carrying a paper-bagged lunch.

Father, oblivious to our fear, parked directly in front of them. My stomach wrung itself as I wished I was Grandmother, back home living in the old ways, my fears clearly defined.

Somebody opened the bus door and we filed out, clutching our books and bagged lunches. Father drove off as we stood there, naked as plucked hens.

There were titters. Ruby and Darryl, used to crowds from their father showing shows, walked boldly forward. I reached without thinking for Wanda and she knocked my hand aside. A big girl, with straight blond hair and a face wider than a pie pan, sauntered over, asking loudly, "Do ye have lice in your heads?"

"Not unless they just jumped from yours," Wanda snapped.

I died.

Everyone laughed. A tall girl with nice cheekbones and dark hair came over, smiling down at Wanda. "My, you're some saucy. What's your name, my love?"

"Butter 'n' cream. Ask me agin, I'll tell you the same."

I died.

The tall girl laughed, looking over at her friends. "Oh, I know she's not saucy." Mercifully, the school doors opened then and everyone funnelled inside.

"Man came from the ape," the history teacher informed us.

I paused, then scribbled down his words.

"Before that we were fish that crawled out of the sea and we grew legs from fins and lungs from gills. We walked on four legs and then stood upright and walked on two. And the reason we have lower back pain is that we haven't been upright long enough for our muscles to adapt."

I stared at him, waiting for everyone to laugh. Everyone kept scribbling. The teacher hunched up his shoulders, let his arms hang down, and walked bowlegged across the room, demonstrating our once primal walk.

Eh, yeah, I could see it.

I wrote furiously. I listened to everything he said and everything the other teachers said and accepted everything I read as absolute. I passed every test and might've become the scholar Father kept forecasting if not for the library—three long planks, painted white and screwed onto the back wall of the canteen and lined with used books—that opened at the start of my second year. And there I met Leon Uris and John Steinbeck and Kurt Vonnegut and Jack London and Joseph Conrad and Mark Twain and a slew of others. Imagination. It brought far more to my mind than the alphabets spelled out in schoolbooks. Their characters took up residence in my head. I read in the classroom and on the bus and on the sofa and at the supper table and on the toilet. When I was reading textbooks or the Bible, my father applauded. When I began reading fiction, he shook his head. "Gawd-damn books, always slouching around, reading. Go help your mother."

"I'm not *slouching around*, I'm reading."

"You'll go foolish," Grandmother warned. "No different than card fever. There's them as can't put the cards down, and the same with books. Mark my words, you'll go foolish reading all them books."

Wanda flourished in her own way. She started hating school and schemed to stay home, forever sweeping and tidying and soaking up everyone's praise. "Claudine got some help there; good as her mother for keeping the house clean," said the aunts.

"That's right, that's right, you help your mother, my dolly," praised Father. "Your mother's helper, you are. Not afraid of the broom or the dishrag."

"Work, work. Them who don't work is the devil's pawn," warned Grandmother from the rocking chair as I sprawled on the couch, reading.

It was too late. The fictive worlds grew bigger inside of me than the world outside. I took to hiding and reading. Under beds, in closets, in the bathtub (which had no plumbing; instead it was filled with coats and made for a comfortable lie-down, providing no one pulled aside the shower curtain and saw me there). *Drucie*, Father took to calling me, after an ancient aunt, long dead, who'd raised pigs and chickens in her house; the only cleaning it got was from her dogs licking the floors. Then I found the best hiding place of all: the store. Father had since expanded it by adding an extension to the side of the house. It was warm and cozy, with only the occasional customer to interrupt. I'd hurry through the cleaning and sorting of shelves, add up the credit sheets, and then stretch out in comfort atop the deep freezer, always as warm as a sunspot. I kept a cleaning rag in my hand while I read should Mom or Dad appear. Once, when I was hiding from the supper dishes and getting in a good read, I drifted into a deep sleep. It got late and Mother came to check on me. It was so dark that she switched on the light, startling me awake. I scrabbled onto my knees and, still holding the cleaning rag, began wiping the wall. She burst out laughing. I stalked past her, back into the house, the book shoved under my sweater. I wondered whether Grandmother was right and I'd grown foolish from all them books.

It was John Fogerty who jolted me from them. Slouched in a chair one Sunday evening, reading, I was suddenly riveted by the sound of a throaty voice belting out something about a fortunate son on *The Ed Sullivan Show*. I was electrified. The hard-edged singing and driving rhythm and crazy hair and skinny blue-jeaned legs made me throw aside my book and hunker beside Wanda in front of the TV. And hunker beside the radio in the kitchen for days, weeks, months after, listening to the staticky strains of songs about some sweet Lord and long winding roads and travellin' bands and troubled waters and houses of rising suns, and a hundred other such wondrous words and sounds.

I lugged the radio through the house, testing out spots for a clear reception. I finally found it after I'd hooked up two extension cords and crawled through my bedroom window onto the roof of the store. When summer came I'd lie out there on a blanket, doused in baby oil and iodine, sizzling with the tar on the roof as the radio rocked to bad moons rising.

The following summer an Anglican minister and his family arrived from Toronto to visit their aunt. They had a daughter named Ruth who spoke English so perfectly I had trouble understanding her. She had straight blond hair swinging down her back and laughing eyes and a collection of little records—forty-fives, she called them. She also had an electric record player that you could play anywhere—and she gave it all to me before she left. Oh my *gawwwd!* I permanently peeled myself off the tarred roof and danced through the house singing *Meee and Bobby McGeee* and waltzing with Wanda's broom, crooning *Hey Jude.*

Mother was on her way to bed one night when she looked into my room; I'd left the door open and was prancing in front of a mirror, wearing a headband I'd made from a fake-leather belt. She paused, looked away, and kept going. But Dad was right behind her. He stared at me in my headband, stared as he'd once stared at a strange nut that fell from his chainsaw. *What's she trying to be—an Indian?* I heard him ask Mom after she'd hauled him into their room. I bolted for my door, closing it against Father's voice. *Lovie,* he continued, *she's losing it . . . too gawd-damn much reading . . . them gawd-damn records . . . beating around the roads up Hampden . . .*

≫—▷

The day I brought home my grade eleven mid-term report card, with its two failing grades in math and science, Mother stood beside me at the sink, drying the dishes as I washed them. "Now," she said, "you can keep failing and spend the rest of your life on the Beaches. Or get your nose back in your books and make something outta yourself."

She didn't wait for an answer. But that Christmas she gave me a gold-coloured three-piece luggage set that sat beneath the tree like a bus ticket. That coming January I'd be sixteen. In those days there were no trodden roads out of the Beaches, no one who'd left for Toronto or Alberta or Boston. Nobody who'd gone to university or even trade school in Corner Brook. At the end of our grade ten school year, one of our teachers had spoken to us about university in St. John's. But the talk lasted ten minutes with just two clear pieces of information coming at us: St. John's was a ten-hour drive, and you turned left on the highway to go there.

Father had one thought. She stays home and works in the store.

Mother slewed her eyes. The day I brought home the failed mid-term report card she fixed it that I would go and stay with her brother who lived in Corner Brook, a city of twenty-five thousand that lay to the right of the highway. And find a job and do night school to finish my grade eleven if I didn't make the grade, then go to trade school and become a secretary.

Father threw a bloody fit. "She's only fifteen, gawd-dammit!" he yelled across the supper table at Mother. "She's not going to no gawd-damn city till she grows up."

"She'll be sixteen in two weeks. What were *you* doing when you were sixteen?" asked Mother.

"Different. That's different, lovie. I wasn't wild. That gawd-damn television got them drove wild."

"How come we're not all wild then?"

"We are. We keeps it to ourselves. She's not that growed up."

"If she goes, I'm going too," said Wanda. I booted her in the shins under the table as Father pushed away his plate and stalked into the store.

While Wanda helped Mother clear away the dishes, I put on a new Doors record I'd just bought through the mail. With Jim Morrison's grave-deep voice rumbling like a trombone through the house, Father barged back through the store door and yanked the record off the player. I let out a bawl and Mom yelled at Dad and Wanda yelled at me for playing the record when Dad was home and Dad was fisting the air and yelling, "They're gone wild, the youngsters are gawd-damn wild!"

"What do you expect?" I shouted. "We all come from the apes!"

Stunned silence. "It's true," I said. "Adam and Eve is just a story. We all come from *apes*. And before that, *fish*."

Father grabbed a tumbler of water off the table and sluiced the water over my face. I ran for the stairs, pushing aside Glenn and Ford—wide-eyed with glee at the goings-on—and stomping into my room. After slamming the door I let loose a full-throated scream at the wall. Then I stared at myself in the mirror: my face was white, my eyes wild, my hair stringy wet, and I was shaking with the hard-edged rage of humiliation.

I didn't go downstairs for the rest of the evening and feigned sleep when Mother peeked in before bedtime. Father's step wasn't as boisterous as it usually was as he followed behind her. And he wasn't singing *Down by the river*, as he usually did before bed.

Little sister Karen, born more than a year before, toddled into my room early the following morning. After clambering onto the bed and dragging her soggy diaper across my face, she crawled over to Wanda (who always snuck into my bed during the night,

convinced there was a bomb ticking in her room's walls) and
plopped her butt right onto Wanda's face. She got knocked sideways, wailing as she hit the floor.

Mother came running. She scooped her up, ordered us out
of bed, and called out to the boys—and soon everyone was rushing to the bathroom, rushing to get dressed, rushing through
breakfast, complaining about the lumps in Father's boiled oats.
Still furious with him, I dallied upstairs. Only when I heard him
leave the house to warm up the school bus did I sneak downstairs and into the washroom. Then I was out the door, ignoring
Mother's call to at least have a slice of toast. I climbed into the
back of the bus and didn't look Father's way till we were dropped
off at the school in Hampden. As he drove off I threw him a
withering glance.

After lunch I mooched from school with Wanda and some of
the older girls, forging a path through the snow-laden hill in front
of the school. We hid among the trees, sitting on sun-warmed
rocks and smoking cigarettes that Wanda always seemed to have
by the pocketful. At one point I stood on a rocky ledge, staring
down at Dad coming up School Road in the bus. Wanda yanked
me back. "You wants him to see us, do you?" she said accusingly.

"I don't care."

"You'll care if he sees us."

We waited till school let out and then ran down the hillside,
melting into the crowd of students bustling through the doors and
then off towards home, those from the Beaches heading for the
bus. I sat in the back again, but when I caught Father glaring at me
in the rear-view mirror I knew he'd seen me up in the woods. It
didn't matter. I was Dickens's Pip, admonished by his harsh Uncle

Pumblechook. I was Steinbeck's Rosasharn, deserted by her own family. I was the unappreciated Cash in Faulkner's *As I Lay Dying*.

At the Beaches, I got off last. But Father was right there behind me, demanding, "What was you doing up them gawddamn woods?"

I glared back at him, eyes as angry as his. Without thinking, I blurted, "Toothache."

"Where? I don't see no swelled face."

I opened my mouth and pointed inside, holding his stare.

"Then get in the car, we goes to the doctor."

So be it, I thought grimly. Damned if I was backing down. Inside the house, I plunked my books down on the table and told Mother that Dad was taking me to the doctor. She dropped whatever she was doing, calling after me as I went back outside. Dad was standing by the gold and green car he'd bought the year before, his face sullen as a cranky youngster's. I got in the car. He got in the car. Mother kept bawling out from the door.

Father drove the four miles to the clinic in Bayside. Neither of us spoke. He parked and then watched from the car as I walked up its steps and went in. Through the window of the little waiting room I could see him gripping the wheel and staring at the clinic door as though expecting me to walk right back out. When Dr. Messik called out from inside his office—it was one of those rare times when there weren't a dozen people waiting to be seen—I walked straight in. His office walls were lined with shelves filled with jars and pill bottles and bandages and small boxes of every imaginable shape and colour. I sat down, stiffening from the strong smell of peppermint and antiseptic. I had some idea of what was coming. If you went to the doctor with toothache, he pulled the tooth. If I left the doctor's office without a pulled tooth, it stood to reason I didn't have toothache. I wouldn't give Father that satisfaction. Truth is, while he had never laid a hand on any of us or even kicked a dog, I was more scared of Father's wrath than of a doctor with a needle and a pair of pliers.

Dr. Messik was sitting behind his huge cluttered desk with its two facing chairs. He was a tall man, red-faced and smiley, with sparse blond hair and a big belly that sagged like a sack of sawdust over his belt. His strong Slavic accent made speaking sound like a great effort.

"*Vhat* is problem with tooth?" he asked, coming around his desk as I opened my mouth and pointed to the third last tooth in, top-left row. I'd noted just that week a speck of black on it.

"Zis tooth eees good," he said, raising his eyebrows. But I shook my head, jabbing at the tooth. He closed one eye, peering closer. "Ahhh, *mabeee* go to Corner *Broook*."

I shook my head again. A one-hour drive to Corner Brook with Father was not going to happen. "It always aches," I muffled.

"It eees *extraction* you *vant*?"

I nodded.

He walked over to a shelf and rustled around, humming some off-key sounds. Then he turned and came towards me with a long needle. I felt the first flickers of fear. The doctor loomed before me. He put his hand atop my head, gently pushing it back.

"Open mouth."

I opened my mouth, and clutched the armrests. As his thick fingers pried my jaw open further, my breathing quickened and my stomach clenched. I thought to escape but didn't know how. The needle pricked my gums and a hot burn started up.

Minutes later he had a foot lodged against the chair between my stiffened knees. Then, with some instrument I mercifully couldn't see, he started wrenching at my tooth. The tool slipped off; he got it back on; he continued wriggling and wrenching. At that point I opened my eyes and looked at his tensed, reddened face, tears of agony streaming down my cheeks. Then came a terrible suction sound, accompanied by a jolt of pain that brought a grunt from deep in my gut. Blood spurted. I felt faint.

Dr. Messik smiled, nodded, and patted my head as he did with all good girls. Humming again now, he inserted a wad of tissue into the hole he'd just excavated inside my mouth and pressed against it with the pad of a thumb that felt wider than a two-inch socket. The blood kept flowing. He pressed harder against the flow; my neck stretched and my butt rose off the chair. Finally he plucked his thumb out of my mouth and I settled back onto the chair, feeling wobbly. Then he passed me an aspirin that I swallowed with blood while he wrote me a bill for one dollar.

I didn't have any money with me. Snatching more tissue from the box on his desk, I held up my hand in a wait-a-moment sign and then scurried out of his office on quivering legs. There was a garbage can in the waiting room; I bent over it, spitting and gagging. Then I put the wad of fresh tissues against my mouth and walked weakly to the car. Father had his window down and was gaping at me. He paled when he saw the bloodied tissue.

"Well the blue *Jeezes*! Your mother's goin' to skin you."

I mumbled through the tissue that I needed a dollar. He pulled out his wallet, quickly handed me five, and then stared straight ahead, silent, as I scurried back in and paid the doctor. He said not a word when I got into the car and he said not a word as we drove the four miles home.

Nor did he say a word when we got inside and Mother jumped to her feet, dropping the spud she was peeling and gaping at my mouth. I bolted up the stairs. Father said not a word as Mother started cursing. Soon I heard the store door slam.

It wasn't till evening that I heard him cursing too as she lit into him again about getting a good tooth pulled. It was one of their worst fights to date.

"What was I supposed to do, lovie? She was lyin'."

"Ahh, you damn fool."

"She wouldn't back down."

"You should've. You're foolisher than she was."

"Gawd-dammit, lovie, she's the youngster. She got to back down, not me."

"Nor should she have. You think now she got that glass of water forgot?"

"What glass of water?"

"*What glass of water!* Get out of me sight."

"I thought she was sitting in the waiting room, waiting. I never thought she was getting her gawd-damn tooth pulled. She never come back out; what was I supposed to do? Go in the doctor's office and yank her out?"

"Better than having her tooth yanked out. Go out in the store, I can't look at you."

The store door banged shut. I listened for more arguing, but all remained quiet. Feeling disappointed that it hadn't continued any longer, I tucked into my martyr's pillow, comforted by the bloodied tissues and murderous throbbing in my mutilated jaw.

BAY GIRL MEETS COOL GIRL

IT WAS JUNE 1972. I was sixteen. Several months after the pulled tooth and two weeks after I'd brought home an end-of-year failed report card (not having managed to improve my math and science grades), Mother and I were sitting in the back seat of a shared taxi to Corner Brook, my new gold luggage set packed and in the trunk. Just as she'd planned, I was to stay with her brother in the city, get a job, and go to night school to finish grade eleven.

Wanda had pouted because she couldn't go with me. Tommy had cried; Ford, Glenn, and Karen had taken no notice; Father had hidden in the store. The aunts, though, had trailed back and forth, nodding their approval and touching my shoulder. I was the first person from the Point to reach grade eleven, no matter that I'd failed two subjects.

Father had emerged two or three times, supposedly looking for something, giving Mother sullen looks as though she were solely responsible for my leaving. He wouldn't look at me and kept going back into the store even though no customers were about.

"Don't mind your father; he'd have you tied to the table leg if he could," said Mother when we were standing outside waiting for the taxi and Father still hadn't said goodbye.

"Did he never want to go anywhere but the Beaches?"

"Big Island," said Mother, referring to a monster rock, twenty miles straight out the bay, with a crop of trees and one inch of soil on it. "That's his dream spot. Providing we all went too."

"What's *wrong* with him?"

"Scared something might happen to one of you. That's better than his wishing you gone, I suppose."

When the taxi came I dashed into the store. He was hunched over the counter, looking as though he was examining someone's bill. My lips quivered, I felt a strong urge to cry.

"See ya, Dad," I said as casually as if I were just going up to Hampden.

"See you, lovie," he said without looking up.

I ducked outside, wiping away sudden tears.

They didn't last long. As soon as the Beaches dust settled behind us, I began to feel sick with fear and excitement. Corner Brook was a mill town, right on the mouth of the Humber River where it flowed into the Bay of Islands, and with its painted houses and surrounding mountains, it was as pretty as anything. Mother had always been wide-eyed over its nice lawns and flowers and bushes.

We took the long way in through the city. Then suddenly, right there in the middle of town, was an acreage of greenery. I'd been to the city a few times before, always with Mother near holding my hand so's I wouldn't get lost, but hadn't seen much beyond a clinic or shopping mall parking lot. I gaped at the sight. Crowds of young people were loafing about on the grass. Hippies. Straight from the television screen. Long hair, frizzy hair, shaggy hair, headbands, sideburns, beards and braids and not one ponytail to be seen. When our driver stopped to let a couple of them saunter across the street, I whipped the window down and leaned out, staring at their leather-sandalled feet and silver pendants swinging around their necks and dangly earrings and clinking bracelets. Whiffs of something like oakum filtered through the cab. Mother hauled me back onto the seat, and when I twisted my neck for a longer look she rooted me with her elbow.

"Get your eyes back in your head. Your father might be right," she added with sudden worry. "Cripes. Perhaps you are too wild for this."

"Gawd, I'm not a beast."

She clicked her teeth as she always did when she had no rebuttal.

We were heading straight for the government building, where I'd be applying for a job. Mother had said she'd go in with me; after that we'd go to my uncle's, where she'd get me settled.

As we walked up the concrete steps towards the big glass doors, though, I wavered. Everything was big and foreign looking. Even the grass growing around the buildings was perfectly cut. *This* was Away.

Mother took the lead. She was wearing her good blue raglan over her good dress. Her short hair was freshly curled and I could smell her Here's My Heart perfume, which always made me sickish during car rides, but the last time I told her that she'd given me a clout in the head, so I kept quiet.

Once inside the waiting room, I started to really feel anxious. The overhead lights, the cold, stiff plastic seats, the phones ringing from all directions, the subdued voices—it made me want to flee, to escape from that rabbit warren of halls and doorways and scurry back to the Beaches. I kept clearing my throat and looking at Mother, who was sitting stiffly as though she, too, was hearing the click of a hunter's gun.

But when a smartly dressed woman with nice hair and lipstick clicked past us in her high heels, calling my name, Mother rose with a polite half smile. I followed her as the woman led us down a short hall and into a small office. Another woman sat behind a desk and half-smiled back as we took a seat.

"This is my daughter; she's looking for a job," said Mother, her English as good as what you heard on TV.

"What kind of job?"

Images of myself flashed before my eyes: brushing down horses; fixing pretty flowers into vases; twirling atop an elephant in a circus.

"Waitressing," said Mother.

"No," I said too loudly. They both looked at me. I shook my head. "No."

"What are your interests?" the woman asked with a curious smile.

Interests. I didn't know what she meant. My mouth was dry. She kept looking at me with questioning eyes. I wanted to slap her. *Why the hell don't you just show us what jobs you got and let me pick one?*

"Cashier," Mother blurted out. "She works in our store. We have a store on the Beaches," she added. Her hands were tightly clasped in her lap. I saw her throat moving; she was swallowing nervously, feeling as awkward as I was, yet she kept her head erect.

"Do you want to be a cashier?" the woman asked, sounding out the words slowly as if speaking to the dim-witted.

I nodded.

"What is your second choice?"

"Working on a train."

Mother looked at me with surprise.

"It was just something that come to me," I argued with her later in the taxi to her brother's place.

"How're you going to do night school, working on a train?"

"Not like she was offering me a job."

"Funny thing to come up with, working on a train," said Mother. "Have you even seen one?"

I didn't tell her about twirling atop an elephant.

⇒—▷

It was during my third day as cashier at the Co-op Grocery in the middle of downtown Corner Brook that I ventured farther down West Street on my lunch break. I passed the Seven Seas, a Chinese restaurant where I'd had chips and gravy twice by then, then a spike-fenced cemetery, then the Holiday Inn. I kept walking— past Woolworth's, a jewellery store, a drugstore, and two more clothing stores. Finally I came to the end of the street and stood still. There they all were. Hippies. Dozens of them, like a herd of seals basking and bobbing and swerving about on a sea of grass, their long hair glistening in the sun.

I leaned against the rough bark of a maple tree, half hidden beneath the swoop of a branch burgeoning with leaves, gazing sideways at the throng so as not to be caught looking. Somewhere in their midst a transistor radio whined out a tinny electric guitar lick. A couple of girls—one in a granny dress and the other in cutoffs—were clapping their hands and singing along. The second girl flashed a peace sign at someone calling out to her from across the way. There were huddles of fellows playing cards. One fellow busted out laughing, throwing down his cards and cussing, and the others threw down their cards laughing and cussing and they all looked and sounded so happy.

I stared and stared. I stared with the same yearning as I'd stared at that *Cat in the Hat* book and the Lone Ranger. I stared with such want that I was quivering. Eventually I shoved off from the maple tree and began walking through the centre of that green, eyes straight ahead as though I were meeting someone on the other side. I glanced neither left nor right as I took in the smells of cigarette smoke and pot smoke and oily sorts of scent I'd never smelled before but suddenly *loved*. I took in their talk as well. *Hey, how's it goin', man. Hey, mutherfucker. Far out, man, fucking far out* . . .

I reached the end of the green too quickly. My lunch break was nearly up; I had to turn back anyway.

I held up one hand and waved furiously at some imaginary person in the distance. There, job done. Reason for being, established. Then I turned, raised my chin, put on Mother's half smile, and started back across the green at a more relaxed pace. I noted the skinny jeans the girls were wearing. The silver skull-and-crossbones ring one of them had. I glanced down at my own faux silver ring turning my finger green and jammed my hands into the side pockets of my speckled wide-legged polyester baggies, all the rage on the Beaches. I sauntered on until I was safely across the green. Then I hurried back to work.

The second Friday, payday, I went shopping. I bought a pair of tight-fitting, straight-legged Lee jeans. A purple-and-yellow tie-dye shirt, leather sandals, and a pair of big white-framed sunglasses. Then a bangle. Saturday afternoon, my day off, I put on all my new clothes and stood before a mirror. Proud was what I felt.

Monday at lunchtime I walked from the fluorescent lights of the grocery store into the bright sun of a summer's day. I was wearing my new jeans and sandals and tie-dye shirt; by the time I'd slipped on my bangle and sunglasses, I was already high. I loped down the street as far as the maple tree, confident as a bird swooping from its perch. I'd been making that walk almost every day now for the past two weeks, going as far as the maple and no farther since that one time. I looked out at the array of folks all decked out in headbands, beads, bell bottoms, and belts. Laughing and jostling about, some playing Frisbee and card games, most just lying on their sides, smoking and gabbing.

I jammed my hands into my back pockets and strolled among them, feeling like a light pole on a flat field. I wondered if they'd all recognize me from that last walk, my speckled baggies. I gazed upwards, feigning interest in the sky as though a solar eruption or something had captured my attention. But then I bumped into somebody and stood back, startled by the long-hair suddenly nose-to-nose with me, gazing through my sunglasses.

"Peekaboo," he said. He had reddish curls falling to his shoulders and a reddish beard. His little round sunglasses were scarcely big enough to cover his eyes, but he pulled them down the bridge of his nose and said, "Get rid of the belt." Then he walked off grinning.

I looked down at my belt. It was white plastic, with a double row of holes dotting its length; I'd thought it looked good highlighted against the dark blue of my jeans. I turned, searching after him. He was crouching next to a fellow who was petting a German shepherd with a red kerchief around its neck. But seeing me looking towards him with a blank face, he nodded to his friend and came back, pulling off his belt. A wide, carpeted thing with a big brass ring for a buckle. A couple of hippies sitting nearby laughed as he approached me, holding out the belt, and I thought of how Wanda would be giving him sauce if she'd been the one standing there. I just turned red. My nose watered. Granny-eyes was speaking again. "Take it," he said, jabbing the belt at me. "Gypped it from a junkie in *Trawna*."

I had no idea what the hell he'd just said, but I took the belt, stared at it.

"What bay you from?" he asked.

"White Bay."

"Ahh. My name's Jerome. What's yours?"

"Donna Osmond."

"Say, who?"

"Yeah. As in, go away little girl."

"Tell me it ain't true. Ohhh, it hurts," he said, his face taking on a pained grin. He beckoned me to follow and sat back down, tonelessly humming what the year before had been a number one hit on the pop charts, "Go Away Little Girl" by teen heartthrob Donny Osmond.

I sat, looking around. The sun burned the top of my head. A floppy hat would be nice, like what some of the girls were wearing. Some of the guys were bare-chested, their T-shirts wrapped around their heads for shade. Everybody was just nodding and grinning and grooving in the sweet warm sun. I whipped off my white belt and put on the carpeted one; it fit perfectly through my loops. Jerome stretched out on the grass, his arms tucked beneath his head. I flopped back myself then, elbows digging into the grass, clouds sifting pink through my Janis Joplin sunglasses.

Just like that, man, I was cool. And Mother was wrong. Away does not cease to be the moment you reach it. It was I, the girl from the bay, who ceased to be.

>—⊳

Thus began two years of never-ending camp for big kids, and with no supervision or rules or bedtime. Pot, pills, psychedelics, and Mick Jagger was the heady mix dragging me through each five-hour workday at the cashier job till I could join my thirty best friends on the green, tripping into the wee hours of the morning. Yet I still managed to get my grade eleven diploma, making my mother proud.

Here's the thing: I remember in exquisite detail mostly everything about growing up on the Beaches, from the flutter of Mother's eyelashes to the squawks of Grandmother's hens to Father's *gawddamns* and his one-line "Down by the River" song. Everything from smoking with my sister and knocking around my brothers to toting babies all about the house. Yet I remember almost nothing from those two years in Corner Brook. Aside from making the loveliest of free-spirited friends, it was a surreal experience, scarcely a lamplight penetrating the psychological landscape I was tripping through.

Only once did that idyll falter, almost six months after I'd started working at the Co-op store. It was Friday evening, payday at the paper mill, and the place was crowded. Customers lined up their loaded carts in front of ringing cash registers as overhead heaters blasted the cold December air swooping through the four main doors every time they opened. The three supervisors were hustling about, smiling for the customers, white shirtsleeves rolled up to their elbows as they lined up carts, helped the packing boys, and hoisted fifty-pound sacks of spuds up onto the checkouts.

I glanced at my watch. Another ten minutes and I'd be off work for the evening. I turned aside, slipping a brown capsule of peyote into my mouth—as prearranged with my buddy Jerome— and swallowing it with a bite of the apple in my smock pocket. Right at six I slipped the strap of my bag over my shoulder and prepared to turn in my cash. One of the supervisors, fat-bellied and with wet spots the size of facecloths on the underarms of his shirt, slammed down two massive containers of liquid detergent on my counter. "You stay here till nine," he wheezed.

I gaped at him, then shook my head. "No. I mean, no, sir. I—I can't."

He shoved aside a loaded grocery cart, veins rippling up his freckled forearms, and rushed past me. When I reached for his arm my hand slipped off, wet with his sweat. I wiped it on my smock, calling after him.

He turned, head and shoulders as one, his eyes small and dewy behind steaming glasses.

"I can't work," I said.

"We got no one to take your place! You're on till nine."

I bent over, hand to my belly. "I'm sick. I have to go. Now." I whipped my hand to my mouth as though pushing back puke. He grabbed another cart, forced a smile at the pinched-face couple standing behind it, then bawled out to another supervisor, scurrying past, "Get the girl from the candy counter." Finally he snatched my arm with his meaty hand and nudged me aside, taking my place behind the cash register. I skittered off, fake-hobbling up the stairs to the staff room and snatching my fur-lined leather jacket off a hook.

Six-ten—the peyote would kick in soon. Perhaps another fifteen minutes. Most likely Jerome would already be waiting at our spot near the cemetery.

I snagged a comb through my hair, smeared on some purple lip gloss, did a mental check for signs of getting high—nothing yet—and dashed out of the staff room. I slowed my pace going down the stairs into the frenzy of ringing-dinging cash registers and customers yakking and packing boys hollering for help. I hunched a little. The supervisor was bustling past; when he gave me a withering look he bumped into one of the packing boys, who dropped a gallon-sized glass jar of dill pickles. It smashed, splashing juice up the supervisor's pant legs and sending dill pickles spilling over his boots like a landed load of little green fish. His roar blasted the packing boy backwards.

Ducking out into the blessed quiet of a mild winter's evening, I turned right onto West Street. And there was Jerome, up past the Seven Seas restaurant, leaning against the cemetery's spiked fence and waving. A couple were coming towards me, taking up the whole sidewalk; I huffed with impatience, making to step past them, all the while fluffing my hair and slipping a brown leather headband over my forehead.

"My God, Donna, look up."

I stopped in my tracks. It was Mom and Dad. I hadn't been home since I'd left almost six months before and had seen Mom only twice for lunch during her shopping trips. I'd never seen Dad this far from the Beaches.

He was scowling, looking warily up and down the street as he clutched Mother's arm. "Where we going to eat? I'm not hungry, gawd-dammit."

"Then don't eat. We were just coming to get you at the store," said Mother, giving me a warm hug. "To have a bite with us. In there," she added, gesturing towards the Seven Seas behind me. I glanced frantically up the street at Jerome as she walked us to the restaurant. They'd been to the bank, Mother continued as we slipped into a booth, and then had gone down to the mall to do some Christmas shopping. "Worse than having a colicky young-ster along," she said, giving Dad's arm a fake punch.

"Hates this place," grunted Father with a pained look on his face.

"Ahh, you're foolish as your mother. Scared someone might speak to you."

"Home. Home," he said, jabbing his finger at nothing. "Where everybody should be." He stared pointedly at me, at the worn black leather jacket I'd bought for two bucks at a secondhand store, at the brown leather band circling my forehead. He stared at my leather wristband and clunky silver ring with a peace sign engraved in black. He stared at my glossy purple lips and hennaed reddish hair and sooty eye makeup.

"Lovie, what's you jannying?"

"Oh my gawd, Dad. *Jannying!*" A Christmas tradition around the outports. People would dress up in odd clothes, wrap a rag around their head with cut-out holes for eyes, and go from house to house rapping on doors with a stick of wood, demanding in raspy voices to be allowed in. And if they kept their disguises going long enough and danced a few jigs around the wood stove with granny, they'd have earned a shot of rum or whisky or moonshine. Then on they'd go to the next house, getting drunker as the night wore on. And that's how I felt sitting there before Father's searching eyes—like a janny waiting for the rum to kick in so that I could kick off down the road. Except it was peyote I was starting to get off on. My insides were beginning to feel warm and squirmy. I shook my head, "I just ate," I said to Mother as the waitress approached.

Mother smiled at the waitress and ordered two hot chicken sandwiches, then pointed Father towards the washroom. She leaned in closer, looking smart as ever in her grey pantsuit and with her lipstick on. Her eyes were dark with suppressed excitement.

"Don't say nothing, but we're buying a store in Hampden. That's why your father's here—we were at the bank. That's not all," she added as I tried to take in what she was saying. "Your father wants to buy one of them trailers—a mobile home—and move it just past Hampden, couple miles further up the road."

"Oh, my gawd, Mom! He must have a tumour on the brain."

"It's my arthritis. I got it everywhere now—in my neck, my shoulders. Doctor says the only cure is to live away from the ocean. Your father thinks that's three miles in the woods."

"Did you tell him the doctor meant Texas?" I sat back, suddenly overwhelmed by the heat spreading through my limbs like slow-flowing lava. Music drifted from the jukebox. *Come on now, baby baby baaaaaby, commmme on . . .*

"Donna?"

I tried to focus in on Mother's face.

"What's wrong?"

"It's the heat." I waved my hand for air, sitting forward again. "My, Mom, buying a store in Hampden?"

"You knows your father now. He wants you to come home. Work in the store. That's why he's buying it: something for all of ye to build on and work at."

Come home? I shook my head and hers started to wobble and the music started drifting around me and I wanted to close my eyes and drift with it and my mother was looking at me, her eyes starting to glow. I began to get up in a panic but she waved me back down, thinking I was looking for Father who was now lurching towards us, his eyes darting about as though escaping an ambush.

"Donna!"

I won't look at her. I can't.

"Oh, hey," I exclaimed with sudden glee, "there's my friend." They turned to see Jerome coming towards our booth. "He's second cousin with Leona," I lied, naming one of my straitlaced cousins from my mother's brother's wife's side of the family who lived in Corner Brook. Father was taking in Jerome's long curly hair and bearded face, his army jacket and blue-tinted glasses.

"Jerome," said Jerome, tipping an imaginary hat towards Dad. Then he turned to me, saying "The bus is leaving" in an urgent tone. I snatched up my purse.

"You hold on a minute," said Father, reaching for my arm.

But I stood back with a foolish giggle. "Trying to kidnap me, he is," I remarked jovially to Jerome. "We gotta go, we're missing the bus," I said, my voice sounding squeaky. I hurried after Jerome towards the door.

Then I stopped and looked back. Mother and Father were both standing now, gazing after me with such concern in their faces that it twisted my heart. Dad slashed the air with his hand, beckoning me back to the table. I laughed gaily, doing a little two-step to lighten the moment, backing up against something spongy and smelling of dill pickles. I hadn't heard the door opening behind me. It was my supervisor, his little dewy eyes staring at me through his steamed-up glasses. I giggled, blew Dad a kiss, and bolted outside.

And I couldn't stop giggling, no matter the tiny voice of alarm whimpering within me: *Not good not good not gooood . . .*

DEMYSTIFYING AWAY

MOST DEFINITELY, HOW I LIVED the next two years was *not good*. A steady diet of pot and pills washed down with Southern Comfort and apricot brandy (my fave drink) on the streets of Corner Brook was not good. Leaving my uncle's house and moving in with the coolest chick in town and best buddy Bernie, whose mother thought *I* was the bad influence and booted me out, was not good. Taking up shelter in CN buses parked at night beside the Holiday Inn was not good. Begging spare change, stealing food, thumbing rides, beating about in rusted-out cars, tripping on acid for days and floating down rivers of colours was not good.

But good things lived inside of me. Like the fear of being caught doing bad things by my parents; like their lectures about finishing school and getting a trade and getting a job—these pulsed hard in my heart. So in the midst of all my carousing I managed to pass one of my two night-school subjects, which allowed me to do a secretarial course at the trade school. Despite being the fastest typist in class I failed at being an actual secretary—but it didn't matter. For along with five or six others I was soon in the back of a blue Volkswagen van owned and driven by a lanky, long-haired guy called Dave. With a lobster pot strapped across the roof, we were heading for Toronto. Lotsa work in Toronto, I told my horrified parents, and promised to call every weekend.

Thus far, since leaving the Beaches, it had been a seductive ride: roadways changing at whim, the rush of new faces, good hashish, different jokes, unfolding tales. And the same endless void with zero commitment to thought, family, community, or self. Well—I did *think* about my family. I thought about them a lot, and would often squat in phone booths with stacks of coins, assuring them of how well I was doing and—after I got to Toronto—how neat my job was, working in one of those new self-serve gas stations, making new friends.

In truth, Toronto was becoming a frightening ride. The river ran wide and fast. Our little group of friends became a band of fifteen or twenty, most of us living in two multi-room houses in the same neighbourhood where walk-in closets became prime real estate rentals providing you didn't host too many parties in there or try to sublet half the square footage. When pot and pills gave way to needles, the river started rioting, its whitewater taking some of us into the deep. Our first casualty was Pete, sixteen years old and found talking to a light pole one sad Sunday morning after we'd all been high. Someone had sold him motor oil for hash oil and he'd been too stoned to tell the difference. I stopped by the subway station later, where his uncle worked, to ask after him. The uncle's eyes searched me over—skinny as a fishing pole, tight ratty jeans, long straight hair streaming past sooted eyes—and he shook his head sadly just as I'd done once when looking at a tattered homeless old woman living on the streets. I found a tinge of pride and straightened my shoulders. Tucked my hair back off my face and walked away.

Pride calls louder than common sense. That little shift in consciousness before Pete's uncle—it gained a foothold in the months that followed as needles made bruised and bloodied tracks down the arms of my friends. I watched as their once lovely faces started shrinking inside their growing habit, their eyes becoming shifty with suspicion and paranoia. I stood aside one night after being abruptly toppled from my bed by a pal stripping its sheets and blankets, shoving the mattress aside, searching for the smack he believed I was hoarding. Another smashed his fist against a brick wall from the agony of withdrawal while yet another hid the deformity of a self-mended broken arm inside his coat and another fed his girlfriend's dog acid just to spite her. All meaning, all values became lost as addiction deepened its insidious hold, planting delusions among a once strong band of friends, forcing them into two warring camps that saw gashed heads and faces gaunt from the beast hungrily feeding itself from their insides. Of particular angst was the night a dark-eyed stranger drifted through our door, and, upon leaving a few hours later, accused me of stealing his leather gloves—I probably had, I liked leather gloves—and my drug-fogged mind couldn't remember ever having seen them. But when something in his eyes burned through the fog, I reached atop the shelf in the hallway closet and tossed his gloves at him. The next night he pulled a gun from his inner pocket and shot a girl dead at a party, then shot himself. I wondered if she too had parked his gloves somewhere and couldn't remember.

More frightening was doing a hit one morning and rising from the couch in a rush of energy and then falling into a choir of singing angels. I awakened to a group of friends staring down at me confusedly, shaking me, and then their belly laughs as I smiled back at them, calling them my angels. It was the timelessness of being high that intrigued me; how a minute could morph into hours inside my mind but remain sixty seconds on the clock. And its reversal: how I once sat for seven hours in a parked car waiting for a friend (equally as high) to come back from some errand we'd been sent to do. The friend forgot to return and I forgot I was waiting. And all the while Leonard Cohen was crooning his heart out at Massey Hall, which was why I was sitting in the car in the first place, I later learned—to get a ride to the subway station.

God knows. God knows why, when we were tripping along the beach near the Scarborough Bluffs and the avalanche of mud that rumbled down off the cliffs, pouring into the lake, buried us *only* up to our thighs, breaking *only* one leg. Or why the dirty blotter acid bought off the street didn't poison us, containing just enough rat poison to bring us to our knees with cramps and vomiting and to colour everything in our fucked-up world purple. Or why the train didn't slice us in half as we tried to decipher what the blinking red lights meant, or why—a *dozen* whys. And a *thousand* grateful prayers to the God of praying mothers. For that remains a question I always ask: why some survive and others don't. Why some dip their toes into the water while others strike out further and still others submerge themselves till they drown. Is it the strength of a good mother and a good father residing big within their heart that anchors them more firmly to shore? A priest once said to St. Augustine's mother as she knelt at an altar, weeping for her wayward son, *It cannot be that the son of these tears should perish.*

By the grace of God go I.

It was Dave, the guy who'd driven us all to Toronto in his Volkswagen van, who threw down the hard drugs and braked on that fast track to hell. He, with two others, packed their bags and headed for Alberta. Before leaving, though, Dave took me aside and warned me to stay clean—he'd be sending a ticket as soon as he found a job and a place to stay.

A couple of months later the ticket arrived.

And it was on that train to Alberta that the concept of Away raised its curious head once more. But first a bit of context here. Newfoundlanders are like mushrooms: find one and a dozen more pop up. Two years in Toronto and I'd seldom been caught outside my group of buddies from home—for whenever I had ventured outside the fold my strong outport accent would provoke curious looks and amusement. Even in Newfoundland's larger communities the bayman accent is a thing noted. It's sometimes challenging to decipher, and among the ignorant it's often ridiculed. I'd started to hate friendly strangers, having them stare at me when I spoke, their patronizing smiles . . .

So when I boarded the train for the two-day ride to Alberta, I made myself small. Hardly ever left my seat except to use the washroom. But by the second day, after sleeping curled like the letter C throughout the night, I was forced to walk about just to stretch my cramped legs and aching back. I ventured up into the lookout atop the car (the "cupola," I later learned) to enjoy the scenery, praying to God there'd be no friendly people. But there they were, eight or ten of them. All looking towards me, smiling. Having a chat, they were, about where they were all from.

I made to dart back down, but one of them, a big-gutted American, spoke loudly to me with a Southern drawl that made my own talk sound half-assed normal.

"And *wheaaare're youuuu froooom?*"

"Eh, Newfoundland," I said.

"New*fouuund*lin. Do you get many *taaaurists* in New*fouuund*lin?"

Tourists! Not a word bandied around much on the Beaches, so I thought he'd said *turrs*: a seabird Father would shoot by the dozen and bring home for supper.

"Oh, sure," I said. "We gets lots of *taaaurists*," I said, mimicking him to be polite. "I was just talking to Mom. Dad shot seven yesterday."

I noted the silence following my words. To cover it, I kept blathering. "We loves them, we do. Soaks them in barrels of brine till their skin turns pink and falls right off their bones."

They were all staring at me as though my words were themselves little baby turrs flapping out of my mouth.

"Well, nice meeting ye," I said quickly, and fled back down the steps.

Flustered, and feeling hungry, I headed for the restaurant car, wondering what the hell had just happened up there.

Once I got settled, I ordered a slice of lemon mirage pie.

"Mirage?" asked the server. "You mean meringue?"

Fawk! "Well, if you've got no mirage," I muttered, with a full understanding now of Father's reluctance to ever leave the Beaches.

Which is what got me thinking more about Away. For the first time since leaving the Beaches I felt like the bay girl again. And during my initial weeks in the more sedate city of Calgary,

I continued feeling that way. But perhaps it was because I was among strangers for a time—mostly straight ones, too—that I stumbled into another conscious moment, and the very idea of Away began unravelling itself.

›—›

Dave and his friends were off working in the camps when I disembarked from that never-ending train ride across the prairies. But they had Lisa, an old friend from Corner Brook, greet me, and it was with her that I spent the following month hanging out.

One evening we sat around with a group of her friends, sharing our stories. "I come from Detroit, a real bad place," one woman said. "Me and my mother, we'd be crouching under the window, listening to the gunfire outside. One day, coming home from school, this junkie put a knife to my throat and robbed my pockets. He took my dime, and when he let me go, I fainted." She told other stories about hoodlums setting her school on fire and her mother keeping her home for days because the streets were too dangerous to walk. I couldn't look at her—in fact I could scarcely keep from rolling my eyes at her far-fetched tales.

Later, after everyone had left, I said to Lisa, "She can stretch a yarn, eh?"

Lisa gave me an odd smile. "Remember the other night?"

I did. We'd been sitting with the same bunch and I'd done most of the talking. Telling them how I'd grown up with no electricity or plumbing and went to a one-room school with a coal stove for heat and had a stuffed baby seal on my bed. I went on about Grandmother closing up gashed hands with cobwebs, and how we were always sucking on brown molasses candies laced with kerosene and white candies she made from her vinegar plant that floated like a jellyfish in a thick liquid she kept in a glass jar on the cupboard shelf. And, oh, I really took my time describing the man who went mad and how they rowed him ten miles down the bay and put him ashore with some grub and a tent to fend for himself. I told them too about how Father was stranded on the ice one night, and a white light, like a torch, steadily came towards him and then passed him and kept on going, leaving him staring after it like it was a ghost. And then there was the time the fairies led my austere grandfather into the woods for three days, and he wouldn't say a word about it after he returned, except that the fairies had led him astray. I finished up by recalling how on stormy nights we all slept by the stove in the kitchen out of fear of the house being washed out to sea by a rogue wave. Plus I told a pile of little things, like my first banana, my first ice cream, my first TV show, and how I thought Mr. Dressup's Casey was an actual little boy and how my jaw dropped when the reception cleared one day and I saw he was a hand in a sock.

"Well? What's that smile for?" I asked Lisa.

She shrugged and turned her pale blue eyes towards the door where the woman from Detroit had just left. "She didn't believe your stories either. Neither did the others."

That shut me up. Till I accidentally found myself squirming at a semi-formal dinner table in Edmonton with a bunch of yuppie types, feeling awkward in jeans next to their funky finery and posh English. The conversation was stilted and boring and I hid in the shadow of a big Italian fellow called Pete sitting next to me.

During a lull in the talk I half whispered to him, "What was it like as a kid where you grew up?"

Oh, man. His face lit up and his brown eyes danced as he told his stories. The table jiggled with laughter as he told us about his big Italian family and their fighting and dancing, their old-time remedies of garlic and herbs for curses and colds, and the Lucifer's horn his grandfather wore around his neck to ward off curses. Never *ever* stick a knife in a loaf of bread for it'll bring you bad luck, he was told. Owls and spirits and dancing spiders—there was no end. Everyone at the table leaned in, keen to tell their own stories about grandmothers and aunts and superstitions true as dirt. And that's when Mother's words caught up with me: "Home is Away when you're somewhere else."

Yes, yes, it is. But whether here or there, Away is simply a landscape broken down into groupings of homes. We were all youngsters once, racing around, shaped by stories and the grace of God. And so I learned to ask that question whenever I found myself feeling squirmy in awkward social situations: *What was it like as a kid where you grew up?* Whether it was Miss Proudy Two Shoes or some hick from the backwoods, people responded. Their eyes would warm and their tongues would loosen and we'd sit together spinning and embellishing our yarns of home, proud of our tribal roots whose colours we each wore through our skin tones, accents, beliefs, and humour.

Without noting it at the time, a light was slowly dawning within me about the power of story. Our tales do more than dismantle social standings and generate camaraderie and entertainment. They create a space for one's past, touching its flesh through memory and shedding a light that illuminates ourselves to ourselves and to others. Without those stories we're only half ourselves; without them that other half lurks inside like a shadow yearning for the sun.

><—▷

One last lesson came to me during that year in western Canada. The paradox of pain. I got pregnant. I was nineteen.

Before venturing further with that thought, meet Dave again, the long-hair who'd driven us from Newfoundland and later sent me the ticket to Alberta. Dave was a rebel. He'd been only nine when he lost his father to a work accident and had fought back ever since—against his sisters, his brother, his mother, anyone moving in too close. My first sight of him was on that green field of hippies in Corner Brook. He wasn't a cool dude with tie-dye shirts and bell bottoms. He didn't fit anywhere; everyone fitted around him. He wore grimy jeans and heavy boots that easily kicked down his motorcycle stand and trampled the grass of any green he trod. His hair was brown and hung straight down his back and his eyes were more fiercely blue than Father's. The only time I ever saw him off that green was, to my amazement, when he poked his long-haired, wind-tousled head inside my math class at night school. He was wearing a grungy jean jacket with a sheepskin lining sewn into it. I was sitting at the front, first row by the door. He sat behind me. Nudged my back and borrowed a pencil. A minute before the class ended he was up and gone. I twisted around: he'd laid my pencil across a sheet of paper doodled to death with nothings, and not a number to be seen. Neither was Dave after that first class—at least, not in the classroom.

Despite having shared a communal house with him for a year or two in Toronto, I knew practically as little about Dave when I met up with him again in Calgary as I did in that math class. Apparently he'd had the hots for me all during that Toronto time but was too much of a dude to ever let on. Which is why he sent me the ticket. Of course, he never fessed up to that. Not even when he received the surprising and joyful news, a few months after our reuniting, of his pending fatherhood.

There's much to say about my being a mother, a wife. Too much for the bones of this story. But I will say what *becoming* a mother meant to me: It meant no more hard drugs. Ever. It meant no more drinking wine or smoking pot or hashish till my baby was born. It meant draping my rounded body in a flowing blue hand-made dress during my eighth month of pregnancy and getting married so that my baby would be born into "our" name (norm of the times). And it meant life could never be the same again. Ever. For I discovered pain—the pain of giving birth, and, when that squalling little red face was laid in my arms, the pain of loving too hard. And for the first time I understood my mother: the suffering she had endured from the loss of her three babies. And, tragically, would have to endure once more.

FORTITUDE

BANKRUPTCY AND BUSTED WIPERS

IT WAS 1978, SIX YEARS since I'd left the Beaches with my gold luggage set. I'd just driven from St. John's with everything we owned loaded into the back of our truck. Davey, nearly three years old, sat strapped in his car seat beside me, clawing to get out. Dave had left St. John's the day before by helicopter, hired from the college where he'd just graduated as a forestry technician, and then flown into the bush near Hampden. My father had since made good on his word to buy a store in Hampden and set up a mobile home nearby, so I'd visit with them during the three weeks Dave would be in the bush. Then I'd drive to Corner Brook and find us an apartment.

That was the plan.

I am not heroic. If to regret is to offend destiny, I humbly bend my knee in weakness before the masters of fate. Because if I could change the future in order to eliminate pain, knowing I'd also be eliminating gifts of grace, strength, courage, and glimpses of God, I would do so. If I could gamble on the outcomes of a different pathway by choosing one day to go back and relive, thereby changing everything that happened after and forsaking everything I am today, I would choose that moment when I braked in front of my father's house with Davey strapped in the seat beside me. I would turn that truck around and drive straight to Corner Brook and find an apartment and offer myself up to a different fate.

But fate wasn't whispered by the October winds that day as I got out of the truck and stood before the swaying spruce saplings in the front yard. It wasn't written on the tableau of my parents' trailer, renovated now into a four-bedroom house and aproned by a trimmed lawn and a two-car garage. Or in the warmth of my mother's eyes as she scooped Davey up, winging him against her bosom. Or in the merriment of my brother Ford's glistening brown eyes as he strolled from the garage, eighteen now, tall and golden-haired, punching me too hard in the arm and guffawing as I punched him back, both of us too shy for hugs.

Perhaps if fate were so easily read none of us would get out of bed in the morning. Or perhaps we'd be so busy switching pathways that a life could never really be lived. Perhaps the ultimate irony is that, no matter how many pathways we take, they're all detours that merge further down on the road first taken. If that is so, and fate is merely the handrail we hold on to as we skid towards a destiny we don't control, then that thought brings me comfort on sleepless nights.

Glenn came out of the garage behind Ford. Fifteen now, he was a head shorter than Ford and still pudgy with baby fat and cherubic cheeks. Like Father he was blond, his eyes the same strong blue and lit with mischief. He was munching on a fistful of cookies and gave an open-mouthed grin to show off his crumb-covered teeth. Ford and I jumped on him but I pulled away when Tommy came running from the house. He was twelve, skinny, bony, large-eyed, and with big front teeth. He was blond too, his hair curly and longish; he looked like Ford, who looked like Dad. As I squeezed him mercilessly against me, he dug his bony fingers into my armpits, trying to tickle me. I looked again at Glenn, who looked like Wanda, who'd since moved to Toronto with her husband and their baby girl whose second name was my own.

"We'll phone her after supper when the rates drop," said Mother, pouring us tea after we'd settled at the kitchen table. Karen sauntered from her room just then—ten years old, with dark hair and sultry dark eyes filled with suspicion as she sized me up. She'd been so young when I left that I wasn't sure if she included me in her picture of who her family was. "I don't babysit," she muttered, yet took Davey's hand and led him outside for a walk. When a runt of a short-haired dog with black spots peered through the door she'd left open, Mother shooed it out. "Jack," she said. "Tommy's dog."

While she put out some food for him, I glanced around the trailer, as everyone still seemed to call it. It was pretty, with creamy lace curtains and a brown carpet, the sofa and chairs cushioned in coral and golds and browns.

"I love it, Mom, it's gorgeous."

"All needs to be painted," she said, closing the door behind Jack. She was forty-two and her face was untouched. I saw myself in the dark of her hair and eyes and in the curl of her bottom lip as she offered a smile. It was her eyes that had changed. They were no longer haunted with sadness. As she looked at me, they stirred with anger.

"What's wrong?" I asked.

She let out a big sigh. "Oh my, Donna."

"Mom!"

"I never told you any of this. Your father didn't want you to know."

"Know what?"

She rubbed the back of her neck. "We lost the store. We had to give it up."

"Nooo!"

She gave a wearied nod. It took her the better part of an hour to fill me in. They'd bought the store with Dad's friend Lonzo and his wife Marie. During the past two years they'd been losing money, mostly because certain people weren't paying their bills. Then came a notable decrease in profits, with neither Dad nor Lonzo talking to the other about it. "Your father thought it was Lonzo siphoning money from the till and taking cigarettes and alcohol from the shelves. He didn't know how to ask him. Turns out Lonzo was thinking the same thing about your father."

She and Marie worked as many hours in the store as Dad and Lonzo did, and they too had been silenced by loyalty. They all loved each other too much to accuse.

Mother tightened her fingers around her teacup with a deprecating shrug. "Turned out, neither one of us took a penny. But by the time we got the truth it was too late."

"Who did it?"

"Ralphie Langford lives right behind the store. He come over one day and told us there were six young fellows breaking in through a basement window and lugging out stuff. *I seen six of them going in*, he told your father, *and the last two was mine*. They'd been doing it for the past two years. Not so much at first, and then—" Mother shrugged again. "You knows how it goes, you gets greedier and greedier. Your father took it hard. He give them young fellows everything. Brought in a pool table for them—something to do in the evenings. Played cards with them, sold them cigarettes on the sly. Then they steal from him. Broke his heart, they did."

"What did he do?"

"He and Lonzo hid in the store one night and caught them. Shamed, they were. Couldn't look at your father. Still, none of them paid the twenty dollars the judge ordered them to pay the store."

"Twenty dollars!"

She nodded, and then, in an undertone of scorn, "They were underaged. That's all they had to pay. But that's not all. We got a bill from taxation for ten thousand dollars. They were bigger thieves than the boys. Wouldn't let us claim our truck for expenses. That's what we bought the truck *for*—loading up and delivering groceries and driving back and forth to Deer Lake for supplies. And they wouldn't let us claim our losses, either. All of that now—the thieving and the taxes and them not paying their bills—took us down. And not just one tax bill for the whole store. We got one and Lonzo and Marie got one. Ten thousand dollars each. Twenty thousand dollars they said we owed."

"Mom, ye should get a lawyer."

"We did. The lawyer told us it would cost as much agin in accounting fees. Seven years we'd have to go back. Still for all, we kept everything, every receipt. Never stole a cent from that store, we didn't."

"And now your jobs are gone too."

She made a disparaging sound. "Wish I'd never gone at it. Too small of a place to own a store. Seeing every day them that owes you for the fridge and stove in their houses."

"You regret buying the store?"

"My, Donna, it's all the same. You regret something when it don't work, you regret it more if you never tried." She gave a piteous look towards the bottom end of the table where Father always sat. "I feels more for him. He don't get over things."

"Hard thing, losing your livelihood."

"Was more than that your father lost. You know what he's like now—face down a bear, he would. But runs from the smallest thing. Took the good from him, the boys stealing from him like that."

She glanced out the window as a car pulled up and Ford bent down towards the driver's side, chatting with whoever was behind the wheel.

"Annie Walsh," said Mother. "Seventy-six dollars. That's how much stuff she charged the last week we were in business. Said she'd be back with her family allowance cheque that Friday. First time I've seen her since."

"Seventy-six dollars," I bellowed at Ford a few minutes later when he came inside. "Next time you sees her, ask for the seventy-six dollars she owes Mom."

"Yes, I knows now," said Mother, giving me a flick behind the head. "She just opened her own store; she'll find out soon enough. Go mind your own business," she said to Ford, who was looking from me to Mother, trying to figure the half of what had just been said.

There were other things I learned sitting there, Mom and Ford taking turns talking. Dad had been about to get hired on cutting wood when something else was put on his plate: a provincial housing program had approved an application from Johnny Bagnell, a good friend of Dad's, to build himself a low-mortgage house. Trouble was, Johnny couldn't get anyone to build it because before the contractor could pay them he needed at least five thousand dollars upfront to buy the supplies and get a certain amount of work done.

Father didn't want to do it. It was October and soon the weather would be too wet and cold to be pouring concrete for footings and basement walls. Plus, it would take everything he and Mom had banked and more. Mother didn't like it either, investing their last penny and with no store to fall back on for food. But Johnny was near destitute, sick and weak, with seven kids to feed, and his house was rotting to the ground. So against Mother's wishes Father had put practically all their money towards cement, rebar, plywood, and other materials needed to do the job. Ford, who'd just graduated high school, was working alongside him; he'd hired another carpenter and Johnny's two eldest boys as well. Now Dad was working twelve hours a day trying to get the basement walls poured before the bad weather set in.

That day I came home was a Sunday. I hadn't seen much of Father the past few years, and when I did it was during some holiday with a crowd around and I'd be gone again in a day or two. And each time I did see him his eyes would be guarded when he looked at me, as though, like Karen, he no longer knew who I was.

But that evening when he came through the door it was I who was staring at Father, scarcely recognizing him. My heart sank. His face was a ghastly grey, his eyebrows and eyelashes coated with cement dust, his hair stiff with it. His shoulders were stooped and he was holding up his hands: rough, dirtied, his fingers chapped along their joints from working the cement without gloves.

"What's you home, lovie?" he said to me by way of greeting, then shook his head at Mother who was tut-tutting at the state of his clothes.

"Not fit," she said, "working on a Sunday, and by yourself."

"Doing some clean-up is all. I got it done now, I got it done. All ready for the mixer tomorrow. A mixer," he repeated, looking at Ford. "We needs a cement mixer. Too slow doing it by hand and there's a gawd-damn storm coming. Might be the only chance we got to get it done for a week."

"Then wait for a week," Mother urged.

"Money," he said. "We needs the money. I got none left. We gets the basement poured this week, we'll get our money back by next." He looked at me and grinned, his teeth and gums gleaming, the only part of his face not coated in concrete dust. "You take care of things here tomorrow and your mother will drive to Corner Brook with me."

"I can't go tomorrow; I've got bread to bake and the washing—"

"Donna's home. She can do that."

"Donna can go to Corner Brook with you."

"No, no, I wants you," Father persisted, following her down the hall.

I half listened to their arguing, shaking my head over Father's resistance to driving in with me. He was still judging me wild, still thinking of the last time I'd come home for a visit and had slipped Ford a joint so that he could be cool in the eyes of his friends. Word had shot around Hampden like the rapid fire of a loaded machine gun: *Nerk's daughter Donna got drugs, Nerk's daughter Donna got drugs.* The visit before that hadn't helped either: we'd all been sitting in the bar when Mom's youngest brother, visiting from Jackson's Arm, kept winking at me and flashing his yellow package of Vogue rolling papers as though we were members of a secret drug cult and the papers were its emblem. Which is exactly what Father thought when he caught sight of Uncle Gene winking away. His face took on the same ferocious look it had when he'd caught me mooching off from school that time of the pulled tooth, when he'd caught me drunk with Wanda on another visit home, when he'd been searching for a smoke and found three joints in my cigarette pack, and a whole lot of other *whens* that had taken place over the years.

"Ahh, go by yourself then," I could hear Mother saying.

"Gawd-dammit, you knows I can't talk to them fellows."

"*Ha ha*, ask him about the butt plane, Sis," Ford bawled out from the living room.

"Took them an hour at Canadian Tire to figure what he was asking for," Glenn bellowed.

"Ye thinks now ye're funny," Father bawled back.

"Butt plane," scoffed Mother. "That's something you sits on, isn't it? Your butt."

"Gawd-dammit, I was showing them the butt of me hand. If I wanted an ass plane I would've dropped me pants."

"Ohh, now you're making sense," I yelled, stomping down the hall and joining them in the bathroom. "I'm going with you," I added firmly. "Don't worry, I'll leave my pound of black Afghani under my bed, all right?"

"Right," Father muttered, his head over the sink, splashing water on his face. "You thinks now I thinks you're joking? Don't trust a bone in your body."

"It's my tongue you needs, not my bones. Here, move aside, Mom, I pours his bath before he turns to concrete."

He didn't like it. Moped about all evening and was still moping when he came home from work the following afternoon, readying to go. He jabbed a finger at me as we went out the door. "Now, we drives straight there and straight back. No stopping to visit friends or the gawd-damn stores or restaurants."

"What? No robbing a casino?"

He made a face, hauling open the truck door. "You thinks now I thinks you're joking?"

We were quiet on the drive. It was the first time since the tooth-pulling that I was alone with him. And sitting there in the silence of the cab, away from the crowded kitchen with Mother and Davey and the boys buffering us, I felt ridiculously shy. I sat as close to the door as I could, looking out the side window and sneaking glances at him. Fished out of the family corpus he looked minuscule and yet felt as immense as God. And I, without the structure of family shoring me up, felt as vulnerable as Job before the wrath of the Almighty.

Within ten minutes of bumping along the dirt road to the highway, Father shoved in his homemade Hank Williams tape. His mood lightened a little and soon we were both tapping our fingers to *Jambalaya and a crawfish pie and fillet gumbo* . . .

It was on the return trip, around five o'clock in the evening, when the winds struck. Till then, all had been good—I'd done all the talking to the clerks; Dad had kept himself in the truck; the cement mixer was now in the back. And the air had been quiet, the darkening trees speeding past us a relief against the dreary greyness of late fall. We had another forty-five minutes to go before reaching home and Dad was flipping over the tape when he shouted, "We're in for it, we're in for it!"

Within seconds we were caught in a maelstrom of swirling easterly winds and snow that jarred the truck. Dad hunched over the steering wheel, cursing. *Gawd-damn the like-a-that, gawd-damn the like-a-that.*

Our speed was reduced to a crawl, vision swiped out by slob snow smothering the windshield. The wipers creaked and scrubbed against the glass, scarcely scraping an opening through the thickening paste. But that wasn't Father's concern; it was the bad weather starting and he with the cement mixer rented for the next three days—the longest he could afford—and finishing the job before having to return it.

"It'll probably blow over," I said.

"Long as I gets that cement poured, then I don't give a good gawd-damn if she blows ten gales."

Eventually we turned off the highway onto Hampden Road. Another thirteen miles to go. When a pair of headlights flashed before us, Dad touched the brakes and the truck swerved on the muddied road, nearly fishtailing over an embankment. He cursed and kept going. Clinging nervously to the door handle, I leaned forward, straining to see more than two feet ahead through the white rain slamming against us. Dad switched on the high beams then switched them off again. He was hunched so far forward his nose was an inch from the windshield. Suddenly the wipers stopped. Completely stopped. We stared at the blanketed windshield, the headlights dulling.

"Well, the dancing Jeezes," roared Father. "Roll down your window, put down your window!" he shouted at me, pumping the brakes. "Where's the road, where's the edge of the road?"

Screwing down the window, I shoved my head out and was instantly slobbered by cold wind and wet snow.

"How far, how far," Dad yelled as I tried to make out the edge.

"Over a bit—"

"Feet! Feet, lovie! How many feet?"

"That's it! STOP!"

He braked to a stop and I cranked my window back up, scraping wet snow from my face and eyes. I shivered down into my coat as Dad opened the truck door and ducked outside, every nut and bolt in the truck jarring when he slammed the door behind him. His knuckles smudged little tracks in the snow-covered windshield as he fiddled with the wipers and then he was back inside, a clump of snow matting his head and shoulders. He hauled his door shut and flicked on the wipers—flicking them on and off, nothing. "Gawd-damn the like-a-that, gawd-damn the like-a-that. I heard that whinny, I heard it yesterday, I should've checked it, I should've gawd-damned checked it."

"What're we going to do?"

He must've heard panic in my voice, for he looked at me and said, "Don't you worry, now. We'll see this out." He bent down and started unlacing his workboots, sputtering about that whine and how he should have fixed it. Then with a loud grunt, and both laces dangling from his hands, he shoved out through the door again. Through peepholes scraped by his knuckles I watched as he tied one end of each lace to the tip of each wiper. Then he was pounding my side window.

"Catch hold of it," he cried impatiently as I rolled down the window, staring blankly at the end of the boot string he was dangling in my face. After drawing it inside I cranked up the window again as he hurried to his side and got back in, jarred down his window, and fed the second lace through. Then he yanked on it—hard. The wipers sprang upright, clearing half an arc of visibility through the windshield.

He closed his door and yelled, "Pull!"

Fully comprehending now, I rolled my window partway down and yanked the lace he'd given me. My hand slipped off the wet string.

"Knot it!" he yelled.

"Hey?"

"Knots, lovie, tie knots in the gawd-damn lace." He reached over, plucked the lace out of my hand and knotted the end, then doubled it and tripled it and tossed it back. "Now, pull!" he ordered again, edging the truck back onto the road as I clutched the string above the knots and pulled. The wipers crept across the glass. He yanked them back; my arms shot up and I yanked them back down. On and on we went in this fashion, each time clearing little bits of the windshield for Father to steer by.

"Harder, harder," he shouted as the snow and wind butted in through the side window, soaking my face and trickling cold down my neck. I heaved harder, my butt lifting off the seat, my wrist scraping across the window edge each time I strained on the lace, bringing the wipers back, bringing them back, bringing them back. We inched forward, bit by bit. I was in awe of Father, perched as he was at the edge of his seat, peering through those little openings, gripping the wheel with one hand and yanking on the lace with the other. "Pull!" he ordered. "Pull!" And I pulled and pulled, gripping the soggy lace with both hands, water squeezing between my fingers.

I muttered a curse as the truck hit a rut and my wrist shredded across the edge of the window and Father shouted, "Pull, pull, pull!" *I AM bloody pulling!* I wanted to yell back. Was it a mere two hours ago I'd been thinking of this man as *God*? We hit another bump and I yelled *Gawd-dammit, gawd-dammit,* whipping my sore wrist to my mouth, sucking on it, when suddenly I noticed Father's silence. He was staring at me, astonished. I realized then that, for all the crooked deeds I'd done, he'd never heard me swear before.

The dark wall of trees opened to my right, revealing the long black blob of Rushy Pond. "Another two miles," he said. "Almost home." The soggy mass of knotted lace slipped more and more from my hands, my fingers too numb to curl and too numb to straighten. As we crept past the Hampden garbage dump on our left—a mile and a half to go—the snow turned to rain. When we passed the sawmill I fell back, unable to lean, unable to heave, unable to lift an arm, unable to uncurl my fingers from around the lace.

Father let go of his own lace, rolled his window all the way down, and half stood, leaning his head out the side window, his right leg straight and pressed to the gas. With the wind skimming back his soaked hair, his eyes squinted against the driving rain until the porch light burned through the dark.

Mother gasped in fright as we staggered through the door, hair pasted wet to our scalps, clothes soaked to our skin, faces numb, lips a thin line of blue.

≫—➤

Later, after we'd washed and changed and were sitting at the table wolfing back bowls of hot turkey neck soup, Father recounted what had happened in full. Mom and the boys hung on his every word.

"I should've known," Father kept interrupting himself to say. "Was only yesterday I heard a whinny in the dash, was only yesterday."

"Ahh, you never takes time for nothing," Mother chided him, reaching over and smoothing a strand of hair behind my ears. "Could've been stuck on the road all night or had an accident."

"But we never did, did we, doll," said Father, looking at me. He rested a forearm against the white of Mother's tablecloth, his wrist reddened and chafed rawer than mine. Despite the burn I'd kept my own sleeves down so that Mother wouldn't fuss. I deliberately pushed them up a bit and as I laid my forearms on the table next to his, I was reminded of the time I'd straightened his boots next to mine to make up, somehow, for our fight over the bike. I'd been comforted by that gesture, just as I was comforted now by the commonality of our shredded wrists as we laid them side by side on the table. Like a pair of relinquished pistols.

"Swear to gawd, Mom," I said to her later, turning off the lights and following her down the hall to our rooms, "I cursed in the truck and it was the first time Dad ever paid attention to something I said."

"That's your father now. Start cursing like him and he thinks you're finally thinking straight."

BETRAYAL, IGNORANCE, AND PAYBACKS

THE SUN SHONE THE NEXT MORNING and for the next two mornings straight. Father managed to get the basement poured, working twelve to fifteen hours a day. When he came home the third evening the joints of his fingers were so chapped they were raw; he couldn't uncurl them for all the stiffness and pain. Mother argued with him for not wearing work mitts and he argued back that he'd used up his last pair. After he showered he lay flat on his back on their bed and rested his hands on his pillow, his palms facing up. The flesh had opened, chapped nearly to the bone on each joint of each finger. He grimaced as I dabbed his wounds with cream to soften them.

"Inspector be out tomorrow," he said. "Get some money back, take a day. Only needs a day, that'll heal up."

He was gone before daylight the next morning. Phase one was completed by noon. At three the inspector arrived in his white hard hat and creased pants and gloved hands; he examined Father's work to date and nodded his approval. And gave Father permission to continue into phase two: getting the basement covered and wired and laying piping for the plumbing. Then he'd be back for a further inspection and, providing everything was good, he'd issue a cheque.

Father stared at him, stupefied. "No, sir," he said. "First I gets paid for phase one, and *then* I starts phase two."

The inspector shook his head. "This is all part of phase one," he said. "It's in your contract."

"No. Phase one was clearing the land, putting in footings, and pouring walls. *Then* we starts phase two and covers it in."

"I'm sorry, sir. That's not our understanding."

Father stood there, the inspector's words sinking in. Overcoming all shyness about his way of talking, he pulled off his hard hat, stepped up to the inspector, and started yelling. "Ye gawd-damn dummies, you don't think I knows what I heard? This is phase *one*. Covering and electrical is phase *two*. That's what we agreed on and that's what we shook on!" As he yelled Father kept jabbing the hammer he was holding at the inspector—once even jabbing him directly in the chest.

All this Ford told us when he came home that day, his face red with excitement.

Father stomped in a few minutes later, his face as red as Ford's, not from excitement but from the flames raging within him. Mother and I fit together the pieces from them both: that no money would be coming just now; that another few thousand was needed to complete phase one; that Father had been told this was phase two back when the deal was struck.

Father fired his cap to the floor and fisted the table as he sat, demanding of Mother, of me, and of God *why* they'd think him so stupid as to sign something that would put them all in the poorhouse?

Mother sat at the table beside him, staring searchingly into his eyes. "You're sure now that's what you signed?"

"I knows what I heard, gawd-dammit. I thought they'd put the same thing on paper as what they were telling me."

"You should always read . . ." Mother began.

Father's rage looked to be veering into a frustration that was no longer as sure of itself.

That's when I pulled out a chair and sat down. "I have the money. Let's go to the bank and get started."

They both fell silent, gazing at me. Father shook his head, looking rueful. "Doll, you can't do that without talking to Dave."

I shrugged. "He won't be home for another two weeks. You'll be paid by then. And it'll be a bigger cheque."

Father gave Mother a hesitant look.

"Done," I said. "Come on. Deer Lake."

I got my bank book from the bedroom, feeling entirely comfortable with emptying out our account. Dave was never particular about where he laid his head. He was as content in a field of landmines as he was in a field of clover, providing there was enough space for his elbows at the supper table, decent beer to be had, and good yarns to be told. And the tellers themselves wearing the scars of their escapades. He'd be fine with knuckling through this unfair situation. Besides, by the time he returned from the bush I'd have our money back and would probably be in Corner Brook with an apartment rented.

I drove to Deer Lake with Father and withdrew the money, bought a mess of groceries, and filled the back of the truck with plywood and two-by-fours and all else and sundry Father needed to complete phase one, which was really phase two, as Father kept reiterating at every turn.

For the next two weeks the house buzzed with comings and goings: Dad, Ford, the carpenter, and the two brothers who made up the rest of the crew. Because there was no money to pay anyone just yet, Father felt it fair to bring the brothers home and feed them lunch. Besides, they were a slack duo and this way they'd be back to work on time.

Mother and I cooked and baked and cleaned and washed clothes and, with the dryer so small, hung out most of them on the line. Meanwhile the prospect of a hefty payment coming kept Father's temper in check each time some little thing went wrong or the wind and rain threatened to slow him down further.

Finally the work was done. Phase one. Which by now we all knew well and good was *phase two, gawd-dammit*.

The inspector came. He surveyed the work; he gave his nod for a job well done. Father threw down the hammer he was clenching in his work-chapped hands.

"Should have your cheque in three days," said the inspector. Then he drove off, never knowing how close he'd come to getting his head caved in.

❧——▷

Four, five days later, the cheque hadn't arrived. Six days. Mother sat by the phone, drawing her finger down a column of numbers in the phone book. Then she lifted the receiver and called the housing corporation. At length she nodded, offered a quick smile, and hung up. The cheque had been mailed the same day the inspector was there, she'd been told. Should've had it by now.

We waited another couple of days. The cupboards were being emptied. We were down to molassey bread and tea, and Father started cursing. He was up at dawn, sitting in his truck by the post office door each morning, waiting for it to open. He came home still cursing. Fired his hat on the floor, flung more bills in the sink, and sat hunched at the table, glowering through the window. The two brothers had vanished—gone to Toronto, we heard. We wondered where they'd gotten the money given how they were waiting to be paid, same as Father.

Mother called again. And again. Then, one last time. "It's been two weeks now," she told them, "since the cheque's been in the mail. Something's not right." She waited in silence for a few minutes, tapping the phone with her finger. Dad and Ford sat at the table, eyes fixed on her. The only sound was Davey zooming his Dinky cars across the kitchen floor. Mother was suddenly nodding. She became still.

"Cashed by who?" she asked. "We haven't cashed no cheque. When was it cashed?"

We all stared at her as she stood with the phone to her ear, the colour draining from her face. She put down the receiver and turned slowly to Father. The housing corporation had a policy whereby it wrote the cheque out to its client, not the contractor. The client was to pay the contractor. The client cashed the cheque over a week ago. The client couldn't write so he marked an X there, and his two sons signed beside his name.

We sat in a stunned silence. It was a silence where everything happened. Where loyalty was betrayed, where honour and brotherly love burned to ashes. We sat in a silence where the heart ached to cry for the one most wounded. For Father sitting at the table, his expression frozen as the meaning of Mother's words worked their way through him. He looked towards the window, turning his face from us. Ford saw. Ford was sitting at the side of the table near the window Father was looking through and now the look on Father's face was mirrored on his own. Father rose, snatched his cap off the floor beside his chair, and bolted out the door. Ford swiped the wet from his eyes and bolted after him. Mother ran across the room and stood in the doorway looking out, her mouth opened to call them back but no sound came, her tongue caught in the contradiction between fearing for their well-being and applauding the rightness of whatever act they would choose to take.

I was left holding the hammer. I seized the phone and called the housing corporation back. I told them what had happened. "How do you want us to deal with this?" I asked politely.

There was nothing they could do, they told me; the problem wasn't theirs. I asked again. "How do you want us to deal with this? How can we help you get our money back?" They could do nothing, they repeated; the cheque was cashed, it was no longer their concern. "But it was your doing, you paid the wrong people, how do you want us to deal with this, how can we help you get our money back?" I demanded again and again and they put me on hold, they kept me waiting and they kept me waiting, and I hung up and I called back, demanding, "How can we help you deal with this?" I asked to speak to their manager and then the manager's manager and they informed me there were no more managers and I informed them of their stupidity in handing over money to a client without knowing who the client is, without considering how poverty feeds ignorance because hunger becomes its own justification for stealing and I hammered and hammered and they put me on hold and I hung up and called back again and they wouldn't answer the phone.

It was Father who told us how to fix it. He'd been gone for an hour and came home with whisky on his breath, Ford trailing behind him. Ford sat and Dad paced the floor. His friend had been fooled by his two sons. They'd coaxed him to go with them to Deer Lake and cash the cheque. They were tired of working for nothing, they told their father. The money was theirs, they told him. They were owed it for the work they'd done. "Nerk got his own cheque," they'd said, and he believed them. And now they were gone, took the money and a train to Toronto. "Gawd-damn little bastards," said Father. But there was no anger in his face as he spoke, only pity for the man who'd allowed his sons to lead him astray. Mother was not so easily turned. "Not like they had a gun to his head," she said with scorn.

Father shook his head and sat down heavily at the table. "Too late, too late for that, lovie." He wiped at his brow, an unbearable look of fatigue on his face. "I'll go to the bank," he said without courage. "I'll get a loan and finish it. We got too much invested to stop now. Not like there's more work waiting." He looked at me. "Got to get your money, back, doll. Dave's back in a couple days?"

"He's being helicoptered out," I said. "Listen, don't worry about us. I'm in no rush. Dave won't be either. We're all fine."

He nodded, then got up. "Thanks, doll." He clasped a thickly calloused hand on my shoulder and strolled down the hall singing in a feigned heartened tone, *Down by the river.*

The next morning I watched as Mother went out the door behind Father, her Here's My Heart perfume wafting back at me. They were going to the bank in Deer Lake to ask for a loan. I watched through the kitchen window as Davey ran out through the gate, Jack the dog barking alongside him. Mother hugged Davey, sent him back inside the garden, and shooed Jack in with him. As I watched them drive off I noted Ford and Glenn standing at the end of the driveway, blond heads bent towards each other, nodding studiously at some plan they were hatching. They dodged off down the road towards Hampden.

I lingered at the window, watching Davey trot with Jack across the yard and through the bushes growing wild at the far side. Most freedom he'd ever had. Spent the last two years of his life on the fifth floor of an apartment building in St. John's.

I sat in Dad's chair at the table. I needed to pack my bags, Davey's toys; I needed to get ready for our pending move to Corner Brook after Dave returned in the morning. I looked around the trailer and its big comfy couch imprinted with Father's shape from his evening naps, his feet resting in Mother's lap as she knitted, his grunts when she poked him for snoring. And the shag carpet all battened down from Ford and Glenn sprawling across it, playing cribbage in the evenings, arguing and cheating, Dad or me taking on the winner. And Tommy poking at us with his bony fingers, trying to get a laugh and getting swatted and yelled at instead, and Karen threatening to murder us all in our sleep if we didn't shut up so that she could hear the TV. Glancing back out the window, I realized I was feeling a camaraderie within my family that I'd not felt before. Despite my added years, during each of my earlier visits home I'd slipped into the role of who I'd been before I ever left. This time around, though, it was different. I felt a sense of importance; I was a cog in the wheel for once and not the baggage it carried. Another light bloomed: the paradox of having to break away from the whole in order to find one's proper fit back inside of it.

The dull morning light had given way to full afternoon brightness when I heard Father's truck coming up the driveway. They came into the house, shivering from the easterly wind blowing a gale outside. Mother looked worried; Father, too. The bank had agreed to their loan, I quickly learned, but not as much as they'd hoped. And it would take a couple more days for the transaction to be completed.

Father kicked off his boots, walked over to the couch, and threw himself down onto the cushions. Mother took off her coat and scarf and went to the sink, fidgeting with the cup towel. I had a small stew simmering in the pot, using the last of our meat and vegetables. I hadn't packed. Dave would arrive with a cheque in the morning. I wanted to offer that relief but it wasn't the moment; to do it then would've nicked their pride too much.

Father got off the couch and walked hard down the hall. Mother kept opening and closing the fridge door. Then Ford strolled in, Glenn behind him, the two of them noisily stomping their feet and yelling, "Anybody home? Anybody home? Where the hell is everybody?"

"What's ye gone foolish?" Father bawled out, marching back up the hall. Ford tottered into the kitchen, Glenn behind him, both of them grinning and loaded down with stuffed brown paper bags and two six-packs of beer. They put down the beer and ripped open the bags; a frozen chicken, a package of pork chops, and some cans of food rolled across the table. Then they ripped open a bag of vegetables and opened their coats, pulling out a carton of Rothman's cigarettes and tossing a bag of candy to Davey who was climbing atop a chair demanding cookies. Pulling a receipt from his coat pocket, Ford dangled it before Mother's eyes. "Eighty-six dollars," he announced. "From Annie Walsh's store. Told her we were buying 'on credit.'" He grinned. "And I figured the extra ten makes up for the interest."

Mother and Father stared at the two of them, then Father busted out laughing. "Well, gawd-damn the likes of ye. Thieves, thieves, I raised a bunch of gawd-damn thieves. Gimme one of them gawd-damn beers. I done something right after all."

"Yes, give me one too," said Mother. Then we all popped a beer each and Mother and I did a tap dance in the kitchen and Father sank back on the sofa, still laughing, and Glennie drank his first beer in front of Mom and Dad.

When Davey was tucked in for the night, and Tommy and Karen had gone off, bickering, to their rooms, and Glenn had snuck over to the neighbour's house to play poker, Mom and Dad and Ford and I talked over the day's events and the progress of the work on the house to date. We cursed the two brothers. Then we ended off the evening talking about Dave's arrival the following morning. Perhaps a fishing trip would be in order, an overnighter at the cabin.

After all hands had gone to bed I lingered on, sipping hot milk and piecing together a jigsaw puzzle Tommy had spread out on the coffee table. Father creaked open his door and came down the hall. He was hesitant as he sat on the sofa, his elbows on his knees, his hands dangling emptily between them. I looked up. His face was shadowed, resembling that tired old man waiting down the road for him.

"Gone too far in the hole building that house," he said, his voice more constrained than a river beneath a sudden freeze. "Got me hove back three years. Your mother was right—should never have took it on."

"We'll make it through, Dad. God, we haven't gone hungry yet."

"Close, by the Jeezes, close. What do you think of staying on for the winter? You and Dave. Don't think we can make it by ourselves."

"I was going to stay anyway. Talking to Dave about it soon as he gets home. He'll say yes, I knows he will. He likes it here."

Father nodded and got up. Then he went off down the hall, singing *Down by the river*, his voice running free again. I started to cry.

BEFORE AND AFTER

SINCE MY RETURN HOME FORD had been ousted from his bed and was now bunking in with Tommy and Glenn. Each morning, just as when they were kids sharing a room on the Beaches, they wrestled each other awake, the common wall between us shuddering from their heads, elbows, and knees thudding against it along with more grunts and groans than a midnight brawl in a bar.

I dragged myself out of bed, wondering how the hell Dave would deal with these murderous awakenings *should he say yes to wintering over.* I pushed back that worry; another two hours and he'd be here; please God he'd say yes.

"Ye're gonna get the shit kicked outta ye when Dave comes," I hollered, passing the boys' door, and then met Mother coming in from the porch holding up Dave's black leather bomber jacket.

"Where we gonna hang it?" she said. "It keeps plying down the hangers and falling to the floor." I laughed. Dave had been wearing that jacket the first time I saw him on the green in Corner Brook. He'd bartered, swapped, or out-tricked it from an old geezer who claimed to have swiped it off a dead bombardier (whose nationality he would never say) back in World War II. Its leather was thick and hard and it had clunky silver zippers and side pockets big enough to hold a small dog. Dave wore it when he was riding his motorcycle and when he wasn't. He wore it in the sun and in the rain. He'd worn it to Hampden the first time I brought him home, my father's eyes widening in wonderment as he watched him coming through the door and unzipping the pockets and pulling out six or eight beers. Mother had flinched when he let it slip off his shoulders and hit the floor with a thud.

The jacket thudded again now, this time onto the floor inside the closet as Mother tried hanging it back up.

"Pass it here," I said, partway through hauling on my boots. I was preparing to go meet Dave down on the dusty ball field by the sea. A helicopter would be dropping him off there. He always left his heavier coat in the camp so as not to be cramped in the chopper.

I loaded Davey and Jack into the truck while Ford, Glenn, and Tom hopped in the back. The helicopter was coming over the hills as we parked. It was sunny but cold, the November winds brisk and roiling the water. Then we were out of the truck, looking up, the roar of the chopper deafening as it hovered overhead, its blades *whop-whop-whopping*. Finally it touched down, windmilling dust as Dave ducked out of the cabin, his clothes flapping as he ran towards us. His hair fell to his shoulders; he was bearded and looked like Jesus, as my cousins on the Beaches would say each time they saw him. Jack ran barking at the chopper and Davey ran with his arms outstretched to greet his father. Tommy ran too, his own arms up to the chopper, begging for a ride. Ford and Glenn called out greetings then dodged on to the wharf down the road. I swapped Dave his leather jacket for a hug and we all ambled towards the wharf, the *chak-chak-chak* of the chopper receding beyond the echoing hills.

Davey rode on his father's back. I trailed behind, wondering how to approach Dave about staying on in Hampden. We weren't the greatest at communicating; we weren't the greatest at anything except arguing. It had been a tough call for Dave to haul himself off the road and saddle himself into a college seat for two years. Equally as tough for me to mother all day then work the bars at night, slinging beer to help pay the bills. But we did it, and now—Oh, to hell with it.

"I wanna winter over," I blurted out, going on to explain about the stolen cheque and Father needing us. My voice trembled with want as I spoke, and Dave looked at me curiously: since I'd left I'd never spent more than a weekend at home. He said nothing, though, and I knew to leave it alone. He'd let me know his thoughts when he knew them himself.

He lowered Davey and, holding his hand, led him across the rotting timbers of the middle section of the wharf that had been washed out. I followed, moodily contemplating the darkish waters gurgling beneath us around the pilings, wondering what I'd do if Dave was opposed to our staying.

A couple of Ford's friends were idling around the end of the wharf where it was sturdier and much wider, heaving sticks big as pickets into the water, watching and whistling as their dogs swam out, clenched their jaws around them, then paddled back to shore. Jack was barking, sniffing around Dave's leg, when without a thought Dave bent down and picked him up and tossed him into the water—too quick to heed Tommy's warning shout.

Jack hit the water and sank. "He can't swim, he can't swim!" Tommy screamed. "Go get him!"

"What the fuck!" Dave knelt at the edge of the wharf as Jack bobbed to the surface, snorting and sneezing. "Swim!" he bawled out. "Swim you little fuck!" Jack pawed feebly at the water, then sank again. Tommy and I were both yelling now, Tommy's shouts growing louder as Jack surfaced and then, no longer pawing at the water, sank once more. Dave cursed. "Have I got to jump in that fuckin' water?"

"Yes, yes, he's drowning!" cried Tommy. Dave cursed again, tore off his jacket, and gave me a withering look. "If I'm going to gawd-damn live here . . ." He stepped off the wharf and dropped like a rock into the frigid water.

He resurfaced, spurting out curses, his arm an iron bar around Jack's throat, and swam to shore. All hands cheered and then busted a gut laughing as Dave hauled Jack onto the landwash and staggered out of the water. Ford handed him his jacket and we all followed as Dave headed for the truck, shrugging the jacket on over his dripping clothes.

"And *that's* fuckin' walking," Dave muttered, shaking a finger at Jack, who cowed as he shook off water on the landwash.

I looped my arm through Ford's. "We're spending the winter," I told him. He tightened his arm around mine as we grinned and half skipped along the rutted dirt road.

It would be a year from then, perhaps even to the day, that I'd be walking that road again. Alone.

The following weeks were full and frantic, our days shaped by Father's. Each morning he rose before dawn, made coffee, and smoked, gazing out the still darkened window. When I couldn't sleep and would wander down the hall he'd say, "Good morning, dolly," without looking up, without breaking thought. Mapping out his day or thinking back on his yesterdays, I figured. Sometimes I'd ask, "What're you thinking about, Dad?" and he'd always reply, "Nothing, lovie, nothing," his voice soft as Mother's those nights when I'd overhear her whispering the Lord's Prayer as she knelt beside her bed. That's what Father was doing too, in his way, sitting alone in the early morning light, drinking his coffee and smoking in silence—whispering his prayers.

Going back to bed, I'd hear him tap on Ford's door and their muffled sounds as they readied for work. Mother would get up just after they left—and soon after that would commence the hellish disharmony of Glenn and Tommy thumping and thudding against their bedroom wall as they bullied each other awake and Karen's wails as she collided with them against the bathroom door, each fighting to be the first inside. From there they fought over their tea, toast, and jam at the breakfast table, their coats, books, and boots in the porch, and, as they slammed out the door, who would catch the school bus first. Holding on to Davey as he bawled at the door wanting to follow them, I'd let Jack out and then watch as he'd barrel off furiously, barking and snarling after the bus, wondering what the hell he'd do if he ever caught it.

After a quick breakfast Mother and I would begin our routine: washing dishes and mopping floors; cleaning bedrooms, the porch, the doorplace, the sooted wood stove. From there we'd start the clothes washing and the bread making and the planning for lunch when they'd all be back again—Dad and Ford and whoever else was working with them that day—kicking off boots, shrugging off coats, shedding caps and mitts and scarves and piling around the table sugaring tea, buttering bread, spooning back soup or stew or beans or whatever it was Mother had laid out for them. They argued and laughed and complained and told bad jokes and taunted and kicked at shins beneath the table. Jack whined for scraps and Davey was forever standing on his chair, butter in his hair, butter on his face, breadcrumbs falling from his mouth as he waved his spoon about. I'd scrape plates with Mother, and after they'd all piled back out the door and quiet had descended, she and I would sit for a bit, sipping tea and eating whatever food was left over. The midday light would wash over our faces as we stood before the window at the sink, squirting detergent over greasy dishes, soaping down the stove, wiping down countertops, rinsing the dishrags, searching through the fridge for something to cook for supper. After another quick sweeping and mopping up water from their boots in the porch and stogging the wood stove, we'd sink gratefully onto the couch and drowse our way through *The Young and the Restless* before heading back to the sink and peeling vegetables.

Undoubtedly it was repetitious. It was drudgery. It was a deafening of our ears and a culling of our thoughts as we worked through the days then fell senseless into bed at night, the day's tensions ebbing from our neck and shoulders into the soft of our pillows. Yet I relished being with family again. And I fretted over its well-being during this unusual and challenging time. Mostly, I fretted over Mother. The winter's cold was brutal on her arthritis. Her knees were swollen in the mornings and her right elbow so puffed out she could scarcely straighten her arm. The pain kept her awake at nights; I'd hear her shifting about, going to the washroom, the kitchen. I witnessed her discomfort each morning as she kept working that swollen and stiffened arm, forcing it to straighten as she sliced bread, sliced cheese, cut up meat. I saw the fatigue on her face from the constant aching and her constant fighting against the pain burning in her joints. I saw her suffering in the dark of her eyes. I asked about medications once but she brushed me aside, saying, "Oh, my, Donna, if I had to take a pill for every little ache."

I was silenced by her fortitude. And daunted by Father's later that spring, when the contracted house was almost finished and the money flowed steadily but was hardly enough for anything other than food, supplies, bills. Yet instead of the cheap linoleum the housing corporation had budgeted for, he lay down more expensive, higher-quality tiles. And he was installing carpet and paying for it out of his own pocket. "You're going to do some-thing, do it gawd-damn right," he would argue as Mother balked at the expense.

Fortitude. Without it, I was to learn, all other virtues wither on the vine.

≫——▷

That winter's end was marked by Jack's passing. We found him in the closet out in the porch, curled up on Dave's leather jacket that had slipped off its hanger. There was a terrible smell, and a terrible mess. Father wrapped the jacket and Jack into a bundle and took it to the woods and buried it deep. An oath was taken by all to *never* tell Dave where the dog and his jacket were buried. On the day Dave was flown in, about a week later, I was in Corner Brook running errands with Mother. When I called home to ask about something, I was told that Dave had just discovered the awful truth and was outside with a shovel, looking for freshly dug ground.

Except for Dave, who was still sour over the loss of his jacket, spring livened our step and danced us into summer. The house was near completion, the loans were paid, and the larders filled. To celebrate, we went to a dance at the club. When the band struck up a medley of rock songs Father astounded me with his hip-swivelling moves to the Beatles' "Twist and Shout," and later, dropping to the floor, his pawing at his sneakers to Elvis Presley's "Blue Suede Shoes."

I simply stared. Mother, staring at him too, shrugged helplessly. "He was loosening up back when the store was doing good," she said. "Having a bit of fun. Wanting to dance all the time, drink a few beers. Then, when he learned the boys stole from him, he give it all up. Lost his courage. I worry about your father, how he won't talk about nothing. *Nothing.*"

"Who do *you* talk to?" I asked.

"My sister Shirley." She looked at me. "Your father's right about one thing—we'd be nothing without family." She gave a girlish grin as Father lurched over and grabbed her hand, the arthritic one. At first she grimaced but then laughed as he yanked her onto the crowded dance floor.

I laughed too, watching Father slow it down for a waltz, his hips still swivelling, Mother swaying along with him as gracefully as a sapling in a summer breeze. Then a barrage of aunts and cousins from the Beaches paraded onto the dance floor for a fast number, clapping and singing. I put down my vodka and tonic, shoved back my chair, and skipped among them. The floor trembled beneath our feet as we shoved each other around, clapping and stomping and twisting and shouting, the walls rocking and all the ills and pain and sins darkening our souls temporarily lost in the joy of childlike love permeating our collective heart.

It was this image of my mother and father, joyous and free on the dance floor, that I would bury in my heart throughout the coming months. A souvenir of what life was before the laughter stopped. Someday, much much further down the road, when I no longer thought in terms of before and after the accident, when I was older than my mother and had learned to abort the two ugly sisters of guilt and shame, when death had become equated with life within the terrible paradox of *being* and I had given up the futile search for meaning and bowed at the altar of the cathedral that was me, I would dig out this picture. And I would nuzzle it with the same tenderness and joy a new mother nuzzles the downy softness of her infant's crown before life hardens it. For some that is a lifetime's journey. For others it's a journey that never completes itself. For me, that night on the dance floor, it was a journey I wasn't even aware of. I knew only that life *was*. But I knew it *not* in the sin of knowing. Only in the bliss of innocence and naïveté.

⋇──▷

It was nearing the end of summer. The house had been completed, the final cheque had been issued, and Mom and Dad had left for a two-week holiday to visit Wanda in Toronto. It was during the last four days of their holiday that the furnace stopped working. Followed by the television. Then the vacuum cleaner and the electric stove.

The night they returned a cold easterly was blowing up the bay. Ford picked them up at the airport as the rest of us, draped in shawls and sweaters, sat around the wood stove, frying hamburger patties. Sitting with us was a friend just home from the oil-rich province of Alberta. Workers from all over the country were boarding this gravy train to riches and Dave and I were exchanging meaningful looks when Mother walked in the door, her face twisted with worry. It had nothing to do with the broken-down furnace or stove that Ford had forewarned them about, I was to learn. Dad followed her in, throwing off his coat, already cursing, *Gawd-damn the like-a-that*, and heading for the stove. As he began hauling it out from the wall, Mom argued with him to leave it till morning, her voice shrill, frightened. She beckoned me to her room and closed the door behind us.

"Your father had what they calls a *silent heart attack*," she said deeply and with a tremor in her voice. She sat on the bed and leaned against the headboard. There were smudges of dark beneath her eyes.

I knelt beside her, half whispering, "A *silent* heart attack?"

She nodded, wearily rubbing her neck. "It's silent because you scarcely feel anything. Then you learns later you had a heart attack—perhaps getting a checkup for something else. That's what the doctor told us."

"So how did Dad know?"

"He was feeling *something* in his chest. Not pain, but . . ." She shrugged. "It made him nervous about getting on the plane. So we went to the hospital and they gave him an EKG and sure enough he'd had a small heart attack. He can have another one," she added. "A bigger one."

My own heart thumped hard.

"He's all right," Mother said quickly, seeing my distress. She sat up, her dark eyes fretting over mine. "No sense in worrying; he's home now."

When Father bellowed something about *the gawd-damn Roberts screwdriver*, she got up and marched down the hall to where he was crouched down on his knees, fiddling with wires at the back of the stove.

"Get up," she ordered. "Leave it till morning. We're not cooking nothing tonight. Get up!" she shouted as he ignored her, bawling at Ford to hold the flashlight closer. She reached over, pried it from Ford's hand, and held it threateningly over Father's head. "Get off the gawd-damn floor or I'll beat your brains out!"

Father gave her a fierce look and then sat back, shaking his head. "Foolish. You're gone foolish." Still, he got up and clomped down the hall.

I stood before Mother and placed both hands on her shoulders. "Tomorrow, you go buy the best stove and TV and vacuum cleaner in Corner Brook. We'll have it paid off in no time. Yes, we will," I said to her skeptical look.

After she'd followed Dad to their bedroom I whispered to Dave and Ford about Dad's silent heart attack.

Then I finally said out loud what Dave and I had been mulling over for days. "We're going to Alberta," I announced.

"Already packed," said Dave. And he was. A few days later he was on a flight and I'd begun my own packing, torn between leaving and never leaving again; petrified of Father's weakened heart and feeling for the first time since Baby Paul's passing the cold finger of death stroking my spine.

Ford came out onto the back steps where I was squinting against the sun, hauling the laundry off the line. He wanted to come with me to Alberta.

I bundled a sheet into the laundry basket and turned to him. He resembled Dad with his wide brow and wide cheekbones. And his eyes, molten brown and glistening, made him look as though he were always smiling inside, even when his brow was troubled, as it was now.

"Don't think Dad will let you go," I said.

He shrugged. "Either I goes with you or I joins the army."

I nearly choked. "Yeah, good fucking luck with that one. If Mom don't string you up I will."

He shrugged again. "So I'll just go to Alberta with you. What's the problem?"

I couldn't help it. I grinned, pleased as anything. There'd been lots of times in the past when he'd sat beside me, asking about the outside world; I'd regale him with yarns of being on the road, feeling like the cool big sister. I friggin loved the notion of his coming with me to Alberta.

"I'll fly up first," I said, "and get settled. Then I'll send you a ticket. Not scared to fly, are you?"

He looked skyward. "Won't know till I gets up there. Don't say nothing yet to Mom. Be nothing but fighting till I goes."

Davey came loping along with three kittens tucked under his T-shirt, their little heads poking up through his shirt beneath his chin. As Ford, muttering his first curse word, chased after him to save the kittens from asphyxiation, I too looked skyward. A jet, just then, was streaking a white trail through the blue.

A week later it was me streaking into the blue of a late summer's day, Davey sitting beside me, his face squished against the window, waving and chanting. *Bye-bye Lucinland, bye-bye Lucinland . . .*

THREE WHITE LICE

GRANDE PRAIRIE, ALBERTA, was a boom town burgeoning with migrants pouring across its borders, filling its apartments, bars, and restaurants and spilling over into encampments along its riverside. Through three sets of miracles, Dave found us a four-bedroom townhouse with a great backyard and secured a job in the oilfields for himself and, within the next couple of weeks, for Ford.

I booked Ford's ticket and drove the four hours to the Edmonton airport, getting there three hours early so as not to be late. When his plane finally arrived I stood, eager for a first glimpse of his gorgeous blond head—and kept watching until the last passenger filed through the gate. Mother must have pulled him off the tarmac at the last minute, I was thinking. Father must have tied him to the couch. Oh, gawd, he probably got off during his stopover in Toronto and was now walking the length of Yonge Street, lost. I was chewing my fingers when he finally stepped from behind a partition, his grin so wide he was showing his molars. "Bastard!" I yelled. We hugged hard and long.

On the drive back to Grande Prairie he told me everything about how Dad and Mom had argued to keep him home. Then, he told me, he'd played his trump card: if he didn't fly to Grande

Prairie, he was joining the army. That silenced them both, and in that small reprieve he packed his bag. Later he went down to Hampden for a last party with his pals, returning home just before dawn. His flight left at six. Mother had his suitcase unpacked and all his clothes put back in his drawers.

"She never."

"Yup. Giving me a chance to back out, was all."

"And you did what?"

"Stuffed the clothes back in the suitcase and ran for the door. She and Dad drove me then, and"—he held up his hand for emphasis—"I promised I'd be home with a new truck this spring." He looked at me, grinning. "She's going to be some purdy, my first truck."

When we reached the outskirts of Grande Prairie Ford had his head out the window, scouting out the rows of new trucks shimmering beneath the sun before every gas station, restaurant, hotel, and motel along the main drag into the city. We cruised through the downtown streets, the smell of wet grass from last night's rain whiffing through our open windows. Throngs of people crowded the sidewalks, virtually all of them young, transient, and looking for a quick bank account. Given the number of Help Wanted signs hanging in practically every shop and restaurant window, that didn't seem to pose much of a challenge.

We swung into a crowded, smoky bar where Dave and a couple of friends were waiting. Scarcely a woman to be seen. It was mostly men—drinking hard, talking hard, laughing hard. Rig hands, roughnecks, truckers, and servicemen, all wearing muddied steel-toed boots, dark, heavy clothing, and ball caps with their company logos. As Ford and I settled at our table, I noted the scarred hands and missing fingers of those men sitting up close, the fatigued look in their eyes.

I looked at Ford's smooth brow, his face bright as a new moon rising, his eyes eager for this new day, and felt my first jitter of nerves. Dave wore the same wary expression as Ford turned to him, the fuzz on his upper lip catching the milky froth of his beer. And there began the first of Dave's lectures. "See that fellow over there," he said to Ford, nodding across the room, "that fellow with the buzzed head and lower jaw jutting out far enough to catch rainwater? That's the boss. Now, here's what you got to know about working rigs, and you better listen up, buddy, cuz this is the most training you're going to get."

The "training" continued throughout the steak and fries we ordered, all during our walk home, and then picked up again the following morning at breakfast. *When you're on that rig floor you keep your eyes bugging outta your head; you sees all ways at all times, you sees what just happened, what could happen, what might happen—and you're always ready to duck, jump, and run like hell. Sour gas, pipes blowing outta the hole, any fucking thing can happen any fucking minute on the rig and those who aren't watching, who're snoozing behind the mud tank or thinking about a rum and Coke, they're the ones most likely to get their fingers hacked off or their heads landing atop the cookhouse two hundred feet yonder.*

"Jeezes, Dave," I kept muttering. But on he went, all through that week and then during the drive to the camp in the week that followed. Davey and I had been invited to spend a few days there, and despite Dave's lecturing we all caught Ford's enthusiasm as he kept sticking his head out the window, exclaiming over the size of the pine trees, the eagles soaring through the blue above us, the bushes and flowers populating the roadsides. Dave turned onto a rutted dirt road and soon we were bouncing into a camp that consisted of three long trailers, a scattering of mud-sprayed trucks, and off to one side, a good forty or fifty metres away from the trailers, the rig itself: a monstrously huge platform with scabs of red paint gleaming through the mud and a creamy-white derrick towering into the air. The whole thing shuddered and rumbled and screamed from the diesel engines and generators powering it, the stench of diesel bringing water to my eyes.

It's what I took to bed with me that night, the distant screaming of that rig. I woke the following morning to someone clinking pebbles at our window and looked out to see Ford's face grinning up at me and Davey trotting through the mud behind him. I grinned back, got dressed, and then joined them outside with the camera. "Hey, for Dad," said Ford. He was wearing a reddish plaid shirt, worn cords, muddied rubber boots, and a grin that would lift our father's hopeful heart. I snapped the picture and we laughed, musing about the look on Dad's face when he'd open a card a few weeks down the road with a thousand dollars in it and Ford's beautiful face smiling mischievously back at him.

It seemed like all we did was laugh during the weeks that followed Ford's arrival. As the sweeping Alberta winds chased clouds across the sky, money orders were sent back home, paying off that new stove and furnace and television and vacuum. Father was working in the woods again and Mother was working too, in a new crab plant in Jackson's Arm. Everything felt right.

One blustery October evening when Ford was back in town he got up from the supper table, rubbed his overstuffed belly, glanced at the phone, and said, "Let's call Dad."

It was the funniest thing. In that second the phone rang and it was Father. All excited. It was the first time he'd made a long-distance phone call without Mother doing the dialing for him. Ford laughed, then paused as he listened to what Dad was saying. He shook his head, gave another laugh, and said, "Naw, not coming home yet. Won't be long though. Coming home in the spring in my new truck." He was silent again, listening to Dad, slowly shaking his head.

When he looked at me pleadingly I shouted into the mouthpiece, "What's Mom doing?"

Ford tipped the receiver towards my ear and I heard the strain in Father's voice. "Come home," he begged. "Come on home, lovie. All of ye, come home."

"Oh my gawd, Dad. We haven't been here three months. Our bootprints are still on the stoop."

He started saying something and then his voice broke off. He was crying. Ford shouldered the phone back to his ear, mumbled a few words, then gave an awkward laugh.

After he hung up I turned to him and said, "You watch yourself out there on that fuckin' rig. Anything happens to you out here, it'll be the two of us gone. Because I'll never be able to go home agin."

He shook his head. "No," he said. "You won't." For a moment, the shine left his eyes.

That night I woke from a bad dream—I was holding three white head lice in the palm of my hand. They were big and sluggish. Grandfather lice, I remembered Grandmother calling them. A sign of death.

I went back to a troubled sleep. Aside from Grandmother's prophecies, I'd never even heard of white lice.

Come morning, I was feeling ill. Dave was hauling on his jeans, readying for an early start, when I told him about my white lice dream. "A sign of death, Grandmother used to say."

He raised a skeptical brow. "Does that apply just to the Beaches crowd?"

I followed him downstairs, making pancakes as he called out to Ford to get up. It was October the sixteenth. The sun spilled through the kitchen window, pooling onto Davey straddling a red toolbox, a plastic fireman's hat on his head that was flashing red lights and screaming like a siren.

Breakfast finished, I stood in the doorway, watching as Dave climbed behind the wheel of the truck. Ford waved to me and swung aboard the passenger side, wearing his sky-blue jacket with the company logo on its chest. I watched as the truck lumbered down the potholed driveway and across the open field beside our house, shortcutting it to the highway.

They'd been gone about four hours. It was midday, the sun brightening the windows, the wind swooshing through the trees and tumbling fat clouds across the sky. I was standing at the sink, my hands in hot dishwater, scrubbing grease off a frying pan. I laid it aside and, flicking water off my hands, darted upstairs to the washroom. I heard the door open downstairs and Dave calling my name. I hurried back downstairs; he shouldn't be home. He called my name again, his voice hoarse, too loud. He was standing in the doorway, just standing there, not looking at me, looking somewhere past me, his chest heaving as though he was struggling to breathe.

"What is it? Oh my, what's wrong?"

"Fordie. He's in the hospital. Ford's in the hospital." He ducked outside and vomited.

I started mewling like a pup. I turned in circles, looking for my boots. I got them on and as I grabbed my coat Dave came inside.

"Is he hurt—is he okay? How bad is it?"

Dave looked at me, his eyes a harsh blue, fixated on mine. Then he spoke, sounding like a winded old man. Something about hooking a toolshed up to the truck. Semi with a highboy. "Just a fuckin' kid driving it—no air brakes on. The truck rolled back—pinned Ford between the trailer and a steel shack."

"But he'll be okay?"

Dave was already running back to the truck. I raced a few houses down to where Davey was playing with his two little friends, my legs trembling so hard I kept staggering. Their mother, my friend Laurene, assured me that Davey would be fine and ushered me along my way. She asked no questions. My eyes told her what I hadn't yet told myself.

Dave said nothing during the drive. His breathing was ragged, breaking into little sobs that he quickly stifled. I kept looking out the side window, not thinking, not praying, not asking for anything except the numbness that was holding me steady, keeping me together. At the hospital emergency they led us into a quiet yellow room, a lamp with a big white shade shining soft, a faint smell of something like new upholstery. Dave sat beside me. We hadn't spoken since we left the house. We didn't speak then. A nurse shadowed the doorway and the smell of new upholstery grew stronger, making me sickish, and I was thinking the smell must be coming off the nurse herself when she stepped closer, looked down at me and Dave, and said, "Who will identify the body?"

Grace, they say, is a gift of God. I felt it in the thickening of the silence walling me in. I heard my breath coming in and leaving me. Dave asked me something but his words were muffled through the silence. He got up and followed the nurse. I kept sitting there after he was gone. I sat, and I stared. I stared at nothing and I felt nothing. The nurse came back, bending down to see into my eyes, but I wouldn't let her in. She asked if I would like something to calm me but I wouldn't look at her. I kept staring over her shoulder at the wall beyond. She straightened and moved away. Dave came into the room and sat, shuddering. We walked stiff as corpses out of the hospital. Some of the rig hands were in the parking lot, parked alongside our truck. A roughneck nicknamed Pickles opened his mouth, reaching out to Dave. I kept walking. I heard nothing. I felt nothing.

When we got home I walked to the bank. I stood at the counter and asked for my brother's money and for them to please close his account because he'd just been killed. The teller stared at me and left her wicket. She returned with the bank manager, who recognized me from an earlier meeting about a possible loan to buy a truck in the coming weeks. I repeated what I'd said to the teller and without any questions she gave me the money from Ford's account and then closed it.

I walked to the liquor store. I bought a bottle of rye whisky and went back outside, standing on the street corner next to a man who was waiting to cross the busy street. "My brother was just killed," I told him. "I haven't told my parents yet. It just happened."

He stared at me the way the teller had, and I turned away. I walked to Laurene's and told her what I'd just told the man on the corner. Then I collected Davey and, against her wishes, walked home. She stood in her doorway, watching after me. When I got home the boys from the rig were inside with Dave. They all hushed when I entered the room. Dave sat alone in a chair, his head down. I smiled, nodding to them, and walked upstairs. And looked at the phone. I would not call. I would not call them that evening. I would give them one more night of peace.

Hours later, when Dave staggered to bed, I was still slumped against the wall, staring at the phone. Before morning's light had fully broken Dave got up quietly and left the house. I listened as he revved up the truck and booted across the field. I looked at the phone. I could not call them. Instead I called Uncle Don, my mom's brother. He was a spiritual man, and, in that moment, I was looking for Christ.

Some hours after that, the phone rang. I was still lying in bed. It was my Aunt Beat, Dad's sister. She was at our house. Your mother can't come to the phone, she told me, nor your father. "They're in their room, my love, they wants to know when you're coming home. They're waiting."

I hung up the phone. A loud moaning started up inside of me. I crawled off the bed. I crawled like a dog inside my closet, pulled the door shut, and hid my face in the dark.

WALKING THROUGH WATER

THERE WAS LITTLE CONSCIOUSNESS of the days that followed. As we flew home I cradled in my heart the horrible knowing that Fordie was somewhere beneath us in the baggage compartment. When we landed in Deer Lake, I stepped off the plane and into a river whose current pushed me back. I pushed forward. My cousin Selma was there to meet us; she kissed my cheek and took Davey. I sat quietly in the back seat with Dave during the drive home. We parked before the house, and when someone opened the car door for me the river rushed in. It pushed against me as I struggled to get out. It pushed against me as I started towards the door. It pushed so hard I could scarcely stretch out my hand to open it. Instead the door was pulled open from the inside. Aunt Shirley was standing there. She took my hands and she pulled me from the river.

Grace is a gift. It filters out everything except what is needed for this moment. It calms the wild rivers and screens out feelings and thoughts. It shoulders us up; it allows the sea of aunts and cousins and friends and neighbours to wash over us and cradle us. Grace is the voice of God whispering in my ear: *I have you, I have you in this terrible underbelly of the life I have given you.* Grace is the courage given to walk down that long hallway and open that bedroom door. It was a gift of which I'd been unaware when I turned my eyes onto the bruised, wretched eyes of my parents, lying there on their bed, sharing the one pillow, waiting for me, waiting for him, waiting for me to bring him to them, their hearts not believing the news that had been given them until they heard it from me. Yet their arms were already open, reaching with grace for the disgraced to enter them. Grace is the exiting of self and the surrendering into the paradox of our awful loving God.

»—▷

Six weeks after we buried my brother I flew back to Grande Prairie. I sat in the armchair by the window, gazing outside for long hours. Davey spent his days down the road playing with his two little friends. Dave was on the rigs. I sat alone for days. I sat alone remembering the past six weeks in images: the dull thudding of my father's heart against my ear as he clutched me to his chest on that bed; the heat from my mother's throat against my forehead as I squirmed over Father to nuzzle into her; Tommy standing quiet beside the new stove, Ford having died on his birthday; Wanda curled against my back that night in sleep; the silence coming from the boys' room in the morning; Karen sitting by her little piano in our living room, the day of the funeral, singing "Amazing Grace" in a pure sweet voice I hadn't known she possessed; Glenn, two miles down the road, standing alone in the dark by the closed doors of their hangout, chewing his fingers, the wind blowing cold off the water. It had always been his custom to walk the two miles home with Ford. Afraid of the dark, Glenn was. Afraid of the bears that sometimes prowled the road leading home. Afraid of home now.

Some images I closed my eyes against. Others I tried to block out but they forced their way through: my mother sobbing that I should have called her when it first happened, I should have called, for she'd been playing darts down Hampden when he was up there, dead; my father, she told me, had been lying in his bunk at the logging camp, feeling frightened and not knowing why, locking the camp door that had never been locked since it was built twenty years before and lying there all night shivering, staring at it, waiting for something to happen that had already happened; Father, the day after the funeral, ripping the door from the side of the porch and rebuilding it at the front of the porch and Mother and the rest of us watching without speaking; Father, hiding inside the old truck trailer in our yard, his choked sobs sounding hard as cement; Mother, standing silent before the sink, her hands soaking in dishwater as she stared out the window; Mother and Father fighting for ownership of his death—Mother believing he'd still be alive if she'd let him join the army, Father shaking his head, "No, lovie, no, I should never have let him go, I should never have let him go"; the both of them looking up and seeing me and Father reaching for me, saying, "Be the same if it was you, doll, be the same if it was you."

These are the words I played over and over, clinging to them. *Be the same if it was you, be the same if it was you.* Guilt, you see, doesn't perch on one's shoulder like a turkey vulture, proclaiming itself. It doesn't bloom into the night so that one can see its blight rotting like a winter's spud within the dark cellar of one's sleeping mind. Guilt is a silent thing. It creeps beneath reason, quietly feeding itself on the language of blame and ignorance. *It's you who are the wild one; he should never have left home, they didn't want him to leave, he'd still be alive if he'd never left, if you hadn't bought that ticket . . .*

I started drinking. Every night. To sleep, and to escape torment. Then the dreams started—hellish, nightmarish dreams too horrid to recount. And then, about two months past Ford's burial, as though a greater consciousness than mine was at work, deeming me worthy of saving, I was given another grace. A dream of a different sort. I was lying beside him upon a bed. He was naked beneath the blankets and I was lying atop them, my face pressed against his chest. His skin felt warm and soft like velvet to my cheek. His arms were around me and he was rocking me a little, whispering, *Shh, it's not your fault, Sis, it's not your fault, it's not your fault, shhh.*

I woke up. My body was in a state of rapture. It was suffused with such an incredible feeling of bliss that I seemed to be floating. I stared through the dark, afraid to move, afraid it might vanish. It stayed. I breathed slowly, clinging to the remnant of that beautiful dream. I got out of bed and stood up. It was dark, and when I looked down such was the feeling of peace within me that I expected to see a light emanating from my body. I'm dreaming, I must be dreaming, I thought. But I was not. I walked to the washroom. It felt as though I were gliding. I turned on the light. I looked in the mirror; I looked ordinary; no light was glowing through my eyes. I rested my head against the mirror, revelling in this respite of peace. I glided downstairs and turned on the light and sat in the chair and each cell in my body floated in an essence of a peace beyond understanding. I sat for an hour, maybe two. I thought to pour a drink but was unwilling to stir from the comfort of simply being. Finally, when I got sleepy and my head started to droop, I got up and walked back to bed. I lay there in a haze of peace and in comfort and drifted back to sleep.

Morning streamed through my window, awakening me, and I nearly cried out with gratitude: the feeling was still with me. Not as strong, but strong enough to bring such sighs of contentment that I could have lain there till the end of time. I heard a thump downstairs and Davey yelling. I rushed down and picked him up from where he'd fallen off the sink, hunting for cereal. I sat for a while, soothing him, and then cleaned the house for the first time since before the accident. The glow of comfort and peace slowly subsided, lasting till mid-morning before completely fading. By noon I was curled into the chair again, unable to straighten my legs for the pain in my stomach.

It was a week later that he came in another dream. This time I was sitting on the edge of the bathtub in a washroom I didn't recognize. He was perched on a window ledge, the light in his hair. *Tell me what happened, Sis. I don't remember it.* He listened as I told him. *Do you grieve too?* I asked, and he nodded and smiled. *Yes*, he said. *We grieve too. For about three years.* I woke up and it was dark and as before I was filled with utter peace. With such feelings of well-being I could do nothing but lie there. And feel it. As though I were on some drug. All throughout the night I lay with it, then finally, just before dawn, I drifted into the sleep of angels. Come morning the bliss was still there, although, as before, a little faded. It faded further with the morning hours till it was gone.

I called my mother. Her voice was small; I filled the line with the exuberance of my own as I told her about my dreams. She listened in silence. When I was done, she said she wished she could have one. Then she spoke of Father, that he was drinking too much. She worried about his drinking too much.

I had one more dream. I was pushing through the crowded hallway of our old high school in Hampden. There was something happening outside, and everyone was pushing to get through the doors. Suddenly he was beside me—*How ya doin', Sis*—and he took my arm, guiding me through the people, guiding me outside where everyone was gathering around Dad, who was having some sort of spell.

In that moment I was awakened from my dream by a shriek from Davey. I struggled to wake up and rushed to his bedside half asleep, the dream clinging to me like fairy dust. Little Davey had had a bad dream; I soothed him back to sleep, reliving my own dream with Ford and the crowded hallway, feeling a tinge of that peaceful feeling within me, but only a tinge. As though the dream hadn't had time to catch hold.

I went back to bed and lay there, clinging to that tinge of a feeling. I drifted into sleep and he was there, waiting. Yes, waiting. Outside the school now, the crowd gathered around Dad, who was still having some kind of spell. *You okay, Sis? Yes, yes, I'm okay.* I grasped his arm. *Go to Dad, please can you go to Dad?* He shook his head. *Can't do it, Sis.* And in the fashion of dreams he zoomed from my side and vanished in a blur of energy. And I awakened with the light glowing within me.

My mother called. It had been three or four weeks since I'd told her about my dreams. She'd had one, she said. It left her feeling the way I had described but she couldn't talk about it, she said; she just wanted me to know she'd had one of those dreams.

I started taking walks during the day. The dreams had helped me find courage. And hope. I cradled them in my heart. There were more dreams through the following months, but they weren't the same. Ford was fading. He looked at me from afar but couldn't come nearer and didn't speak. He was sitting on a log, looking away from me. He was sitting in the back seat of a car and he was driving the other way. He appeared by my side in the old schoolhouse on the Beaches; I was so delighted that I gave him a broom to sweep the school, it would be his job now and he'd be safe, but he sadly shook his head and without speaking walked away. In each dream he felt further and further from me, and there was a fatigue to his being. As though it were costing him too much to continue coming. And each time I woke up I felt a tinge of the light, but just a tinge. I knew what was being asked. To let him go. But I couldn't. I was a junkie for the light. I craved its peace. There was a spore of rot inside of me that the light couldn't reach, couldn't eradicate. It had no edges, I couldn't touch it or feel it or see it, but like one's shadow beneath a full sun at noon, it was there. Directly underfoot. Dormant. Waiting for some distant moment to release itself into being.

Meanwhile, something nice happened. It was my twenty-third birthday, January 13, 1979. Three months since Ford's passing. Wanda called from Toronto. She had quit her job. She needed to be with me, she said; she no longer knew how to be with herself. And I said, "Come."

Two weeks later she arrived in Grande Prairie. With her husband and five-year-old Nikki and several suitcases. Everything else she owned she'd either sold or given away.

Within a week her husband was working in the camps. Sister sat with me, gazing out the window. We talked quietly. She shared her pain and I shared my dreams. One day she came home with a picture puzzle. One thousand pieces. We went down to the basement where the floor was spacious enough to lay out the entire puzzle. It was warm down there, with a big old furnace rattling out heat; it was darkish, too, with an overhead fixture dangling its yellow light above our heads as we sprawled beneath it on cushions, fitting together the pieces. We bought another puzzle, and then another. And another. We cocooned down in that basement for the duration of the winter, putting together puzzles within the warmth of that rattling old furnace and the yellow globe of light. We ate chocolate bars and drank coffee during the daylight hours, and we ate chocolate bars and drank whisky at night after the kids were in bed. We talked about everything. We talked about Mom. We talked about Dad. And we talked about *him*. We talked about *him* and about *him* and about *him*.

><—>

There's another piece to the story. If I were writing fiction, a good editor would cut it, claiming that another white lice dream is over the top, and that it's too taxing for the reader to experience another tragedy on the heels of my brother's. This isn't fiction—although our friend Baxter, with his riot of curly blond hair and radiant blue eyes and raucous laugh, was like a character out of a novel. I'd been in love with him since grade seven, as was every other girl in school. And Joanie, his beloved, was the sainted one in her goodness, the quietude of her smile, the beauty of her dark hair and kind eyes. I'd loved her since grade seven, too—ever since we got off Father's bus that first day and stood in a shy, huddled group.

Joanie had approached us and with a welcoming smile said to Wanda, *My, you're some saucy. What's your name, my love?*

Baxter and Joanie were living in Toronto when our brother passed; I visited them on my way back west after Fordie's funeral. They were so compassionate, even offering to visit us there should we need them. Angels, I thought. Then, a couple of months after Wanda moved to Grande Prairie, they stunned us by moving there too. Baxter brought a cribbage board and a deck of cards into our kitchen and stoked the dying embers of our hearth. He sounded laughter through our silence. He brought bags of candies and bars and snuck them to Davey and his cousin Nikki, evoking shrieks of glee from their hushed rooms. Joanie made pots of tea and baked cakes with buttery icing. She told us stories of old. She saw things in me that I didn't see, good things. She coaxed us into new beginnings. Together Baxter and Joanie opened the window of our grieving hearts onto the light of theirs, allowing us to feel love again.

When spring thawed the frozen Alberta mud, Wanda said to me, "I can go home now. Someone's got to be with Mom and Dad." I closed my eyes and nodded. Frightened of being alone again. But mostly grateful for the comfort she'd bring to our parents' days. As she had to mine.

It was perhaps another five or six months after Joanie and Baxter's arrival that I again dreamt of three white lice. They were sitting in the palm of my hand. When I awoke I sat up; the room was in darkness. Then the phone rang, and a coldness crept through my limbs. It was Wanda. Baxter had just been killed in a truck accident. A terrible, terrible accident.

Trauma. It is a violent upheaval of the soul. It changes how you see the world. It changes something within your DNA and puts you on permanent alert forevermore. It coloured our Joanie's hair from black to grey. Trauma. It was another wound to sit atop that of my brother's and was too shocked to bleed. Then, when it did, it bled fear.

About the dream of the three white lice twice presented to me: I don't understand how or why that was. Nor do I have the imagination to come up with a theory. I've not dreamt of them in the forty-one years since.

PLUCK

THE SUFFERING OF THE SUFFERING

IT WAS TOWARDS THE END OF August 1986. Seven years since my brother's passing. I was living in St. John's, Newfoundland, now; Davey was eleven. He was wiry and dark, with brilliant blue eyes and a passion for Dungeons and Dragons, history, quantum physics, and an aversion to homework. His sister Bridgette was five. Equally as wiry, and with yellow fluffy hair, her brother's eyes, and a lover of beetles, snails, slugs, cats, and a penchant for doodling all creatures great and small over the pages of her school books. I had a job in the fish plant on the south side of the harbour. It was morning, just before the workday started, and I was standing in the break room, finishing off a cigarette and busting a gut laughing at a coworker who'd just hauled a fresh cod fillet from the leg of her rubber boot and was staring at it with astonishment, saying, "How the hell did that get in there?"

The buzzer sounded, sending fifty or sixty of us swapping our coats and caps for rubber aprons and hairnets, scurrying to our workstations on the assembly line. I stood nearest the end, hauling a pan of codfish off a conveyor belt rattling along before me, pulling a filleting knife out of the leg of my rubber boot, and hacking the codfish into fillets. It was hellishly noisy—skinning machines screaming, steel doors clanging, the babble of two hundred workers outshouting each other. I always chose the end station nearest the skinning machines. The noise made it harder to chat, and I preferred losing myself amid the loud hum of machinery and the hypnotic cut, trim, flick of my knife; plus, I made a bigger bonus that way. Money was tight and time was sparse and each passing moment had to count towards something, for Dave and I were paddling different rivers by then.

I had the house we'd bought with our Alberta riches, and I had our kids. It had been a year since the divorce. The psychological parting, though, had happened long before. Despite the depth of Dave's heart, the orphan rebel shield he protected it with had become a tiresome thing to battle every day. Perhaps I could've battled harder in those earlier days, when I first became pregnant and drew boundaries around my own self. And perhaps, as I tightened those boundaries after my second pregnancy, I should've worked harder to draw boundaries around our home life as well. But Dave didn't take well to boundaries. He needed the rough-and-tumble of the road, his buddies, the parties—as did all our friends. As did I, until one day I didn't. That was the day the eleven-year-old daughter of our good friends found their stash of hashish and snuck a gram to school. It must have been one hell of a show-and-tell moment. The police were called and the Department of Social Services. For days our friends lived in anguish that their daughter would be taken from them. She wasn't, but something was taken from me. I became frightened. Davey was ten. He was absorbing everything that was happening around our very liberal household. Smoking pot—among other things—was as common as smoking cigarettes. I fought for change. It resulted in a divorce.

There is, of course, no proverbial last straw. When one looks back, all the other straws must be given equal time, as they too have contributed to the weight. More important to me than whose shoulders to lay blame upon was survival. And that job in the fish plant was my financial lifeline.

I stepped away from my station as a supervisor passed out leaflets ordering us to get a tetanus shot before returning to work after the weekend. "Bad fish," he said when I queried him. "Get your shot."

I went back to the line with something else on my mind: my son's reaction early that morning when I'd mentioned changing our surnames from Morrissey to my maiden name, Osmond. He'd shaken his head and said adamantly, "I'm David Morrissey."

Then he'd spun off to his room, leaving Bridgette staring up at me. "If I change my name will David still be my brother?"

"Nobody's changing their names. Let's just forget that." I took her hand and led her outside for the drive to the babysitter's.

"Will I have a new mother?" she asked.

"You have a mother."

"But if Daddy gets married again?"

"She won't be your mother; she'll just be your dad's wife."

"She'll be a princess."

"Hey?"

"Daddy will marry a princess next."

"Okay. Who will Mommy marry?"

"A farmer."

A farmer. I could take that. Although I would've preferred a mechanic, I thought as I punched the time clock at the end of that long, tiring day and started up the '68 Pontiac, wondering if it would get me home. Among other things, strange knocks had been coming from beneath the floorboards.

A cop pulled me over ten minutes from our house. I looked worriedly over my shoulder at the back right door. It was shut tight, not bad considering it was held there with a scarf, one end attached to the inside handle and the other levered around the driver's headrest. It was also the only door that opened.

Before the cop got out of his cruiser, I clambered into the back seat, harbouring the implausible thought that if I was quick enough he wouldn't notice which door I exited from. Not quick enough. He was already peering through the driver's side window, a perplexed look on his face as I popped up on the opposite side. "Yes, Officer?"

He took out his ticket book and pen and began inching his way around the car, writing furiously, wrinkling his nose at the stench of fish coming off my clothes and rubber boots as I followed his steps. While I waxed on about being a single parent, no extra money for a new car but was saving for one anyway, he kept writing, staring at the Pontiac as though it were some ancient beast. Finally he handed me a wad of tickets. "Cash in your liability for a tow truck," he told me, "and never put this thing on the road again."

"May I please get a ride home, sir?"

No response—he just got back in his cruiser and then merged into the bumper-to-bumper traffic idling along. Nothing to do but start walking. But it was a suffocatingly hot August day, I was still in my rubber boots, and the smell of fish was strong around me. Any minute every feral cat on the docks would be sniffing at my ankles. I got about twenty feet until it was all too much. *Screw you*, I thought and trudged back to the car, got in through the back door, climbed over the front seat, levered the scarf around my neck to keep the back door shut, and drove home. Thankfully I was about to begin a two-week holiday; I'd be taking Davey and Bridgette on the CN bus across the island to visit Mom and Dad. I'd deal with the car when I returned.

Undoubtedly, looking back at the rutted road thus far travelled, the biggest upheaval had been my brother's death, with its subsequent pathways through grief, its handrails of grace and small mercies along the way. But even then I saw no further than my own experience, receiving those graces as a child would receive a Christmas gift—with awe and gratitude and yet with no sense of being a giver oneself. That was about to change. A whole other world was about to open before me, one that would shake the last vestiges of sleep from my eyes and plunge me into a darkness I could never have imagined. And it was there, on that dark and loneliest of roads, that I'd be granted yet another grace: that of fortitude. And through it bump up against the immensity of God.

It was a nine-hour drive to Hampden Junction, where Mom was waiting to meet us. Davey was almost as tall as she was; Bridgette, toting three stuffed cats, tottered to her waist. I looped my arm through Mom's and we walked excitedly to the car. She looked great, colour in her high cheekbones, her eyes laughing behind fashionable, round-framed glasses.

We pulled into the driveway. The house had been repainted and entirely refurnished since the days we'd all lived there, although traces remained—the dark cupboards, the wooden beams in the living room. The long hall. Ford's room. I no longer ducked into it when no one was watching just to stand there, listening. Smelling. Searching through his clothes drawers. It was Tommy's room now, with photographs of Tommy on the wall; photos of Ford had been tucked aside, one of them propped on Mother's dresser. No one spoke of him. Once, during an earlier visit, I'd been counting off the dinner plates by naming them—something I'd always done in our growing-up years—when I accidentally named Ford's. Dad laid down his cup of tea, left the house, and didn't return till after dark.

I stepped into Mother's room and touched the crucifix placed just above Ford's picture. God. Before the accident I'd been too caught in life to think about God. After the accident I'd been too caught in grief. God existed only in clichés—*God be with you, God our Father in Heaven, Ford's with God, it was God's will.*

Those dreams of Ford had given me huge pause for thought. But life marches on, and perhaps I hadn't paused long enough to consider their implications—they'd just become stories I'd sometimes share with a close or a grieving friend. Standing now in Mother's room, I wondered, not for the first time, why it was the crucifix she'd hung there and not an image of a loving God. Perhaps it was the son of God she felt a greater connection with, in that he'd lived in the flesh, his blood dripping from unjust wounds just as hers dripped from her broken heart. Or perhaps she was holding Jesus ransom for God's long-held promise of resurrection from suffering and death.

I left Mother's room thinking less about Christ than about the soreness of my neck from the long bus ride from St. John's. Which reminded me of the tetanus shot I needed.

The clinic was just a five-minute drive away; no one else was waiting; I was called directly into the doctor's office. He was youngish, mid-thirties. South Asian. Gentle brown eyes and a bright smile, his words deeply accented but clear. I sat down and asked him for the injection. I told him about the bad fish, about our hands getting nicked from the filleting knives, about the fish plant requesting that everyone get a shot.

He nodded and rose from his desk, walked behind my chair, and asked me to lean forward. Touching firm fingers to each side of my neck, he moved them up and down, pressing against the sore spot, making me flinch. Then he went around to his desk and sat back down, gazing at me more gravely than an errant priest receiving his last communion.

"I'm afraid it's too late," he said. "You already have it."

I cocked an ear. "Have what?"

"Tetanus."

"Tetanus?"

He nodded deeply, his eyes fraught with concern. "The pain in your neck is your first symptom."

"Ohh, nooo," I said, smiling. "That's just the way I was resting it on the bus."

He shook his head slowly but firmly.

"Seriously? You think I have tetanus?"

He nodded again. "Yes. I am sorry."

"Oh. Well, uh—okay then. What do we do?"

"There is nothing we can do. It is *terminal*."

I stared at him. His words came to me as though they'd been spoken through water; they bobbed against my ears. I laughed, the sound gurgling from far off. The steady gaze of the doctor's eyes held mine, held me in place as his words started clicking inside my head. When he saw my comprehension he got up, went to a drawer, and began peeling away the wrapping from a needle.

"This tetanus shot will help you," he said. "It will probably be another six to eight months before the more serious symptoms develop."

As he pricked the needle into my arm I wanted to ask questions. I wanted to ask *Why give me a tetanus shot if I already have it?* I wanted to ask—I don't know what I wanted to ask—my mind couldn't think and something was happening, a stirring deep inside, a sickish feeling in my stomach, burning cold through my veins and rushing through my brain, flashing out images of that little yellow room in Grande Prairie and the lamp with the soft white light and the smell of new upholstery; the doctor's words *It's terminal, it's terminal* bouncing around with the sound of Joanie moaning into the phone, begging them to allow her to wash her Baxter's hair just one more time; and perhaps there was another smell in there too, perhaps the smell of soap from little brother Paul in his little white coffin as my old friend fear leapt from its deepest of hiding places and raged like fire through my belly.

I looked at the doctor to tell him I was sick, that my belly was burning, but he was talking again, his words bubbling from his mouth. *I am very sorry. You must go to a hospital. You have some time, between six and eight months, but there is no knowing when you will experience your first attack.* He walked me to the door and opened it. His eyes were tender, perhaps even a little curious as he asked whether I lived here or was home on holiday.

I carried myself to the car. I drove home and went inside. Father was sitting at the table, smoking and drinking tea; Mother was at the sink cutting up a salmon for supper. I draped my arm around Dad's neck, giving him a hug from behind, then sat beside him at the table.

"You got your needle? Your mother said you were getting a needle."

"I think I'll bake that salmon, Nerk. Too hot to heat up the frying pan. What would you rather, Donna?"

I stared at their mouths, heard their words.

"Lovie, what's wrong?" asked Dad.

Mom came to the table and gazed down at me. "You're white as a sheet," she said. "What is it?"

I fought to find my voice. It had receded so deep inside that it sounded raspy as I told them what the doctor had said.

Dad stared at me. Mother stared at me. Then Dad gave a hard laugh, shoving his cup aside on the table.

"Lovie, lovie, you haven't got *tetanus*. Nobody here gets *tetanus*. Unless you walks through cow shit with a hole in your foot."

"The doctor said—"

"The *doctor*," he mimicked with such scorn it soured his face. "What *doctor*? We gets gawd-damn fools here, the ones they don't want nowhere else."

I clung to his words.

Mother shook her head. "He can't have said that. Sure, you got all your needles."

"If it's not possible, why's the plant asking us to get boosters then?"

The phone rang and we all looked at it. Mother picked up the receiver. It was the doctor calling me back.

"Because he knows he made a mistake," Father said. "The gawd-damn fool."

Mother hung up and unhooked her sweater from the back of the chair. "He's up from the clinic," she said. "He wants to speak to you. We'll walk over to his house. Nerk, you mind the salmon."

The doctor's residence was within sight of our house, just down the road. A few minutes' walk and Mother and I were at his door. She knocked and he called out for us to enter. Inside the walls were white and bare, nothing of colour anywhere except a blue cloth on the arm of a chair. The doctor was standing beside a table, peering intently at a heavy book open in his hands; he beckoned us to come in as he continued reading. Then he closed the book and laid it on the table.

"It is as I said." He looked at me. "With this disease, you have up to eight months." He pulled a chair aside and motioned for me to sit. Mother stood, looking uncertain, watching as the doctor once more examined my neck from behind. She wrung her hands, her eyes darkening with the dread of memory, the knowing that death was real, that death had touched her four times already; why not five?

I flinched as the doctor's fingers found the sore spot. It was more painful than before; it seemed to grow more painful as I sat there. The doctor nodded, as though confirming to himself what he already knew. Then he reached across the table for a fat pill bottle and passed it to Mother, speaking rapidly and convincingly.

"I advise driving to the hospital with her immediately. Take these pills should she have an attack during the drive. It is unlikely this early in the diagnosis, but we want to take all precautions."

"What kind of attack?" I asked.

"Muscle contractions. Lockjaw." He led us urgently to the door and watched as we hurried without speaking up the road towards home.

Father was slicing onions to fry with the salmon. While Mom ran down the hallway to get her purse, I told him what the doctor had said.

"Bullshit." He jabbed at the air with his knife. "Bullshit, he haven't got a clue, not a gawd-damn clue."

I kicked off my dirtied sneakers and pulled on a pair of shoes. Dad kept ranting about cow shit and holes in my feet from rusty nails but his words were strained and his cheeks held the same flush of fright as mine and Mother's—he too was remembering that death was real, that death happened to real people. Still he kept ranting, hammering his words too hard; I rushed out, frightened he might break just as I was breaking inside, just as Mother was breaking inside, and that we'd have neither the time nor the strength to fix him.

Davey was down by the basement door, fiddling with a fishing rod. "Where's Bridgette?" I yelled.

"Right here."

"You watch her. I'll be back in a couple of hours. *Davey!*" I screamed when he didn't answer.

"I'll watch her. Jeesh!" he yelled back.

I ran to the car; Mother already had the motor running. She drove. Fast. My stomach was now churning. I wanted to lie down on the ground and roll about. I wanted to lean forward and wrap my arms around myself and rock. But the two of us endured that one-hour drive to Corner Brook with a superficial calm; we spoke sparingly, and when we did it was about the traffic, the weather, and whatever else required no thought, no discussion. Outside the city Mother pulled over for gas and I got behind the wheel; she didn't know its streets as I did.

The wait time at the hospital was mercifully short. The doctor listened. He was a big man with a reddish face, a big friendly smile, and wide-open eyes that widened further as I told him my story.

"You say he gave you a tetanus shot?"

I nodded.

"Are you sure?"

I rolled up my sweater to show him the little red prick mark.

He shook his head. "Well, I can tell you right now you don't have tetanus. If you did he would've killed you with that shot."

I blew out of the hospital on a wave of euphoria. At a highway restaurant we called Dad, rolling our eyes at his tirade about how he'd known all along it was nothing and how he was going over to punch out *that gawd-damn doctor*. Mother begged him to wait—she wanted to *punch his gawd-damn lights out too*—and I laughed and Mother laughed and I could hear Father laughing at the other end of the line.

After that Mother and I sat down at a booth and ordered coconut cream pie. We drank coffee and talked and laughed and talked as our hearts settled down to their routine beat. We were relatively calm driving back home, both of us humming along with Ricky Skaggs's "Love's Gonna Get You Someday." But something wasn't right. Something was squirming deep inside my bowels. And everything was still gunning just a little too hard— my heart, my thoughts, my reactions. Shock, I figured. Still feeling a bit shocked.

DARKNESS

I'D BEEN BACK HOME in St. John's for ten days when the darkness descended. It was early September; Bridgette had just started kindergarten and Davey grade six.

One Saturday night I hosted a small gathering of old friends, hoping to reconnect. After the last soul had left I went zipping through the house, singing along with the Stones, washing ashtrays and wineglasses, reflecting on the evening. It hadn't been the greatest. I no longer did drugs of any kind and felt further and further estranged from those who did—which was practically everyone I knew. It was late, perhaps midnight before I headed up the stairs, still humming. I was partway up, foot lifted for the next step, when it happened. When something struck me *inside* so hard that it brought me to my knees. Terror. Instant terror. As if suddenly awakened in the middle of the night by a cold sinister breath on your face. But I hadn't been sleeping. And the lights were on. And the sinister cold was within me.

I bent over, my chest too tight to properly breathe. I felt no pain, only fear. I could see just fine; everything was the same: the beige carpet, the green wall, the window at the top of the stairs with the straggling red geranium on its sill. I could move. Holding on to the banister, I pulled myself upright on shaky legs. I made it to the top and then to my room; I lay down carefully on the bed. I tried to examine the fear. To feel around its edges, to prod it. But there was no beginning point, no ending; it simply *was*. Suffused throughout me. My fingers ached with it. My whole being was locked in cold, hard terror.

I curled up carefully on my side. I held on to myself and rocked gently. Waiting. For it to leave. It didn't. It didn't leave me. It stayed. I started to pray. I started mumbling the Lord's Prayer over and over and over in one mad desperate mumbling of syllables. Then I began to rock to them. And I rocked and rocked and prayed myself to sleep.

The next morning I jolted awake. It was still there. Cold, cramped fear paralyzing my body. Light filtered through the curtains, birds chirped. The gentle hum of early Sunday traffic. Davey was moving about in his room; Bridgette called to Darby, her cat. I lay rigid, seized with terror. Then I got out of bed, hobbled to the bathroom, and threw up. I stood in the shower under the hot water, trying to loosen the fear, to scald it out. It didn't slacken. Bridgette brought me the brush to fix her hair into a ponytail, chatting away. She didn't notice anything different about me. Nor did Davey when we spoke on the landing. My voice sounded outside of myself, but I stretched my mouth into smiles. I kept taking deep breaths, trying to open my chest, unknot my stomach, create openings for the fear to leave. I kept peering into the hallway mirror each time I passed, looking into my eyes for the fear; it could not be seen.

I went out on the deck and sat in the cooling September sun. The backyard was scented with crabapples starting to rot on the ground. I now knew madness. I now knew suicide. I closed my eyes, cowering. This was why, oh this was why. It was as though a hole had been busted through the side of my world and I was staring into a whole new realm of being I hadn't known existed. And that nothing—no matter if the fear paralyzing me suddenly vanished like a drop of dew beneath a hot sun—nothing could ever patch that hole back up.

There'd been times, after Fordie died, when I'd look back with longing to *before* his death. Everything was measured in terms of *before* the accident or *after* the accident. And now, hunched over with fear on the deck, I was already lamenting another *before*. *Before* that awful moment on the stairs, *before* that awful doctor and his diagnosis—for I knew those two moments were connected; that the doctor had tripped my mind and that this terror was the fallout. I intuitively knew, too, that the trauma triggered by the diagnosis was directly linked to the trauma of Ford's death. And little Paul? Had I suffered trauma back then? How far back did *before* go?

God has infinite wisdom, it is said. And if divine consciousness is represented by those perfect golden discs haloing the heads of deities, it must be a battered, dented, misshapen thing circling the heads of us mortals as we're dragged screaming and protesting through the trials of this world. For that day on the deck, trying to figure out what to do, I had no wisdom at all. Call somebody? Who? I had no family in St. John's; I had no close friend to trust with such knowledge of me. Doctors? What would one say? *Hi, I'm Donna, I've gone quite mad. Hello, yes, may I speak to someone— you see, I seem to have gone out of my mind.*

Then what? Pack a bag for the mental institution? What about Davey and Bridgette? I listened as they ran through the house,

Davey laughing, Bridgette shrieking. Their father lived on the west coast of the island and was usually gone for long periods of time on foreign ships; he was a fisheries observer now, monitoring catches. Who would care for my babies? What about my mother, my father? I lowered my head with the horror of it: that I should go this way. Through madness. Then I looked up, wringing my hands—*Who thinks like this?*

Bridgette emerged onto the deck; in her red rubber boots and carrying a white bucket, she began collecting snails from the rotting pickets behind the apple tree. Davey poked his head out his upstairs window, calling out to a neighbour friend to come finish their Dungeons and Dragons game. A crow startled the air with its harsh caw, another cawed back. Clouds drifted with the warm breeze and the hum of traffic out front grew louder as morning deepened. Come lunchtime I was still sitting there. I didn't know what to do. The terror inside me was so huge I felt nauseated by it. Bridgette kept wandering back onto the deck, sitting beside me, wandering off. Davey kept poking his head out, looking down at me then vanishing back inside. They didn't know what was happening, but they sensed something. Never had their mother *ever* sat so quietly and for so long.

At some point Davey came out on the step, his hair swept across his brow, his young face taut with concern.

"We have to change the kettle," he said.

"The kettle?" It was one of those that whistled as it steamed.

"Bridgette's afraid of it. That it's going to start steaming when she's by herself in the house. And she'll have to take it off the stove and burn herself."

"She's not allowed to boil the kettle."

"Even when it's not on the stove, she's afraid it's going to boil."

"Seriously?"

"She phones me at school, scared of the kettle."

"She—?" I stared at him, aghast. "She phones you at school?"

"I had to run home the other day. The teacher doesn't like it, Bridgette calling me at school."

"But—she's never at home alone."

"Sometimes she gets out earlier than me."

"And she calls you?"

He gave an impatient nod; he was holding a can of unopened cat food and I could hear Darby meowing inside. There was a smell of burnt toast. He was feeding them both, Bridgette and the cat. Davey had become his sister's father, caring for her after school, during holidays while I worked or ran errands—making her snacks, dragging her around with him on his paper route, buying her treats.

"Uh, Mum, there's something else. Bridgette said her teacher ripped her shirt. You should talk to her." He gave a decisive nod. I felt in him then a maturity, one born of a sense of responsibility beyond his years.

He went back inside, making nurturing sounds to the cat. Presently Bridgette rounded the corner of the house, lugging the white bucket filled with snails.

I called her over, asking about the ripped shirt.

She put down the bucket and nodded.

"Why?" I asked.

"I left my pencil at home and she grabbed after me."

Images suddenly came to mind, things I hadn't registered at the time: Bridgette always checking her book bag for her pencil,

Bridgette running down the stairs after she'd gone to bed to check that her pencil was in her bag.

"She yells all the time. I hide beneath a desk sometimes so she doesn't see me."

Ohhh, gawd.

"Will you go see her, Mummy? I'll go with you," she added as I stared. Her eyes were the same earnest blue of her brother's. She stood erect, her shoulders straight.

I nodded. "Tomorrow morning."

After she went inside I finally stood up. Then I did as Davey was doing, as Bridgette was doing. I moved. I started getting my clothes ready for work the next morning. I called a friend of Dave's and told him I needed a car. And so it happened that, in the ways of Dave's world, a ten-year-old black Lincoln Continental was delivered that afternoon, its bonnet as long and wide as a rowboat, its beige leather seats faded and smelling of old rain, its missing registration accompanied by a story. "Just drive it," one of the fellows who delivered it said. "Don't get stopped by the cops, and she's insured if you have an accident."

Night came. I poured a glass of whisky and took a huge gulp, feeling it burn through my knotted stomach. After another gulp I went upstairs with it, leaning against my bedroom window frame, looking down at the darkened empty street. A hunched figure appeared around the corner, bundled beneath a raglan and with a bandana wrapped around her head: Mae, the reclusive elderly woman whose house stood kitty-corner across the street. Every time I looked there were different cats peering from her window-sills, before her closed curtains. Brown paint flaked off Mae's little bungalow, her windows rheumy with street dust, her doorplace speckled with droppings from the pigeons she fed daily and that roosted on her roof at night. I'd spoken to her a few times when passing her yard, but she would always turn her back and scurry inside.

She looked around guardedly this night as she hobbled past, the front of her coat all bunched out. She was hiding something. I kept watching as she crossed the street, holding on to her bundle with one hand as she used the other to open her gate. Shuffling up her steps, she pushed open her door then bent forward, a cat leaping from inside her coat and into her house. She'd rescued another stray. I wondered how many cats she had in there. I wondered how she'd become so solitary. I wondered whether her descent had grown out of a normal day that suddenly went bad. I wondered if she too needed to keep moving to keep from descending further. I wondered how much further down there was left to go. And I wondered which of us would strike bottom first.

⋙——▷

The following morning, once Davey had called out goodbye after breakfast, I walked with Bridgette to her school. The terror had lessened into a fear that prowled around in my belly, shallowed my breathing, and stiffened my legs. Bridgette took my hand as we walked. She sensed my fear, and must have believed it was her teacher I was frightened of, just as she was.

We were admitted into the principal's office. Mrs. Harrington was rotund, with dimpled cheeks and little dimpled hands. She promptly sent for the offending teacher, turning to us with a kindly smile: the epitome of a storybook educator. Ms. Logan, on the other hand, when she appeared at the door—with her reddened face, the hard-set line of her mouth, her dazed eyes—was the very picture of an angry heart medicated, I guessed, with alcohol.

Ms. Logan turned her steely gaze directly onto Bridgette as I held up the torn shirt.

"Are you accusing me of tearing your shirt, Bridgette?"

Bridgette nodded, her eyes huge and solemn, non-wavering as Ms. Logan stepped closer.

"Bridgette, I did not tear your shirt."

"Yes, you did, Ms. Logan." Her voice was small. I stood then. I was breathing too rapidly. I grasped Bridgette's hand and turned to Mrs. Harrington, my mouth dry as powder.

"Are we the first to complain about Ms. Logan?"

Mrs. Harrington remained sitting. She reached for a pen, saying in a reassuring voice, "There are forms and paperwork needed, if you wish to pursue." She looked at me appealingly.

I felt she wanted me to take the incident further. But right now I had to get out. The air was being sucked from the room. "We want a different classroom," I said.

Mrs. Harrington had already written the door number on a piece of paper and was passing it to me. "Miss Fraser's. Room 1C."

I ducked outside, still holding Bridgette's hand, and hurried down the corridor, gulping in air. There were kids running about, teachers herding them along. I was hailed by a group of women. They knew about Bridgette's ripped shirt from their own kids in the class. "She's been suspended in the past for drinking," one woman said to me, her voice quiet. "She slapped a child in kindergarten about two years ago. We're getting her out. Your help would be appreciated."

I nodded. I could scarcely hear them; I was wheezing like an asthmatic. I turned from them, saying to Bridgette, "Which classroom? Do you remember what she said?"

"It's on the paper."

"But what did she say?"

"Miss Fraser's."

"Where? Which door?"

"I think it's that one down there."

I squeezed her hand. "Let's go home. We'll come back after lunch."

"There's Brendan. *Brendan!*" shouted Bridgette. "I can go with Brendan, Mommy. He's in Miss Fraser's class."

I let go of her hand and she ran along with her freckled-faced friend and I hurried for the door, escaping into the open air. I walked hard up the knoll in front of the school and towards home, berating myself with every step. *Shameful, shameful. To abandon my daughter. I am better than this, I am better than this.*

»——▷

That evening I rolled around in bed, anguishing through the moments, searching for a respite from the fear. Then, thinking of Mother's crucifix hanging over Ford's photograph, I reached for my own. It was small, pewter, and entwined with thornlike leaves that dug into my hand as I clutched it. Perhaps it was that—the solid feel of the cross in my mother's hand—that had caused her to choose it over the abstraction of God. For it rooted God to flesh and bone and other worldly materials, giving a stronger sense of holding on to something to keep from running screaming into the night.

>—▷

At the fish plant I stood at my customary station at the end of the assembly line, my turbulent insides finding a little comfort in the raucous, rhythmic roar of the skinning machines, the vibrations of the conveyor belts as they rattled along. I took my breaks, played poker through lunch, autopiloted back to work. Sometimes the fear got so strong I'd flee to the washroom to hide before I crumbled. Sometimes I'd go to the nurse on site and murmur something about a bad stomach and she'd give me a thick liquid to drink from small paper cups. Those little acts of mine brought brief moments of control, and those moments of control brought courage for the moments to come. Nights I sought some semblance of release through a strong shot of whisky. But only at night. There were times when I'd look at that bottle in the mid-morning, in the mid-afternoon, but no. I was a mother. I could not abandon Davey and Bridgette any more than I already had. I prayed instead, I prayed repetitively through those moments when the fear intensified, threatening to overwhelm me. *Dear God, take it, take it from me, our father who art in heaven hallowed be thy name* . . .

Within weeks I was no longer me. The madness had taken over. My mind started playing tricks. It started focusing on one little thing—the vase on the table, say—till it broke apart into pixels; my heart would leap with fear as I'd blink it back together. Someone's voice as they spoke would become garbled, losing meaning in a flow of syllables, striking a deeper fear into my heart. Air would suction itself from the room, leaving me gasping for breath. Should a door slam or the phone ring the sounds would shudder through me like a 747 barrelling overhead, sending me fleeing into the smaller confines of a washroom, where I felt I could command the space more easily and keep myself together.

Weeks turned into months. I thanked God I had no family in St. John's and I discouraged calls from my few remaining friends. I seldom left the house except to work, pick up groceries, pay bills. I'd often think back to the days before this madness struck and the little things I'd taken for granted—reading a book, strolling through the park. I thought too of those wretched moments of grieving after Fordie's death. Without pause I would have traded that terror inside of me for a lifetime of grieving. Hard as they were, they were soul based, not hell. And anything that isn't hell is heaven.

A GAME OF CARDS

I STRUGGLED THROUGH THAT WINTER then fell into a fatigue so deep that, come spring, simply getting out of bed exhausted me. It became harder and harder to get to work on time, to stand at my station. During lunchtime in the cafeteria I'd lay my head on my folded arms and, in the midst of a hundred people talking, yelling, laughing, and arguing over games of poker, I'd sleep. Coming home from work, I could no longer walk up the stairs; I'd fall to my knees and crawl up. I'd sit in the shower, unable to stand. The fatigue was growing stronger than the fear.

One morning I was roused from a deep sleep by Bridgette's cat Darby springing onto my bed, digging her claws into my arms as she scampered across the sheets. I opened my eyes onto Bridgette gazing down at me, her blue eyes beaming with pride as she pointed out the walking harness she'd just made for her rat, Merlin, who was sitting on her shoulder. The rat, too, was gazing down at me, its whiskers twitching.

"For cripes sake!" I yelled, leaping out of bed. "The cat's gonna eat that thing. And it should."

Davey too was yelling, from downstairs. Snails—something about snails. I ran into the hallway . . . and screamed. There were dozens of them, all slithering down the stairwell wall. Darby sprinted from the room, lunging for them; Bridgette screamed at Darby; Davey screamed at Bridgette and I screamed at Bridgette and then came a bedlam of screams as we all screamed at each other and the cat and the rat.

A frenzied ten minutes later—the snails now scraped off the walls, dumped back into Bridgette's bucket, and flung out into the backyard—I rushed through a shower and then the making of breakfast, the making of lunches. Davey dashed out the door; I dropped Bridgette off at her school and then sped down the narrow road towards the fish plant. I was late. How late? I looked at the dashboard clock, contemplated the time, and then hit the brakes with a sharp intake of breath. *The fear was gone. It wasn't there, inside of me. It was—just—gone!*

Instantly, before the thought had completed itself, it flooded back in. I parked by the side of the road and sat, stupefied. But it *had* gone, if only temporarily. I got out of the car and gazed out over the harbour. The air was briny, the sea a choppy dark blue. Dozens of gulls flapped and squawked above the fish plant and the trawlers docked alongside. For a whole half hour or more the fear had disappeared. As if I'd awakened too quickly and raced too hard through my morning for it to catch up. Till now.

I started to cry. For the first time in eight months, ever since the terror had struck, I cried. If it can happen once, it can happen again. It wasn't meshed into my bones or webbed onto my liver. It wasn't a part of me. *It can go.*

I got back into the car and turned it around, heading for the mini-mall I passed every morning en route to work. There was a clinic there. I'd paused a hundred times trying to find the courage to go inside, but I'd had no notion of how to present myself—*Hey, what's happenin', Doc. I'm frozen with fear. Can you fix me?*

Inside the clinic a few people sat waiting. They looked up as I entered. They stared. I caught sight of myself in a mirror and stared, too—an apparition in my white smock, my hairnet under my black ball cap, my filleting knife hooked on to one of my rubber boots.

The door leading into the doctor's office opened. A receptionist stood there with a file in her hands, her lips parting as though to call someone's name. She saw me and closed her mouth. I don't know what she saw in my eyes. Perhaps glints of hope bordering on mania. Perhaps just the mania. When her eyes dropped to the knife she stepped aside and ushered me in. No one in the waiting room protested.

The doctor was bent over a cabinet, thumbing through files in an open drawer. He looked up at a sound from the receptionist, then beckoned her to leave and for me to sit. I sat stiff as a nail. The doctor pulled out another drawer. He took out two cherry suckers. He tossed one on his desk towards me then unfurled the other's wrapper and popped it in his mouth.

"Just when you think you've had every kind of day, eh?" he said.

The statement was directed at me. I gave him a shaky smile, unwrapped the lollipop, sucking on it hard to keep my lips from quivering.

I saw a framed photograph of an old woman with curly grey hair and a small face sitting on his desk. "She looks like my great-aunt Emma," I said, my voice unsteady.

He nodded. "She actually *is* my great-aunt Emma."

"Mine's from Jackson's Arm."

"So's mine."

I looked up. His eyes were kind. He was youngish, late thir-
ties. Fair-skinned.

"Mine's married to Uncle Kenneth Lush," I said.

"Mine too. Guess that makes us cousins."

I pulled the sucker out of my mouth. "That's why I'm here.
I'm looking for a kidney."

He grinned. I told him my name; he told me his. Cousins
through marriage. On my mother's side. I closed my eyes, rubbing
my forehead. There was a smell of home about this man, enough
to make me trust him. I told him everything. About Ford. The
misdiagnosis. The horrible feeling of terror—how it struck, when
it struck, how it clung to my insides like tar. And how it had vanished, for a short time, that morning.

He sent me for blood work and we discovered that I had
mononucleosis. A virus that causes extreme fatigue, flu-like
symptoms, sore throat—all those things I'd been plagued with for
the past month but had brushed aside as minor ailments. Hope
soared. Perhaps it was this virus that had caused the fear. Perhaps
the fear would leave after the virus had run its course. Hope.

Of concern was the doctor's orders to take a leave from work.
How to cope without the routine of movement? He made an
appointment for me to see a psychologist about the fear—or, as he
called it, anxiety. A new word. It had a name. More hope. He suggested that I check out programs at the hospital for group therapy,
and wrote me a prescription for a drug. But I couldn't imagine
sitting within the confines of a group, nor would I risk taking a
drug—fearing it might interfere with my thin grasp on reality. I

would later learn that this latter fear is a common symptom shared by most individuals suffering from chronic anxiety.

Driving home late that afternoon, I slowed as I passed Mae's paint-peeled house on the corner. Cats lined the outside window ledge, purring down on her—and on Davey, having a cup of tea on her front porch steps.

I pulled over to the curb and rolled down the window. "Nice day," I called out. Mae stood. She was tiny, thick grey curls cropping her brow and little brown eyes blinking nervously from their crinkly beds.

"Mae's got about ten cats in there that I counted," Davey told me at supper that evening. He'd been inside her house several times, he added, having tea with her. It had been through his paper route, passing her flyers, that he'd first struck up a conversation. There were always at least five or six cats drifting about the living room at a time, he went on. "But there's always one I never seen before."

"Do you think she's crazy to have them many cats?" I asked him.

He shrugged, sauntering off.

"Wait, how come she invites you in?" I called after him. He shrugged again and vanished up the stairs.

Right. Because you're eleven, I answered for him. Because you're young and you don't judge her and so she trusts you with her vulnerability. She locks the rest of us out, fearing we'll think her crazy and take away the things that matter to her. Just as I'd been locking out the world from the fear of being thought crazy and perhaps having my kids taken. The only difference between me and that old woman was our birthdates. And that the symptoms of her madness were more visible than my own. Except, of course, to those people sitting in the doctor's waiting room that morning.

>——▷

I went to see the psychologist the kind doctor had recommended. She's one of the best, he'd said. Getting great reviews. I spilled out the entire convoluted yarn. I told her what the fear felt like, the churning of thoughts, the cycling of thoughts, negative thoughts spiralling out of control and into panic, into soul-numbing terror.

Stress. She said it was stress.

Stress. Not being educated, I asked her what that meant.

Stress, she said, was a normal response to too many pressures happening at once.

Normal. I was as normal as a rubber boot in a microwave oven. I never went back and garbaged her prescription for vitamin B.

>——▷

Winter that year hit early and hard. I fretted through a snow-storm one night, listening to the wind hurtle against the windows, my insides roiling up their own storm of anxieties. The winds stopped by morning. I sat up on the side of the bed and lowered my head, breathing through the fear and fatigue. Davey had a dental appointment and I'd already missed two that the dentist had charged me for.

Screwing up my courage, I got dressed and went out to shovel the driveway. It was bitterly cold and the snow was up to my knees.

I started shovelling. Everything hurt—my neck, my back, my arms. I kept shovelling. Within twenty minutes I was sniffing and snorting like a workhorse. Once the car's back wheels had been bared I tossed aside the shovel and, pushing wet strands of hair off my face, got in and started the engine, hoping to barrel my way out. The front tires spun. They spun and spun. I opened the door, leaning out for a look. Ice. The tires were on ice. I accelerated hard, trying to burn through it; the tires kept spinning. I accelerated harder. The stench of burning rubber filled the air and white exhaust fumes clouded the car, nearly choking me, but nothing moved, nothing fucking moved—not the car, not that quivering mass of anxiety consuming my insides, and not the rigid policies of that gawd-damned dentist who'd soon be charging me for another missed appointment.

I tore back inside and down to the basement. Snatching the axe off the chopping block, I swung back through the house and out the door and started swinging at the ice beneath the tires. I swung and swung like a madwoman, and that's what I was, *mad, mad, mad,* cursing with every swing and shutting my eyes against the ice splintering back like needles and striking against my face.

A neighbour, Len, called out, "Come for a bite and a drink this evening."

I looked up. He was swinging a pickaxe on his own driveway in a leisurely fashion. I waved. Called out some excuse about work and then went back to splintering ice. I hadn't socialized since that gathering back in September when hell had descended. Just one more thing tormenting me of late: my growing sense of isolation.

"Maybe," I added absently.

"I mean it. Me and Deb are having friends over. Come!"

I missed the appointment by six or seven minutes. The dentist had gone; his receptionist passed me a bill. I refused it. "Call the fuckin' cops," I yelled and bustled Davey out of there, ignoring his look of utter horror. Six minutes! Bastards!

By evening I was so anxious that I started readying for Len and Deb's dinner just to have something to focus on. I had no intention of going. But still I showered, hauled on a clean pair of jeans and a T-shirt, skewered red lipstick across my mouth, mascaraed my lashes and traced liner beneath my eyes. I kept glancing across the street through the dark to the warm yellow light spilling from the windows of their house. I took a second look in the mirror, then dabbed specks of lipstick on my white face and rouged them in. I loosened my hair from its elastic grip and curled the ends with a curling iron. I stared at myself in a full-length mirror. Five six and a hundred and thirteen pounds. I was gaunt. And the neck of my T-shirt was stretched. Fuck it. I told Davey and Bridgette I'd be away for the evening, pasted on a smile, and walked across the street with a mickey of whisky.

I was late; they were already at the table when I got there. I quickly did a seat count: eight, plus me. I knew no one; I scarcely even knew Len and Deb. But I sat down; introductions were made; the conversation resumed. I smiled and smiled and answered a few questions and feigned interest. They all looked so lovely—the men with their trimmed hair and beards and cuffed shirts, the women all loosely attired in flowing garb, dangly earrings and bangles, chic haircuts. They sat with poised expressions, chatting and laughing and tossing around banter like confetti. Feeling like someone off the streets with my stretched-neck T-shirt and frayed jeans, I began searching my mind for a plausible way out. *Oops, left a fire burning in the bathtub. Gotta go, there're feral cats pissing on the couch . . .*

Another woman emerged from somewhere in the back of the house, thanked the host for the use of her phone, and took a seat across from me in a flourish of slinky black silks. She was slender and blond, a sleek blunt cut grazing her shoulders. She settled next to a bearded man, introduced as her husband, and narrowed her catlike eyes at me.

"What did you do all day?" she asked pointedly, coiling her legs beneath her.

"Ran through the house with an axe," I replied.

She stared at me for a second, then burst out laughing and held out a lovely manicured hand. "Hi, I'm Karen."

I hesitated, then held out my own knife-nicked, nail-bitten, rougher-than-grade-B-sandpaper paw.

She looked at it, then at me. "What da fuck you been doing with your hands?"

It triggered something in me, her candour; it felt like being with my sister Wanda. My turn to bust out laughing. Then I downed a shot of whisky.

I spent the rest of the evening swapping yarns with her: mine about the goings-on in a fish plant and hers about being a designer in CBC's celebrity-heavy dressing rooms. When it was time to leave she invited me to go shopping with her at a secondhand store; she bought vintage clothing for her vintage characters there, she told me, and could sometimes score cashmere sweaters for four bucks apiece.

I went home and threw out every stretched-neck T-shirt I owned. Within a few months, with the help of my new best friend

Karen, designer extraordinaire, I became a professional bin-digger, queen of fashion in the hood. And through her I made two more best friends, therein learning how friends can be the caregivers of our hearts. They fill the empty chambers and warm them with cheer. They revive the spirit through hope and transform pain into learning and learning into laughter. They seek treasures from the dark and create structure out of chaos and chase the she-devil victim from our stoop. Their instruments are acceptance and understanding and they shield us with love. I told them of my neurosis; they scoffed and said, *Ohh, fuck, Don, we've all had that.* They hadn't, but just sharing my fears would help lessen them. I was so grateful. For the first time since the crumbling of my marriage three years before, I was rebuilding a social life.

"You're so smart," said Jude in a crowded bar one night over drinks and smokes. We were sitting in a booth, the four of us leaning into each other's talk. "I'm serious," she added as I made a face. "You should go to university."

"I'm not *that* smart," I said, but I was tickled by her words. Jude, a fourth-year student at Memorial University of Newfoundland, looked like Brooke Shields with her thick dark brows and wide eyes but felt as comfy as a cushion with her granny skirts and glasses.

"Why do you think you're not smart?" asked Karen.

I'd failed high school. I'd failed secretarial school. I think I even failed an IQ test I'd taken along the way.

I leaned back, spared from answering by a waitress reaching across our table, removing our empties and cleaning the ashtray. I looked around the bar. The air was thick with talk, smoke, and music. Just the kind of place where I coped best with my anxieties.

It overwhelmed the senses. I talked, laughed, drank, smoked, sashayed around. I engaged in conversations where I had to think, respond, shout above the noise to be heard. I ate popcorn, fixed my hair, fixed my lipstick, posed just right for some dude across the bar—which is as far as it ever got. There was no room for intimacy in my fear-constricted heart.

That evening I fell into bed and slept dreamlessly through the night. Sleep. God's vacation from Self. But those nights when dreams did break through my sleep, they were variations on the same frightening theme: matter swirling in bits—bits of words, bits of people, bits of everything swirling around me like a tornado and me swirling inside of it, struggling to escape from being sucked into its vortex.

≫—▷

The next morning, after Davey and Bridgette had gone off to school, I turned up the radio, just as I always did, to disrupt the repetitive thinking chasing itself around in my mind. Except this morning it wasn't the usual *You're losing it, my gawd you're losing it*; it was Jude's *You're smart, why aren't you in university?* funnelling around in there. The lovely doctor who'd diagnosed me with mono had mentioned my signing up for courses somewhere, but I'd tossed his words aside just as I'd tossed aside his prescription for tricyclic antidepressants. The thread holding me to sanity was so thin I feared taking any drug that risked breaking it. But taking courses—that just felt like a joke to me. I couldn't concentrate on Bridgette's primary books, let alone read a textbook. The only thing that relieved my anxiety was to keep moving.

I baked bread and cooked up a pot of beans. I washed the dishes and swept the floors. Finally I darted kitty-corner across the street with a bowl of leftover turkey soup for Mae. Through little such offerings I had earned her trust; she would often invite me in now. Mae had emphysema, which meant she was always winded and spoke in a dry, wheezy voice. Her prime subject was her cats; there were typically three or four strolling about. They each had a name, and she would scold them as we sat. *Now, Bobby, you leave Willaby alone. Oh, he's the devil, that Bobby is. Oh, yes, my dear, he's the devil. Willaby's going to set him straight one of these times; I tell you, I see it coming.*

That morning Mae sat slight as a girl on the edge of her couch as she told me about the old feral tom she'd been trying for the past two years to rescue from the streets. "He'll come as far as my gate, Donna, and no farther. Except to dash in for a bit of food I puts out. Then he darts into the bushes to eat it. My dear, I don't know what they done to that cat, but I've never seen anything sadder."

We sat quiet for a moment, each of us radiating an unrelated sadness of our own. I knew mine; I wondered about hers. How was it that she so identified with the forgotten and the abandoned? I didn't feel I had the right to ask.

I went home thinking again about what Jude had said. I'd always considered myself quick to catch on to things. Back in high school, it was only math and science I'd failed. Those were province-wide exams, and with each one, after seeing that most questions were on material we hadn't even covered in class, I'd marked an X across the entire exam and then walked out. Night school in Corner Brook had been lost in a haze of pot and other stuff best not remembered, and yet I'd still managed a passing grade in science. Secretarial school had been a nosedive into disaster the minute I stepped into the classroom, when the instructor stared at my jeans and told me dresses or skirts were a requirement. Right. Hadn't worn either since I was six and Mother stopped dressing me. Plus, I didn't own any. Plus, my skinny legs, bony knees, and knobby ankles were *never* to be shown in public. Plus, that had been one of the coldest winters on record, snow up to our butts and me with a two-mile walk there and back.

Failed. The only things I'd failed at were stupid things. When did I start thinking *I* was one of the stupid things? Perhaps I *should* go to university. What was there to fear? The mother of all fears already lived inside me.

I wrapped up a loaf of hot bread from the oven, ladled out a bowl of beans, and trotted back to Mae's. She was sitting at her kitchen table stacked high with cans of cat food, some half empty and smelling like yesterday's gravy.

"What's your biggest fear?" I asked, taking a seat across from her, watching as she cut stale bread into perfect little squares with a pair of scissors, tossing them into a bowl for the pigeons.

"My, Donna, I don't know." She patted her chest; her emphysema was acting up and she was wheezing.

"Your lungs?"

"No, my dear. I'm used to this. I'll tell you now, Donna, what my greatest fear is. My cats. I worries a lot about my cats. If something happens to me there'll be no one to feed them."

Oh, Mae. That was my own greatest fear—that something might happen to me and there'd be no one to care for my children. Oh Jeezes, Mae, *that* is the greatest of all fears, not some silly exam in a classroom, even if it is a university.

The stars aligned. That evening an old family friend of Dave's dropped by for an unexpected visit. Marion, a public servant with a master's degree in political science, didn't have kids of her own and enjoyed chatting with Bridgette and Davey. We ordered a pizza and sat around the table sharing food and a game of cards— Crazy Eights. It was then that I had an *ohh haa* moment.

Davey patiently explained to Marion, for the third time, the rules for Crazy Eights. She caught on to the suits, but not the runs. She caught on to the runs, but forgot the suits. She remembered that deuces meant *pick up two* but could never remember that the deuce of spades meant *pick up four*. Or that, to change suits, yes, you had to play an eight, but that any card in your hand matching the one just played can also change the suit and that *No no no, you can't pick up four with the deuce of diamonds, only the deuce of spades . . . Ohh gawwwd, how'd you ever graduate university with a master's!*

And there it was. The *ohh haa* moment. *If you can do it, I can do it too.*

Oh, the paradoxes. Of having to leave home to find it. Of having to go mad to find a sane thought. Of becoming impoverished to find one's riches. Of playing the devil's game to find the angel at the table.

The Beaches; the house I grew up in is third from the left. Dad built that big two storey with his brothers.

Me on the left, holding my sister Wanda's hand. My raised arm was for protection—I was extremely shy.

Wanda and I (I'm on the left), standing near Uncle Art Osmond's house, where we saw our first picture show later that year. We would have been ten and nine.

My children, Bridgette and David, during my first year of university. Bridgette is five and Davey twelve, just a few years from Wanda's and my ages above.

Me in grade two. I hadn't met Dr. Seuss yet. My clenched lips are hiding my missing front teeth.

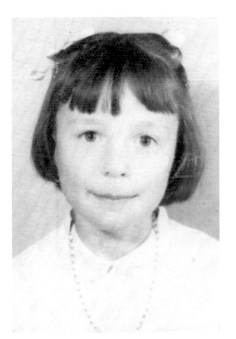

Our one-room school on the Beaches. One of my uncles is posing in front.

Our only family portrait, 1973, the year I left home. Tommy and Karen are in the back; the middle row is Ford, Dad, Mom, and Glenn; Wanda and myself in the front.

Ford asked me to take this photo of him in 1979, so he could send a picture back to Dad.

My father, Enerchius Osmond, and my mother, Claudine (Ford)
Osmond, sometime in the mid-80s.

My dearest friends accompanied me in those horrible years of darkness. Above is Karen, who introduced me to a new circle of friends, and below dearest Mae, our neighbour in St. John's who inspired two of my novels.

My graduation from university in 1992. With David, Mom, and Bridgette.

My siblings and I in 2016: from left, Wanda; Tommy; myself; Karen; and Glenn.

Me with my stack of novels, inspired by my life in the Maritimes.

ALL IS GRACE

BY SEPTEMBER OF 1987 I'd gotten a student loan and was enrolled in three courses at Memorial University of Newfoundland, with a plan to graduate with a degree in Social Work, the *only* degree that didn't require math. Plus, given my background in drugs, the streets, communal living, and re-entering the education system as a mature student, perhaps I'd have something to offer. I was thirty-one. It had been eight years since my brother's passing. A year since the misdiagnosis that had tripped my mind. Four months since the mononucleosis diagnosis that had ended my job at the fish plant. Davey was thirteen; Bridgette was six.

My first assignment was in a history class: a composition essay on colonialism in South Africa during the 1800s, written from the perspective of someone who'd lived through it.

I came home and stared at the history textbook, along with the six other books I'd signed out from the library for research. How does one *research*? What da fawk was a *composition*? I found a dictionary. A composition can be a short essay. Essay. Mmmph! Got an A once on an essay in grade six. Lesson number one: look beyond big words to find their simple meaning.

I read all the books. I read and I read. I started taking notes, feeling grand that I was *taking notes*. I kept reading and noting and scribbling till it started making sense.

Two days before the assignment was due, I was standing at the sink soaping down dirty dishes when a *voice* came to me. The *voice* was that of a crooked Afrikaner involved in stealing land from Africans for the diamonds it held. The *voice* started talking in a twangy sort of accent. I wiped my hands on the back of my jeans, grabbed a pen, and began catching the words as they fell through my mind. I wrote fast to keep up with the *voice*. That night, the essay was written.

A week later I received the paper back with an A. Loaded down with more books, I ran the two miles home, bolted inside, dropped the books and grabbed the phone, and called my mother. I got an *A*, I said breathlessly when she answered. I blathered like a fool. I told her what the essay was about and what I'd written and the perspective I'd written it from and I blathered and blathered. I was so proud. My mother was prouder. "I wish I lived alongside you; I'd be going with you. Now, don't you give that up. Whatever happens, you keep going."

I kept going. I signed up for four more courses come January and studied through the summer and all through the next year. It was tough. The mono was gone by now, yet the fatigue persisted.

And the anxiety was constant. My coping behaviours were ludicrous: arriving for each class ten minutes early to get a seat by the door in case I needed to flee the pending scream; plotting escape routes upon entering any room; ensuring there were brown paper bags in my pockets should I start hyperventilating; walking up and down six flights of stairs in the library, thrice a day, loaded down with books rather than chance the small suffocating space of the elevator; jiggling my foot so hard during classes that my whole body vibrated as I kept myself hidden beneath coat, scarves, and loose clothing; rocking myself to sleep at night, whispering the Lord's Prayer over and over and over; bounding from bed immediately upon awakening and before my monkey brain kicked in; putting a stationary bike in my bedroom when depression started setting in and pedalling furiously for three miles each morning for the energy and courage to get downstairs and make breakfast; twirling my fingers through my hair, often tugging it hard enough to create physical pain as a way to escape the mental pain; constantly monitoring my cup of tea or coffee in the university cafeteria in case someone might drug it and I'd lose my thin grasp on reality; carrying out progressive relaxation exercises during classes, during conversations, during any fucking moment. I'd caught on to another great trick, too: focusing on my big toe. During those long classes in which I'd be jiggling away, anxiety threatening to overwhelm me, I'd concentrate all my energies on that one part of my entire body and feel it coming alive with sensations, often feeling it swell to the size of my head, feeling the blood pumping through it, the tingling. Such a silly little act, but sometimes it had the power to push aside the most crippling anxiety.

It was during exam week of my third year that I started hemorrhaging—or so I thought. It was an hour before my first exam: English literature, *King Lear*. I made it to the hospital's emergency, panicking. *Oh, Mae, who will care for my babies?*

After a brief examination, the doctor told me to get dressed and then brought me to an office and had me sit down. She asked a few questions about who I was, what I worked at. I kept staring at her, hands clenched, waiting for the diagnosis.

"Donna," she said. "You've started your period. Why would you think you were hemorrhaging?"

My period. Menstrual cycle. Been happening to me every month, twelve months a year, for the past twenty-odd years. I started to laugh. A hollowed sound. How incredibly ridiculous.

The good doctor was not laughing. "You're underweight," she said. "You keep twirling and pulling your hair as you sit there. You're breathless. You're jiggling and rocking. You're a thirty-three-year-old woman so disconnected from your body that you forgot about periods. What is going on with you?"

"Stress," I said, getting up. "I gotta go, I'll be late for Lear. Thanks."

She shook her head as she stood. Then she gave me her card. "Will you come see me in my office?"

I took her card, nodded my thanks again, and fled. I had thirty minutes to get across town for the exam. I nailed the exam and hurried home, heart pounding so hard it was skipping beats. I lay back on the sofa, holding my hand over it to soothe it. Bridgette would be out of school soon. I had to go get Bridgette, go get Bridgette . . .

»—▷

Towards the end of that third year Wanda came to visit from Toronto. To cover for my hyped-up behaviours, I told her I was having a mono relapse. It sounded so legitimate: mononucleosis. An illness with a proper name. So dignified.

Sister kept staring at me, shaking her head. Aghast at how skinny I'd become. And the fatigue: she'd never known me to be tired. One Saturday after running around downtown for an hour, we were back inside the car and I was so wiped out I could barely lift my hand to fit the keys into the ignition. I looked at Wanda and faked a grin. "Let's go to the mall, hey?"

She readily agreed. "Then after I'll treat you to lunch."

My insides shrivelled. It was a way of measuring my fatigue. Of assessing how sick my body was compared to her healthy one. Later that evening I overheard Wanda crying to her husband on the phone: "*There's something wrong with her, she's my sister, I knows when there's something wrong with her . . .*"

Yes. There was something wrong with me. But I was making it. Next term I'd be starting my fourth year. I was handling the anxieties. I was handling the workload, and I was getting mostly A's. I just needed to gain some weight.

I started making healthy breakfast drinks with yogurt and eggs and nutritional yeast and berries. I took up yoga at home to relax my body, stretch it out. I kept going. When I found myself adding up every odd number as a means of getting through a particularly anxious moment, or spelling words backwards, or cowering at what I'd become and panic threatened, I'd focus on my big toe and carry on.

⇒——⇨

Mothering. I was failing. The possession of my body and mind through fear and obsessive thinking sucked all joy from my world. Its sound was that of a screaming snared rabbit drowning out my son's words, my daughter's laughter. It smothered my patience, blinded me, injected a rage inside my head that projected itself outwards. *Forgive me forgive me, you're both so beautiful . . .*

›—›

It was during my fourth year that I found a diagnosis. I was sitting in a quiet section of the library, drinking coffee and leafing through the text for a course I'd just signed up for: Abnormal Psychology. I knew I'd find myself in there, but I'd been avoiding it. Afraid. Of what that diagnosis would be—*psychotic; worsens with age; no treatment; your children will inherit your madness . . .*

And there it was—third chapter in. First page. Generalized Anxiety Disorder. Followed by Post-Traumatic Stress Disorder. They were basically one and the same: high levels of anxiousness, fear, obsessive thinking, panic, hypersensitized . . . and on and on.

I closed the book. I sat back, breathing deeply. This was it. This was the thing that inhabited me. It had edges. It was real. It had a name.

I opened the book back up. I read voraciously, seeing myself in print, seeing myself validated. I was not mad. I was ill. An illness with a name, a specific name with specific symptoms. I raced through the pages like a demon searching for a cure. There wasn't one. But there was hope.

I made an appointment with a psychiatrist. This time I was better prepared. Her office was in a hospital. She sat at a small cluttered desk, wore a white jacket, and kept looking towards her office door and apologizing: she may have to leave any minute; she was expecting an emergency call. I talked as fast as I could. I had all the right words. Big words with simple meanings. Anxiety Disorder. Post-Traumatic Stress Disorder. Phobias. Panic. All of them equalling the one thing: a constant state of heightened fear and its resounding symptoms—racing heart, circular thinking, depression, fatigue. Et cetera.

She nodded knowingly. She suggested talk therapy and cognitive therapy and— In the middle of explaining what cognitive therapy was, her buzzer sounded: the emergency call. Before she dashed off she scribbled me a prescription for Valium. Chapter Four: Addictive Drugs. *Valium: The most overprescribed addictive drug for women on the market.*

"Make another appointment," the psychiatrist instructed me on her way out the door, "and we'll talk about cognitive therapy."

The earliest appointment, said her receptionist, was four months down the road. Four months. By then, if I started the Valium, I'd be a drooling addict as well as neurotic. I ripped up the prescription and headed for the car, Father's voice chasing after me. *Well, gawd-damn the like-a-that.*

⋙—▷

During that fourth year I also took a course on community development. Near the end of the semester, at the end of a class in which I'd been particularly disruptive with my smart-ass comments, Professor Burns beckoned me to her office and gestured for me to sit. She wasn't much older than me—perhaps two or three years—but the space between us was immense. She was tall and imposing. Womanish, but downplayed by nondescript pants and blouses. She ran her hands through her thick dark hair, snapped it into a ponytail, and sat back, staring at me through deep-seeing eyes.

"I know you," she said, speaking politely and intently. "I once *was* you. When you walk into a room it's as though seven people walk in with you, such is the distraction of your energy. And that energy is going to destroy you if you don't learn to harness it." She walked over to one of her shelves, selected a slim paperback, and passed it to me. It had a one-word title: *Enlightenment*.

I didn't know what it meant.

She sat down. "I'm taking a chance on you," she said calmly. "That you'll trust my privacy. I'm inviting you to a closed group at my house. Tomorrow evening, for a session of guided imagery."

I'd never heard of such a thing.

She nodded as though hearing my thought, then went on to explain how the group sat in a circle and she, Professor Burns, guided them through a sequence of visualizations. Would I come?

Yes, I would. I was curious. And I kept my mouth shut, as promised, except for telling my friend Karen about it. She wasn't a student; I was sure it was okay.

Doctor Burns didn't look so sure when she opened her door to my knock on that warm summer's evening, ten minutes late and with a friend at my side. She hesitated, then accepted Karen's proffered hand and led us inside. We followed her into a spacious living room snug with thick carpeting and colourful, abstract artwork adorning the walls.

She introduced us to the six other women already sitting in a circle on the floor. They nodded in return, smiling, looking deeply relaxed—I recognized them as senior professors from the university. I sat next to Karen, close to the door, feeling awkward about being in the confined space of my professor's living room.

Professor Burns showed no such discomfort. In a voice that was quiet but assured, she welcomed us and then turned down the lights. Soft music drifted through the room.

I started feeling agitated—the room too small, too quiet, too many people. So I kept my eye on the door, took deep breaths, and forced myself to concentrate on Professor Burns's words. She spoke quietly, slowly, as she led us into a meditation. *You are in a room* (I saw myself in a room shelved with books from floor to ceiling). *You take something from the room* (I took a book). *You hold the something in your hands and gaze at it* (I walked to a wooden study table and stared at the cover. It was a history book of sorts).

And so the experience went. For twenty minutes we each migrated through a room of our own visualizing and with minimal guidance.

Afterwards, when the lights were up and we were stretching and looking around but keeping to our places on the floor, we each shared our experience with the group. There were no two alike. The spaces visualized ranged from my book-lined room to a rustic farmhouse to a sewing room. After each description Professor Burns delivered a little talk about it. Mine, she said, reflected that of a student, where learning was structured around libraries and classrooms. And how eager I was for learning, she noted, given how I'd chosen a history book and settled with it at a study table.

I began to understand how such visualizations could act as a window into the mind of the visualizer, and how something seemingly insignificant, like choosing a book, could carry a deeper meaning.

As we walked home after the session, Karen was keen to chat. Hers had been the sewing room; Professor Burns had been dead-on in interpreting Karen's taking its tape measure and scissors to a more spacious room as indicating a desire to quit her job and start designing her own clothing.

"I've been thinking about that for the past *year*," said Karen, and with such vigour that I laughed. "I wasn't acknowledging just how *much* I've been wanting it. This is great, Don. What a process."

The following week we were back. The lights were dimmed, the music drifted out, the sweet smell of burning incense suffused the air. Professor Burns started talking, her voice soft, leading us into a deep relaxation.

I was with her from the start this time, my chest slackening, my breath deepening. *You are walking along a road.* I saw the gravel road leading into Hampden, the trees walling it in, the sky a dimming blue above it. *There is someone walking towards you.* In his faded plaid work shirt and his beat-out brown cords, Ford approached me. *The person is holding out a gift.* Ford was smiling; with both hands he held out a small dark box; the word *forgiveness* radiated from it. *Forgiveness, forgiveness, forgiveness.*

My breath quickened; my heart was pounding. I opened my eyes: the door was right there, close by. I glanced around the room. No one was looking, no one saw my discomfort. I closed my eyes and tried to slow my breathing. The door was near. I felt Karen's nearness. I kept myself sitting there, doing deep breathing exercises till Professor Burns gently called everyone awake.

Finally the lights were up and the women were stretching out their limbs. I headed for the washroom, sat on the toilet, and leaned over, letting my head swing down to open my chest cavity and help ease back the threatening panic. Then, once I felt okay, I stood up and looked in the mirror, flicking my fingers through my hair, flicking a bit of cold water on my face. I smiled as I opened the door and returned to the circle.

When it was my turn to share I made up something about a stranger on a road giving me a map. Afterwards I said nothing to Karen about what I'd actually dredged up, and scarcely heard anything she had to say about her own visualization—the clamouring in my head was too loud.

The two ugly sisters, shame and guilt. Why was he forgiving me? *He thinks it's my fault he's dead.* What else was there to think?

>——▷

It was a week of rioting anxieties and near panic attacks. *If he doesn't believe me responsible, why was he forgiving me?*

Karen phoned the following week, a half hour before leaving time.

"I'm not going back," I told her.

"What? What do you mean?"

I apologized about not letting her know earlier. Then, after more resistance, I babbled something about not feeling comfortable with the group, not wanting to be *opening cans of worms*. She hung up. Within fifteen minutes she was sitting at my kitchen table in a loose cotton shirt and stretchy black pants, ready for the group. With her hair tucked firmly behind her ears, she stared at me through her old woman's eyes.

"What's going on, Don?"

I let out the weariest of sighs. I walked over to the living room and, assured that Davey and Bridgette were caught up in a TV show, I went back and sat, trying to meet her penetrating gaze. Where does a story begin? I'd told her the rudiments of my sad tale: Ford, the misdiagnosis, the resulting anxieties. But how to explain the depths of it? How to explain the sisters? How to trace back an infection through its multiple toxins that cloud the mind and grip the body?

I kept it simple. I told her about having visualized Ford. I told her, as best as I knew how, about my fear of fully removing that scab and stirring up old pain. "Besides," I said, "Ford's death was years ago. I'm over it now. No need to be going over it again."

"Don, if you were over it, there wouldn't be a scab."

I shrugged with impatience. "I have other things going on now."

"Then do a different visualization."

"That's just it. I didn't plan to visualize Ford, it just happened so fast."

"Tell me again—about the box—"

"No." I shook my head vehemently. My chest was tightening; she saw my struggle to relax it.

"Okay." She got up and held out her hand. "I went with you, now you come with me. Because I want to go back."

"Well, you go then. I don't have to."

"No. You're my ticket in and I really need to go."

"I really don't want to."

"Get your boots on."

"But I won't feel comfortable."

"Fake it. We're going."

Fake it. For sure I was bloody good with that. I grudgingly put on my boots, complaining.

Karen wasn't listening. She was having a quick snuggle with Bridgette and talking with Davey. Davey was sixteen, Bridgette nine. Since I'd started university Davey had been taking care of her more and more when I had night classes. I worried that I depended on him too much. I *did* depend on him too much. I shouldn't be going out. I began saying so to Karen, but she was already directing me towards the door.

As before, we were the last ones to arrive. I took my usual place, but when Professor Burns began her guided meditation, I tuned out. I kept my eyes closed and reviewed the key concepts of social learning theory for an approaching test.

When Dr. Burns finally called everyone back from their meditations, Karen gave me a snooty look. "I counted every one of your sighs," she muttered.

We probably would've argued all the way home if not for what happened next.

As everyone was leaving, Professor Burns discreetly took my arm. "Wait here," she whispered. I nudged Karen and we both pulled back as Professor Burns waved off the last guest.

Stepping back inside, she closed the door. "Have a cup of tea with me?"

As she moved about the kitchen, I sat on the edge of a cushioned straight-back chair, feeling even odder to be in that house, more intimate now with the other women gone. Karen seemed to feel nothing of my awkwardness; she was crouching before a carved sculpture, chatting about whether it was basswood or tupelo.

We returned to the living room, Professor Burns passing us our cups of tea from a wooden tray. Then she sat forward on a settee, shoulders erect in their teacher pose. She lifted her teacup, examining it as though it were a textbook, then looked at me decisively.

"I need to share something that happened here last week after everybody left," she began, her words cutting through me with their sharp edge of clarity. "I'll be honest. I'm going for tenure with the university, so I don't feel comfortable sharing this. Talk can become skewed. But I have to trust you." She looked from Karen to me, but mostly at me.

"Someone made a connection here last week. No one has come to me—whoever it was, they probably didn't know how deep they went. But—" She hesitated. "This might sound strange to you." She hesitated again and then plunged forward, her words coming fast now.

"After everyone left there was a presence here. A young man, around nineteen years old." She paused at a tiny gasp from Karen, at the stunned look on my face. She kept her teacher's pose but her voice softened as she spoke again of a presence, a young man. She never saw him, she said, just felt him. Felt his age, and heard the one word repeated three times. *Forgiveness.*

Her voice faltered, as though questioning the validity of what she was saying. Then she gathered herself and finished telling us her story. She'd called her spiritual adviser, she said, and, on her advice, went through the rooms of her house, repeating, *You can go now; your message has been received.*

She kept talking—something about having slept with the lights on that night—but I was getting up now, my arms out in front of me as though I'd been blinded and was searching for an exit. I heard Karen call my name and Professor Burns calling her back, allowing me to escape outside.

I sucked in the night air, trying to absorb the profundity of the moment. Ford had come before through my dreams; now he had come again. All these years later, he had come again.

The spattering of stars across the cool night sky seared like pinpricks of ice with each thought zinging through my mind, thoughts that had always been there, somewhere, clouded but coming through now with absolute clarity.

Not all of them, though. It would take many reflective hours and long walks and deep readings to come to terms with what had been given to me on that night. That there is no one moment. That my dream of the three white lice had foretold what would happen. Ford's death was already approaching as we lay in our beds the night before the accident, other worlds advancing towards ours, their coming together so deeply rooted in the past that there was no beginning. From before his conception Fordie had been moving towards his death—forgive him that moment of standing behind that truck; forgive that young fellow behind the wheel whose life had brought him to that moment of distraction; forgive the collision of their worlds in that moment that continues living through the lives of others. *Forgive.*

Forgive me my smallness of mind in believing I could have or might have or should have changed the course of a moment that had been careening towards us for thousands of years and forgive

God for shaping us all within the confines of the one transcendent moment that stretches through to eternity.

Some of these thoughts came in flashes as I walked madly away from Professor Burns's house, Karen close behind, her presence a prayer containing me through that painful but wondrous questioning of the two ugly sisters, guilt and shame. How could I have experienced the bliss of divinity through dreams and then groped for more? How could I have kept looking with longing to *before* while missing the graces bestowed on me *after*?

The road from Professor Burns's house ended at the Cat 'n' Fiddle, a pub in a posh hotel downtown. It was crowded. We pushed our way through to the bar and leaned against it, Karen ordering us vodka and tonics.

"Jeezes, Karen, what just happened back there?"

"Fucked if I know, Don. Except that it happened."

≫—▷

After a night of fitful sleep, I knocked hesitantly on Professor Burns's half-open office door. She looked up and nodded, as if expecting me. Then she fastened her thick hair into a ponytail and turned her chair around, facing me.

"Sit," she said as I closed the door.

I sat. She looked calm but had a hint of worry in her eyes.

"Can we talk about it?" I asked.

She shook her head with the finality that comes from having thought something through. "I don't think it's a good idea. Donna, don't put anything special onto me, okay? What happened was because of you, not me."

"I know, but my God, how do you explain—"

"I don't. And I can't bring anything more to you than what I already have. Listen, this is your journey. I played a very small part. Given my role with the university, this is as far as I can take it."

"But—" I reached towards her, wanting her to explain how such a thing could happen. If it had happened with her before. She was shaking her head again; she knew my questions. There was a light in her eyes.

"If you don't trust me, why did you share it?"

"I was obligated. I couldn't hold back that message."

"I understand." Reluctantly, I got up. "Thank you. Thank you so very much. I promise I'll never *ever* speak of this to anyone."

She grinned, "That's a big promise to keep, given its nature. At least wait till I get tenure, alright?"

"Deal."

She stood too now, and touched my arm. "Listen," she said in a half whisper. "Anything more I can say about last night could muddy your story. It's *your* story. Only you can figure it. That way, when you come to a truth, no one can touch it. It wouldn't hold the same conviction if it came from me or someone else. Does that make sense to you?"

"It does. Thank you." Before I turned to leave, we grasped each other's hands.

≫—▷

In the months to come I made a new friend, Angela, who was studying psychiatry. One day, sitting on her sun-bathed deck and admiring her potted red and pink geraniums, I shared with her my anxieties, my possible PTSD, and she told me about a new class of drugs for anxiety disorders known as selective serotonin reuptake inhibitors, or SSRIs. Serotonin, she explained, is a chemical that nerve cells produce in the brain; sometimes, through stress or malfunctioning or other reasons, the brain can stop producing it, and when it did, anxiety and depression can be the result. She described an experiment in which rats, when deprived of serotonin, curled into quivering balls of nerve, and how, when it was reintroduced, they relaxed into their natural way of being. I listened to her. I listened and listened. I watched the chickadees flitting about her bird feeders, their chirping receding as I thought back on the trauma of my brother's accident. The hard-edged anger incurred for months during a broken marriage. The poverty that followed its fall. The trauma of the doctor's misdiagnosis. I understood then how it had happened. How that night when terror struck it had brought me to my knees. It was *physical*. For years I'd been a car running out of motor oil. When it finally emptied, I'd blown up inside.

I looked at Angela, her coppery hair shining in the sun. I was unable to speak. I bowed to the knowledge she'd just given me. I bowed to the SSRIs. And I walked home that day, armed with that knowledge and yet hearing whispers of doubt. *What if they don't work? What if they work for everyone else but not you? What if they cut the fine thread connecting you to sanity?*

Screw the whispers. I recognized my fear of the fear itself. And I knew that the fear was nothing more than a symptom—a symptom of an illness that pills can work with. Just as insulin works with sugar diabetes. *May God bless pharmaceuticals.*

And yet. I wouldn't go to a doctor for a prescription. What if the pills broke my hold on reality? I'd lived the past four years without knowing what was happening to me, I told myself, and I'd been able to control it to a large degree. Perhaps what I'd learned from Angela would give me an even greater sense of control. And if I ever began sinking too deeply into that black hole of fear and despair, I'd get the prescription.

There. I had a plan. A trump card for future use. I was good.

A bee buzzed too close to my ear, sounding like a buzz saw hacking through my brain. I leapt in fright and then calmed myself. A misfiring of synapses. And the resulting anxieties flooding through me nothing more than a bloody awful stupid fucking symptom.

METAMORPHOSIS

SKELETON WOMEN

MISS ELLY O'ROURKE WAS A maelstrom in human form. She changed everything. I met her in a class at St. Francis Xavier University, Antigonish, Nova Scotia, two years after graduating from Memorial with a Bachelor of Social Work degree.

After a short stint working with juvenile delinquents, I'd arrived at the unalterable conclusion that they all belonged in boot camp with one meal a day. In another short stint, this time working with an elderly blind couple, I'd narrowly missed being hauled before the courts for getting drunk with them. Then came a few more stints working with abused women—and snarling into supervisors' faces, snarling with clients, snarling at board members and government officials. It seemed I was no more trainable than my clients. But around that time, coincidentally, I learned of St. Francis Xavier's six-week summer program in community development for adult learners. Adult education. I liked the idea of that, and signed up.

Having dropped off Davey and Bridgette with their dad for the summer, I boarded the ferry for Nova Scotia. About twenty other students were sitting in the room, all mid-forties and up, when I took my seat nearest the door for the first class. Ten minutes into the lecture the door swung open and a tiny, wiry woman rushed in. "Sure, here you all are," she said in a strong Irish lilt. "Where's the signs?" she pointedly asked the professor. "I been walking through corridors for hours."

In a swirl of skirts and scarves she waltzed to a seat next to me, her auburn hair pinned messily atop her head, wispy bits floating around her pixie face. She was about fifteen to twenty years older than me, her face heavily lined but her eyes bright as stars. When she turned slightly, caught my eye and winked, I nearly giggled. She smelled of cigarettes and secrets.

At lunchtime she lit up a smoke and leaned over the cafeteria table, grinning back at me. "Yes, Donna girl, the well-behaved women never makes history, do they, luv? Tell me what you're doing here. I'm thinking myself mad for taking this on at my age."

We talked and chain-smoked through lunch. Her name was Elly O'Rourke. Back in her twenties she'd left Belfast for Canada and was now a retired university professor with a PhD in world religions. Never married ("I'll always be a Miss," she said), no kids, and with a plan to start an outreach program for the spiritually needy living in isolation. She'd studied Jungian psychology, she told me, and for two years had immersed herself in analysis. Now, through correspondence with a Jungian in Zurich, she was continuing her personal work in dream analysis.

"And you?" she asked. "You have the look of Tamar about you."

"Tamar?"

"She tricked her father-in-law into bed with her by pretending she was a harlot."

"I remind you of a harlot?"

"Like someone pushing hard to get what she wants. From the Bible, luv. Tamar was a widow needing a son. Today he'd be called her old age pension. Did your mother never teach you the Bible?"

"Virgins, not harlots."

"And look what the Virgin done to get a son. Tell me about yourself."

I laughed. Daunted by her accomplishments and strong sense of self yet drawn into her warmth, her heartening grins, her keen-spirited eyes. And flattered to no end that she'd chosen me to sit with.

"Eh, the skeleton woman," Elly said dramatically after I'd told her some bits about my mother and me and our trials. "We've all been her, Donna, luv. She walks the floors of a hundred frozen oceans. Fish pecking the flesh from her bones. But there's always a thaw, girl, if she wants to get out—providing there's enough left of her to get out. You're married?"

"Eh, I got out."

"Hah, as old as time." Elly raised her arms as though invoking the universe. "Our stories are as old as time. Speaking of, it's time to go, Donna girl." She tossed back the last of her coffee, gathering her cigarettes. "They'll have the doors locked on me yet."

"So when you say 'I'll always be a Miss,' it sounds like you planned never to be married," I said, half running to keep up with her as we rushed back to class.

"That's right, luv. I've never felt that calling. Perhaps because I was born from a broken heart—in other words, illegitimate. And premature. I wasn't expected to live and my dear mam pushed me away, not wanting another broken heart, I expect. It was my poor old granny who looked after me. Wrapped me in towels and kept me in a basket on the oven door. Been running around half-baked ever since. You see this, girl"—pointing to her bony wrists—"and here"—pointing to half moons of shadow beneath her eyes, carefully made up—"they come from fighting too early in life for life. Yes, luv, I hid in the bushes most of my growing-up years. The ugly duckling. We all have a myth, Donna girl, and I'm still waiting to become the swan—*hah*. Had that ever happened, perhaps I would've been someone's Missus. Hah hah, no worries there, luv. We're not all the marrying kind."

I followed her around as if she'd been imprinted on me. She quoted scripture and poetry and laughed at herself and at me as we cozied into corners, smoking and speculating about people around us, comparing them to certain characters in literature or film. She shied away from talk of her personal life, focusing on mine, especially the dreams about Ford. Often, when we'd walk along trails or sandy beaches or hunker over mugs of coffee in cafés, she'd take the time to analyze some of my dreams, teaching me how to identify symbols and meaning. "Always the unconscious, luv; when you dream of water, it's always about what's beneath. Draw it up, Donna. Always draw up the deep, girl, or it'll take you down."

I started relating some of my experiences with mental illness. She took me to a secondhand bookstore and loaded me down with books on saints, self-help, and Jungian psychology—and five George Eliot novels. "Read, luv. Find yourself."

Towards the end of the program we were sitting at a sunny picnic table on campus, partly shaded by a massive oak, working on our final project together when Elly said, "You're the writer, Donna. You write and I'll take on the research."

"I'm no writer but I'll do it," I said.

"Sure, I thought you said you were a writer?"

"Social worker."

"But I'm sure you said you were a writer. I've been meaning to ask what you wrote."

I shook my head, giving her a bewildered look. Elly was staring at me, her brow puckered. She swatted at a mosquito and said adamantly, "Then you *should* write. Those stories you tell, Donna luv, you're the first person I've met I'd rather listen to than talk to. That's the truth of it. So there you have it. Straight from Elly's scriptures."

I grinned, *muchly* flattered. Then wrote up the nicest research paper.

Our day of parting came. When we were saying goodbye, Elly pleaded with me to keep in touch, to write her letters.

I promised.

"And come visit me in Halifax."

I gave a half-hearted nod. I'd learned the night before through a phone call home that my mother, who had recently been diagnosed with ulcerative colitis, wasn't doing well and I was keen to get home.

My worries were well-founded. But it wasn't colitis that took her down; it was breast cancer.

⋙——▷

A year after my return from Antigonish to St. John's I flew out again, twice within a month, for the airport in Deer Lake. When the second flight touched down I got off the plane and into the driver's seat of my mother's car. She was already packed, her suitcase in the back seat. Her operation for a mastectomy was in two hours' time at the hospital in Corner Brook, fifty kilometres down the highway.

My anxieties, always scarcely kept in control, had intensified. Mother sat in the passenger seat as I started down the wet winter's highway, praying she wouldn't notice how hard I was gripping the wheel just to keep my hands from shaking. I practised my deep breathing exercises as she repeated what she'd already told me on the phone just the day before. That she'd discovered the lump three weeks ago while pacing the hospital's waiting room as Father fought for his life in the operating room. He'd just suffered a massive heart attack.

Dad was okay now. Resting comfortably at home. But I need to back up a bit here.

They'd been at the cabin with friends, having ridden in on Ski-Doos the ten kilometres through the woods, leaving their trucks parked on the highway. Mother could see it on Dad's face the moment it happened. He was standing in the middle of the cabin, laughing at something, when suddenly his face twisted. Then he bent over and fell across the table. They strapped him to a toboggan and hauled him by Ski-Doo the ten kilometres back through the woods. It was cold and snowy that night and they were driving so recklessly that she was afraid they'd hit a moose on the trail. Once they reached the truck they drove the thirty minutes to Deer Lake, Father propped up beside her, buckled over like a piece of cardboard. He was barely breathing; she clung to him as he clung to life. After they'd roused a doctor out of bed, he plunged a needle into Father's heart then directed them to the hospital in Corner Brook, another thirty-minute drive further down the highway. But first he took her aside and said "Prepare yourself. I don't think he's going to make it." "The first words your father said to me when he woke up," she told me, "were *That gawd-damn doctor, made me extra worry for nothing.*"

She'd told me all this on the phone the day of the heart attack, and told it all again after I'd arrived at Dad's hospital bedside— just as she'd told it to Dad when he finally woke up and just as she'd told it to the doctors and nurses, telling everyone till the telling became tiring and she was leaving things out until finally, through the telling, she had transposed much of the trauma out of the tale, rendering it to a manageable size alongside her other harboured sorrows. All of this she now told me again during our drive through the growing snowstorm to Corner Brook for her mastectomy. Along with the story of how she'd first found the lump in the hospital waiting room while the doctors were work-ing on Dad.

She'd been wearing her Ski-Doo suit. Her arms were out of the sleeves, the sleeves dangling down around her, when she clasped her hands under her armpits, digging her fingers into her flesh to divert her attention from Father and onto herself, when she felt the lump at the side of her breast. It didn't hurt, she said; it felt like a frozen pea. She recognized it as cancer the second she felt it but wouldn't tell any of us.

"Why? Why didn't you tell us? Carrying this all by yourself."

"Your father was enough for ye to worry about." She let out a small laugh at what she'd said the day she called about Dad's heart attack: *Donna, this is your mother, Claudine.* She tutted now at the foolishness of it. "As if you didn't know your own mother's name." But she'd been mad with fear, she said.

I flicked on the windshield wipers and looked at her. She was silent now.

Just as she'd been throughout the whole hour they worked on Dad when she first got him to emergency, Tommy told me. Tommy had been there with her. Watching her leaning against the wall beyond which they'd taken Dad. Where she was still standing when I arrived three hours later, her body a hard line with it, her eyes vacant. She had left herself. She'd put herself on the other side of that wall and into Father as he lay there, and she'd fought with him against the tyranny of his busted heart. Just as she was putting herself inside me now as I sat behind the wheel, driving her to the hospital. Protecting me from the tyranny of her cancer.

"I wasn't going to call till it was over," she said. "But your father threatened to call you himself if I didn't. This old stuff. Now you had to fly all the way back here agin."

I struggled for words. There were no words. Nothing humbles more than the magnitude of a mother's heart. I fought to keep from crying but couldn't stop a tear from squeezing through. She saw. Her face softened as she relaxed away from the door and tutted, "Don't be so foolish."

The weight of a tear. That it can bridge such yearning hearts.

≫—▷

I parked, took her suitcase from the back seat, and followed her across the hospital parking lot. Her steps were short but firm, her eyes fixed on the doors ahead.

When we stepped out of the elevator on the third floor a nurse came bustling towards us with a chart. "You're late, Mrs.

Osmond," she said, as though she'd been standing there waiting for us. "We thought you'd stood us up. Give us a moment, please," she said to me.

I gratefully escaped to an empty waiting room, watching through its door as my mother stood beside the nurses' station, ticking off items on the chart. I lowered my head, deep breathing through the anxiety that was threatening to choke me. But then I raised it again and looked back at Mother.

I'd been learning something more about my chronic anxiety. It started the day of Dad's heart attack. After Mom called that day I managed to catch an emergency flight on a little propeller plane with twelve seats and roaring engines. The plane was only half full, but its small, closed-in space, along with my fear of flying and cold fear for Dad's life, overwhelmed my already racing heart. I began hyperventilating.

Directly behind me sat a man who looked to be in his mid-thirties. "Talk to me," I gasped over my shoulder. "My father may be dead, I don't know, and I can't breathe."

That kind stranger leaned forward and spoke quietly into my ear as I struggled for breath. He told me about the lions he'd seen during a recent trip to Africa. He described the tall savannah grasses and the smell of mud and the colours of birds. I clung to his words. I closed my eyes and matched my breathing to his.

Then we hit heavy turbulence, the plane rocked, and I lowered my head—it was too much, it was too much—and I gave over to the fear. I did not sink into the abyss. I remained right there in my seat, clutching onto its armrests with terror like everyone else in the plane. It was then, in that moment's quiet desperation, I noted that my fears were of those things *outside* me—that my father might die, that this tin tube rattling us through space might crash. *Normal* fears.

I offered a quiet prayer of gratitude to that voice still speaking quietly into my ear of jungle sounds and smells. I whispered yet another prayer for my father, and for the passengers in the plane whose faces were as pale and frightened as my own. I prayed for the pilot, that it wasn't yet his time to be taken. And for the first time since I'd became ill with the anxiety disorder, I noted that my prayers were for others, not me.

So now, sitting in that waiting room as I watched my mother complete her chart work, I drew a shaky breath, recognizing that my anxieties were for her. *Normal* anxiety. And this understanding—that the frightening symptoms of my anxiety disorder wouldn't compound with the added fears of threat to those I love, but in actual fact, felt banished by the new fears—gave me courage.

But the anxiety for my mother kept heightening. When she passed the chart over to the nurse and started towards me, tucking a blue hospital gown over her arm, I averted my eyes. Worried she would see the fear in them. More worried that I would see fear in hers.

Picking up her suitcase, I followed her down the corridor. Then we turned into her designated room and stood, shoulders touching, looking around. To our right, lying light as a feather in her bedding, was a tiny-faced elder smiling sweetly towards us. To our left was an empty bed, my mother's. And on the far side of that bed was a third. A biggish woman, perhaps in her seventies, sat to the side of it, facing us. Her one leg hung down, purplish as though cold; the other was a bandaged stump above her knee. She was leaning with both elbows across the tray that stood on wheels before her, her big head drooping as though to show us her thick, coarse curls, each individually separated as though the rollers were still in them. She peered up at the sound of the suitcase touching the floor, her jowls heavy, dark bags sagging beneath her eyes.

"Whom be the patient?" she asked in a husky voice.

I beckoned to my mother and hurriedly pulled the curtain around her bed. Then, as Mother laid her hospital gown on the back of a chair and started undressing, I unpacked her suitcase, feeling oddly uncomfortable. I was thirty-nine years old and had never seen my mother in her underwear. To give her privacy I took my time hanging her few clothes in the closet. And when I heard her pushing her pants down over her legs I busied myself at her nightstand, fumbling with her comb and hand cream.

"You can look now, Donna," she said impatiently, pulling on the gown. I flushed with embarrassment, and with a small laugh stepped outside the curtain.

The elder across the way raised a thin wrist, giving me a feeble wave. "Excuse me, dolly," she said, her voice so soft that I stepped closer. "It's Mrs. Hailey." She pointed to the woman on the other side of Mother's curtain. "She can't breathe very well with your curtain closed."

I looked over at Mrs. Hailey. She was still leaning forward, both forearms resting on her tray. She raised her eyes to mine. "I'm claustrophobic," she said in a harsh whisper, nodding at the curtain two feet from her face.

"My mother is dressing," I said politely but firmly.

But Mother heard and instantly pushed the curtain back around her bed. "I'm done with this now." She smiled at Mrs.

Hailey. "Hello, ma'am. I'm Claudine."

"Claudine. I'm Bernadine. And over there is Mrs. Shepherd. From Flowers Cove."

"Julie, my dear," said Mrs. Shepherd. "Everyone calls me Julie."

"You look well," said Bernadine to Mother. "What brings you on this floor?"

Mother was seating herself at the side of her bed nearest Bernadine. She inclined her head like a queen and spoke with a quiet assurance.

"I have to get my breast removed." She touched her right breast lightly. "I have cancer."

I cringed, hating my mother having to expose herself like that. I turned to swoosh the curtains back around her to protect her. But both Mrs. Hailey and Mrs.—Julie—were making sympathetic sounds. Mother made one of her own, adding, "Not as if I'll be having more babies to feed," ending with a small laugh.

"No, my love, that's right," said Julie.

"I used to dance all the time," Bernadine said, glancing at her stump. "I loved waltzing with my husband. I won't do that no more now. But you can still waltz."

"Sure, you still have your lovely figure," offered the soft-spoken Julie. "That operation won't make much difference to you."

"I was always proud of how I kept myself," said Mother, looking at Bernadine. "All seems like vanity now. Compared to you losing your leg."

"I'll be all right, my dear. That must be your girl, is she?"

My mother smiled towards me and I gave an awkward nod, surprised by her ease with these women, sharing with them her most intimate situation. The sun struck through the window, lending a bit of cheer to the room; they could have been three friends chatting over tea in a parlour.

"Mrs. Osmond?" The nurse's firm, jovial voice sounded a second before she entered the room. "We've to get you ready. It's time, dear."

I patrolled the corridor like a sentry as they prepped Mother for her surgery. One other thing I'd learned about fear—*any* kind of fear: it cuts through all else, anchoring you to a moment where there's only room for you. *Nothing* exists before or after it; there is only the now.

And that now seemed like forever as they wheeled my mother from her room on a gurney and we started down the corridor. When she reached for my hand it gutted me seeing her looking so vulnerable in that hospital gown and lying in a bed—hadn't she just *walked* in here?

Mother tugged at my hand. "Look what I have to wear," she said with a small grin, holding up a puffy cotton cap.

"She's some proud, your mother is," said the nurse. "Don't want to be seen wearing her granny cap. Isn't that right, Mrs. Osmond?"

I wanted to clamp my hand across the nurse's gob for sounding so *gawd-damn* pleasant, as if we were going to the movies. But when I saw Mother dancing the cap around on her fingers, grinning up at her, I silently apologized, even feeling grateful for the nurse's big-mouthed banter as we descended to the second floor. We turned down a short corridor and stopped before a double set of doors, each with a porthole window at eye level. The pre-op room, the nurse called it.

"I'm afraid you can't come any further," she told me. "We'll have your mother back to you in three to four hours."

My breathing was so shallow my lungs involuntarily hiccupped for air. I was still holding on to my mother's hand. It felt cold. Or perhaps it was my own that had grown colder—I couldn't tell; I was clutching hers so tightly that I couldn't feel where my flesh left off and hers began. I forced myself to look into her eyes. I looked deep. I saw no fear. Only concern for me.

"You got the blood nipped off in my fingers," she said. I couldn't even smile. When I bent over, stiff as a picket, to kiss her, she whispered, "Now, go for a walk or something. Don't go waiting around here."

"I will," I said, and quickly kissed her cheek.

She tugged on my hand, forcing me to look at her again. "If you're here when they wheels me out, take this thing off my head."

I tried to grin but buried my face into her neck instead.

The nurse touched my arm. "We'll have her back in no time."

I pulled away. The doors closed and I cupped my face to the porthole window, catching one last glimpse of my mother's pale face. She saw me and waved, and then she was gone.

I was seized with rage—and kicked at the door so hard it hurt my foot. Then I limped off to a washroom, locked myself inside, and gave over to a convulsive sobbing. After I emerged I spotted a little chapel down the hall; I went in and knelt there in the quiet. An hour passed, maybe two. When my knees were numb and my tears had dried up I left the chapel and, on my way back to Mother's room, stopped before two women selling daffodils and bought a bunch.

Julie was sitting now, propped up by pillows. Bernadine was lying back on hers.

"Here, my dolly," said Julie, pointing to a glass vase on her side table with three wilting roses. "Throw them out and use my vase."

"Thank you." I refilled the vase with water, arranged Mother's daffodils, and placed them on her nightstand. Then I lay down on her bed and pulled her blanket over me. Bernadine murmured a comforting sound, then Julie. I curled into their soothing tones, burrowing deep into Mother's pillow.

≫—▷

I was pacing the corridor outside Mother's room when they brought her back. She lay limp on the gurney, her eyes closed. I was shocked at how pale she was, how lifeless. The same loud nurse was there, pulling the curtains around her bed as two aides lifted her from the gurney, her head lolling like an infant's. When she gagged the nurse held a silver pan, shaped like a kidney, beneath her mouth. "There you go, my love. You all right now, Mrs. Osmond? I'm right here." She looked up at me and gestured towards the washroom. "Bring a cold cloth for your mother."

When I did the nurse got up, bidding me to sit in her place. "Keep it to her forehead," she instructed. "Mrs. Osmond, I'll be right alongside, dear. Press your call button if you need me. Is your nausea passed?" She didn't wait for an answer; she hadn't expected one. She was already bustling outside the curtain, giving orders to the aides with the gurney.

Sitting beside my mother's bed, the side closest to Bernadine, I thought about her claustrophobia with the curtains closed. But my mother was so pale. I clamped the wet cloth to her forehead and held it there; I wouldn't look at her bandaged chest, I wouldn't look. She opened her eyes onto mine then peered down, trying to see her chest.

"It looks good, Mom. It all looks good."

She shook her head, closed her eyes, then glanced at the flowers and gave a faint smile. "Daffodils, don't they smell nice?"

When I brought them before her she rested her eyes on the yellow velvety petals; I held them there till my wrist ached. Then she started retching, leaning away from me and onto her side. I bent over her, holding the silver pan beneath her chin, making comforting sounds as she spat up. She lay back and groped for my hand. I held on to hers; it felt soft as a handful of cotton. She closed her eyes, whispered something about the curtains, Bernadine.

I pulled the curtain aside. Bernadine and Julie were lying quietly on their pillows, looking towards my mother, their eyes full of concern.

"She's fine, she's fine," I whispered; they made the crooning sounds of mothers. I was so grateful for their presence, so grateful for their shouldering me through this moment as I shouldered my mother. Suddenly I knew why Mother had been so impatient with me earlier: she was needing me to show my vulnerability so that she could show her own. My eyes grew wet and I rested my head beside hers, comforted by and immersed within the amniotic waters of women.

≫—▷

When I arrived the following morning Mother had her curtain closed. Bernadine sat on the other side of her bed, a nurse's assistant combing her thick curls. Julie, too, was being bathed and groomed by an aide. I slipped inside my mother's curtain. She was dressed in a fresh nightgown but was lying, face down, in her pillow.

"What is it?" I asked. "Mom, what's wrong?"

She stirred, looked at me. She'd been crying. I sat beside her, half lying against her.

"What is it? Mom?"

She spoke so softly that I strained to listen. "It's God punishing me."

"What? Punishing you for what?"

"I dreamed about them last night. My babies. I was on the beach and saw them. The three of them. Lying beneath the water looking up at me." She shivered. "If I'd gone to the hospital, they might've lived."

"Oh, my, Mom, what about poor little Paul, then? You took him to the hospital and he still passed away. Was that your fault, too?"

She was silent.

"Mom? You hear yourself, don't you?"

She wiped her nose. Gave a small nod. "Does sound foolish."

"You *are* being foolish. My lord."

"I'll never look at myself agin."

"Look at her, then," I said quietly, nudging the curtain a bit to the side. We both looked at Bernadine sitting in her wheelchair, wrapped in a bright, flowery housecoat, her thick curls brushed to a sheen, her stump resting on a cushion on an extended leg rest, her other foot cozied inside a furry red slipper. "Do you think she's ugly with her scars?"

"She's beautiful," my mother whispered.

"Well, then, if you think your scar is ugly, you must think her scar is ugly."

"I'm being foolish. Self-pitying."

"My, who can blame you, all you been through."

She wiped at her nose. "Get me a cloth," she whispered.

I got her a cloth; she wiped her face; together we fixed her hair and put a little powder on her cheeks. Then she sat up and I pulled the curtain aside. Bernadine was conversing quietly with Julie, who was sitting up on plumped pillows, her hair nicely brushed too, fluffed around her face.

"How are you this morning, my dear?" asked Julie.

"Feeling a little tired."

"I suppose you are," said Bernadine. "You rest now; nothing like a good rest. You been through a lot, too."

"Yes, my dolly," said Julie. "We gets through it, don't we?"

"Yes, maid," said my mother. "We gets through it."

⋙—⋗

She was discharged three days after her operation. And with no need for radiation or chemotherapy, she was told: the surgery had gotten all the cancer. I left my mother to the care of Wanda and Karen, who'd flown home from Toronto.

On my first day back in St. John's I walked across the street to Mae's house just as she was putting out food for the feral tom lurking in the grass outside her gate. I went inside and sat with her, shafts of sunlight, teeming with mites and cat hair, funnelling through her half-closed curtains and across her living room. Cats prowled all about, tails curling around my legs. Her favourite,

Bobby, was sprawled across her lap when I asked her, finally, to tell me her worst thing.

Her wizened brown eyes snapped from Bobby onto me. The wheeziness left her voice as the girl she used to be uncoiled from her heart and she began telling her story with the same horror she'd felt back when it had all happened. When she was a baby, she said, her mother had a cat named Kit who used to sleep with Mae in her crib. Whenever Mae woke Kit would scamper into the garden where Mae's mother was weeding or planting, and that way she'd know Mae was awake. She would come and feed her, and then bring Mae back with her to the garden. Kit, said Mae, filled her first memories as much as her mother did.

When Mae was about five or six, her mother became ill and died. Mae huddled with Kit for days, she said, in the curl of a sand dune, near the ocean. Her father later married another woman who wasn't kind. But Mae had Kit, and Kit smelled like her mother. Mae slept with Kit each night and woke with her each morning, and it was to Kit that she told her secret things.

One day Mae was coming home from school when she heard a fierce meow coming from Kit somewhere down on the beach. She ran through the bushes and down to the shore and saw her father standing at the water's edge. He heaved a large paper bag into the sea and Mae started screaming as Kit clawed her way out of the bag and began pawing at the water. Her father picked up a big rock and landed it on top of Kit's head. Mae screamed. She screamed and screamed. She plunged into the water, knee-deep, and grabbed one of Kit's paws and dragged her ashore. But it was too late. Kit was a soggy puddle of fur in her arms. "It was a long time after that, Donna my dear, before I ever took to another cat."

I moved closer to Mae, my shoulder touching hers as we sat quietly now, in the reverence of her greatest sorrow. It gave me comfort to comfort her.

So vividly did Mae's story imprint itself upon my heart that I later wrote it, almost just as she'd told it, into *The Deception of Livvy Higgs*, the second of two novels inspired by Mae.

THE WRITING LIFE

A BLUSTERY OCTOBER WIND was kicking up dust one evening, stripping the last leaves from the crabapple tree out back. A year and some months had passed since Mother's operation and not much longer than that since I'd started my job as a caseworker for a non-government agency. I was crouched by the wood stove, poking the fire, when the doorbell rang. At first I didn't recognize the tiny wan face peeking at me from beneath a furry hood. Then a flurry of words in a lilting Irish accent greeted me.

"Sure, let me in, Donna. I'm half froze to death."

I let out a shriek. "Elly! Miss Elly O'Rourke!"

I pulled her inside and we sat like girls, exclaiming over each other and hugging.

"I'm here for a conference. Don't ask me what it's about, for the devil will strike me dead, it's such hogwash. Terrible, it's terrible girl, what they slap God's name on." It came rushing back to me—her study of religions, the outreach program she wanted to launch for the spiritually needy or isolated, I'd forgotten exactly—but I didn't want to interrupt.

"Anyway, never mind that lot. You never did write, but I kept your address on that bit of paper you wrote it on. The cab driver knew the address right away—next door to Archie's fish 'n' chips place. There it is, your claim to fame, luv. Now then, I've only got an hour. I've come to hear you read."

"Read? Read what?"

"Your writing, Donna. I've never forgotten the stories you told. They reminded me of growing up near Galway back in Ireland: the fishing boats, and everyone's grannies out on their stoops, ordering around the young ones."

"Elly." I was shaking my head. "I don't have writings. I'm not a writer."

She looked at me with such an air of crushed expectation that I felt I was failing her.

"You must've written *something* in university, luv. Did you keep anything?"

"*Research* papers?"

She nodded emphatically. "Read me one, hurry."

I stared at her. Perhaps she *was* a madwoman? After all, I'd only known her for six weeks.

She checked her watch. I didn't know what to say or do—but I did have one paper that was kind of storylike. I'd thought it clever, at the time, to take a personal story (about my first period) and tie it into Émile Durkheim's theory of socialism, relating it to the massive amount of emotion invested in creating folklore within one's culture.

Elly was looking at me, nodding encouragingly. I darted up the stairs, fished through a box of essays at the bottom of my closet, and pulled out the Durkheim paper. "The Clothesline Patch," I'd called it. Back downstairs I held it out to Elly, more than a little embarrassed.

"Read it, luv," she said.

"Out loud?"

She closed her eyes and tilted her chin as though she were at the opera.

I laid the paper on her lap, shaking my head. "This is as far as I take it."

She opened her eyes as though I'd shocked her. "But I must hear your voice, luv. How can I hear your voice if it's me doing the reading?"

"But—the words are the same."

"It's your *voice*. I need to hear your *voice*. I don't have much time, Donna."

I retrieved the paper from her lap, took a deep breath, sat back, and began reading. Quickly. It was ridiculous. The whole thing was ridiculous—this older, eccentric Irish woman, the paper, reading it out loud. Seriously, a girl's first period and *Durkheim*?

Eh. But it was clever. And I heard, as I struggled past the Durkheim stuff, the girl's voice. Not mine, but the *girl's*. As though she were an entity separate from me, from my words.

Elly kept nodding as I read, her eyes scrunched shut with concentration. After I was done, she opened them and smiled. "I knew it," she said breathlessly. "You're a writer."

I blushed, feeling pretentious.

But later, after we'd said our heartfelt goodbyes, after I'd watched Elly hobble against the wind to the cab she'd had waiting all this time, I closed the door and picked up the paper. The *girl's* voice. The very fact of it stayed with me.

What if I were to take out the Durkheim stuff? I walked over to the kitchen table, sat down, and began to rewrite it. I added more details—uncomfortable details concerning pads. Like, how do you get rid of them? As I remembered more and more things about that wretched time I wrote them in, too. I wrote and wrote till the words flowed like a story. A friggin' story! Not that I'd ever *show* it to anyone, what with the burning of the pads and all. But I was intrigued. I was intrigued by the *kind* of words that flowed through the pen as I wrote—our old way of saying things back then on the Beaches. Things like *Leave him be, maid, leave him be* and *He got the milk cans squat on his boots agin.*

I started writing letters to Elly, just as a kind of practice exercise. Long, elaborate letters that never ended and were never posted, so grand and high-flown they were. *My dearest friend,* one of these began. *The sun rises slowly over the South Side hills this morning as the gulls—each a little black pod upon the still waters of the harbour—gaze towards its rays.* I led off another with *Oh, my dear, the rain washes the windows this cold winter's morn, and the pigeons huddle beneath the eaves; Dearest of dears, The river runs deep this night, surging against me with the force of a thousand grieving hearts . . .*

I wrote a dozen letters. Two dozen. Thank God I never mailed them.

One evening at a crowded, noisy party I huddled in a corner with an intriguing woman who'd introduced herself as an author; we talked about writing, and at one point she recommended a book for beginning fiction writers. Off I trekked to the shop the following morning; I found two. Clasping them beneath my arm, I took them to work and then delved in during my lunch hour at the food emporium. *Write for ten minutes on your grandmother's garden,* one of them instructed. And so I began . . . *Stretching my arm between the pickets of Nanny Ford's fence, I snapped off a Sweet*

William and held it up close and sniffed its scent so hard that I suc-
tioned the petal right up into my nose and then ran off fast, ran with
my sister through the tall grass . . .

I wrote without pause for an hour, my pen so firm on the page
that the table jiggled. It was exhilarating, all those lovely images
and memories welling up from the past. I could smell that garden,
the grass, the horse manure coming from the barn. I stopped only
when I had to go back to work.

I got up an hour earlier the following morning and every morning after that. Then, before the office crowd descended from their
upper-level offices into the food emporium for their lattes and muf-
fins, I—along with the homeless, the derelict, and the misguided—
would already be sitting at our favoured tables. We'd sit apart, heads
down, brooding over our coffee cups. I'd station myself by a huge
window that overlooked the harbour, and I'd write. I wrote about
my mother, my father. I wrote about my brothers and sisters. And
when I'd come to the end of a thought I'd keep going until a sound
or something penetrated from the outside and again the words
broiled onto the page: *a child screams, he throws himself to the ground*
and screams and kicks and if I were a child I'd do that right now, I'd
throw myself down on the floor and wail and holler and kick and scream
until there's nothing left inside of me, till every tear is shed and every
fear is the simple fear of some fish house with an old woman ghosting
through its rooms at night searching for the home she once had . . .

Home. It came to me in a flash as I sat scribbling out words at the
food court. I needed a new home. It was early spring, 1996. One

by one my wonderful, beautiful friends had left St. John's that past year, seeking their fortunes elsewhere. I was devastated and alone. I'd also become disillusioned with my role as a social worker, and that was exacerbated by my extreme mental health issues.

But that flash of insight made me sit up with knowing. My mother. Breast cancer had a high recurrence rate. What if her cancer came back and she needed chemotherapy, radiation, intensive care? Karen lived in Alberta, Wanda and Glenn in Toronto, Tommy in New Brunswick. How would we take care of Mom?

It all fell into place before me. I would move to Halifax. It was a city of more than three hundred thousand, big enough for us all to relocate there and find work and be ready should our mother or father get sick again and need us. It was time. It was time we became a family again. Incredibly, all my siblings thought it a worthy idea to work towards.

Still, it was tough. Bridgette cried. Davey kept biking around the neighbourhood as though engraving its every curve and rock into his brain. I walked the harbourfront, embracing the strong winds and the smell of salt and brine from the fishing boats tied up along the wharf. But Halifax had fishing boats, too. Halifax had a harbour. It would be fine; it would be fine.

It wasn't fine for Mae. The day before I put up the For Sale sign I went to her door to tell her we were moving. She looked so tiny and shrivelled that I was afraid she'd float away like a dried-out husk. She stared at me steadily through little brown eyes wet as sea pebbles. I held my hand to my heart as she ran from me, back inside her house.

I followed. She sat on the couch amid yawning, stretching cats and stared out through her living room window. It looked fully onto my house. I sat and stared alongside her. As she dabbed at her eyes I could smell her shampoo; her thick grey hair had continued to flourish no matter her shrinking body. When I touched it lightly she shuddered and I wondered how long it had been since someone had held her. I wanted to put my arms around her, but the rigidity with which she held herself kept me back.

"I'm sorry, Mae."

She shook her head. "Oh, my, Donna," she half whispered through her wheezing. "You don't know how many times your light got me through the night. I lie right here." She patted a pillow behind her on the couch and pointed to my upstairs bathroom window where the light was left on every night. "When I can't breathe, I knows you're right there—you and that Davey and that Bridgette. I don't know—" She broke off then, weeping into her hands, and I convulsed towards her. I put my arms around her thin shoulders and I held her. I wept with her, thinking of the nights I'd lain in my own bed, staring through my own darkened window at the moon and the stars, clinging to their light to make it through till morning.

I gave her my phone number for Nova Scotia. I promised to write to her. I promised never to forget. Never.

Then I went home and continued packing. Over the next weeks I took her blankets and warm clothing and a cupboard full of groceries. She kept coming to my door, standing there, then scurrying home. I was gutted.

The last thing I did in St. John's was stand outside her house as she stood in her doorway feeding her pigeons. I snapped a picture of her with the sun shining off her white hair. She looked up, squinting towards me. I waved. She gave me a quiet smile and waved her hand in farewell.

A STORY IS SEEDED

I WAS WAITING FOR ELLY beneath the yellowing katsura tree in the public gardens, its leaves whiffing of cotton candy and corn. It was early September, the sun giving heart to the heavily drooping dahlia blooms.

It had been three months since I'd left Newfoundland. And it had been hard. I missed the friendships I had known there. I missed the narrow winding roads and paint-splashed houses of St. John's. I missed the greeny-blue waters of the harbour on a windy day, the smell of fish 'n' chips from Archie's takeout next door, the landscapes drenched with familiarity. When I walked outside my Haligonian door neither left nor right drew me; no known destinations were awaiting me anywhere.

I looked for work, passing out reams of résumés. And hung out in cafés, smiling at anyone looking my way, hoping to make a friend outside of Elly. I strolled along the boardwalk around the harbour, loitered in the library, sat on bar stools sharing small talk with whoever or whatever happened along. Meeting people was easy, making friends was not. Loneliness, I learned, exudes a scent of neediness. People back off. Not having a job confounded the issue: people were confused when they couldn't place me, when they couldn't define me.

It was easy to lean on Elly, no matter how discomfited I felt in her home. She lived in the old-money part of town. The first time I arrived at her door there was a mailman ringing the bell with an envelope that needed signing—or something. Elly opened her door and before the mailman had chance to speak she was ushering me inside, closing the door firmly behind her as she dealt with him. I felt intrusive, as though I'd happened on a private moment.

I was struck by the grandeur of her house; with its huge stone fireplace, high ceilings, and gleaming hardwood floors it looked like a relic of a more dignified, elegant past. Heavy drapes darkened the windows; heavy antique furniture crowded the rooms. It smelled of wealth. I wondered how, as a single woman working for the Church, Elly had come by such prosperity. After she'd finished with the mailman that day she bustled back inside and poured me some lemon water from a crystal jug. I held the crystal glass with two hands for fear of dropping it, feeling like a misfit in my jeans and T-shirt. But when she pulled on her raglan and her little black beret and we gussied through the park a block from her house, sharing stories, sharing dreams, I felt on even footing again.

Always she astonished me with the depth of her knowledge of mythology, Christianity, philosophy—nothing was too big or sacred for her to draw from. *Yes, luv, whether you're the biggest trollop walking the block or the minister's daughter, we're all virgins when awakening to Christ. At least, that's what that lot will have you believe. Think about it: man or woman, we're all virgins in waiting. Now you lights a candle from that, luv, while I lights a smoke.*

Now I sat forward on the park bench, catching sight of her coming up the pathway in the public gardens, raglan flapping, pigeons taking flight as she hurried through them. I had news. I'd just been offered a social work job. Despite my dissatisfaction with myself as a fit within the profession, I needed a job. Besides, the field of social work offered many different pathways; I simply needed to find the correct one for me.

She perched beside me, tossing down a tote bag and pulling out a pack of cigarettes. We each took one and she cupped a lighter to hers, wisps of curly reddish hair escaping her beret, fluttering around her diminutive face.

"Ever think about quitting?" I asked as she sucked in a mouthful of smoke and held the lighter to mine.

She giggled. "Soaked every match in the house last night, luv. What's up? You're reminding me of myself when I got a secret to tell."

I told her about the job offer and was surprised by her look of reluctance.

"I had other things in mind," she said when I pressed her. "Don't mind me, luv. Perhaps this is best, but I missed chances in my past, Donna. Going after stuff I thought I wanted. When in the end it got me nothing but heartache." She nodded, not looking at me, and took a deep drag on her smoke. "You got talent, girl. I hear it each time you open your mouth. I think you should write, Donna."

"You mean, not take the job?"

"I don't want to be influencing you."

"You are. Look, I love this stuff—writing. I just don't think I can write—you know—books. Lord, it sounds pretentious just to say the word *book*."

"Get over yourself, girl. I tell you, Donna, you're the most innocent person I've ever met, and at your age that's not a compliment, luv. Listen to me. I've heard your voice. It's what you're meant to do. I know this stuff."

"How? How do you know this stuff?"

"I used to be an editor—a summer job I held for years when I was in university." She leaned in. "Harlequin Romance. Don't be flapping your gums—it's not something I highlighted on my CV when working for the Church, much as they love virgins. But I know about writing, Donna. I've heard your voice and I've read your words and I'm telling you—you can write. You have a voice. It's all about voice. You don't know what I'm talking about, I can see it on your face, but you'll learn. You already are learning; I can tell by the way you're talking to me—colouring everything up with your Newfoundland lingo. Sure, you didn't do that when I first met you. No, you were trying to be grand. Don't argue with me. I can see through you like a book—if you'll pardon the pun, hah! Now then, I'm going to put something to you. But you must take your time thinking about this one."

She looked hesitant. It wasn't like her to be hesitant.

"Just tell me," I prodded.

She nodded. "All right, then. You know I've been working on an outreach program with the Church. I'll be doing a survey soon—within the next six months. Be grand, Donna, if you could work it with me. I'll be needing interviews set up and carried out. With your social work degree, sure, you're the perfect fit. Plus, I'll be travelling all over Atlantic Canada and I'll be needing someone to drive—I've never driven a car in my life and I don't expect to be starting soon."

"Oh my gawd, that all sounds so great."

"Yes. Yes, it does. Like it was preordained, us meeting when we did. Do you believe in fate, Donna?"

"I'm learning to."

"I'm quite serious. Now then, we must be frank with each other. Do you have money, luv, to tide you over? It'll be six months or longer before the project is up and running, please God. Then we'll be good; we'll work it together. It's not just the project, Donna. It's about your writing. I've got a plan for it, but you'd have to trust me."

She was lighting another cigarette, giving me time to answer. I was besieged with doubts—I had limited resources. I had two kids depending on me. I'd never written anything but early morning scribbles. I felt Elly looking at me, her eyes with the knowing of a seer. Waiting for me to catch up with what she seemed to already know.

"The sister archetype," she said as though hearing my thoughts. "I think you got inside me through the sister archetype. I've often thought of it, Donna, why I've let you in. You don't see anybody else around my door. No, and you won't," she said as I shook my head. "I've worn myself out with tea parties and fancy dinners. I've no more time for it, but I've time for you. I never had a sister, Donna. Or a brother. I've always felt the loss of that. I would've liked a sister like you—younger and smart, and who loves looking under rocks like I do."

I felt myself blushing. Sisters I had. But a wealthy, educated woman who'd travelled the world (she'd shown me souvenirs—more like art pieces—displayed throughout her house) and who had faith in me—a bumbling bay girl who'd never left the country, never had a job that paid over minimum wage, was half mad with anxieties, could probably still be arrested for shady dealings during those days on the road—yeah, I was flattered. She had faith in me. I, on the other hand, had no faith in me. So I put my trust in her faith.

"I've got a year from the sale of my house. Maybe two if I don't eat meat."

She grinned. "Good answer, Donna. Now, listen then. I've got a plan." She picked up the tote bag and emptied it on the bench between us. A dozen Harlequin Romance novels fell out. "Get that look off your face. These sell by the millions. They publish twelve titles a month and they're each the same bloody recipe. Trust me, from my time in the Harlequin offices, I learned that. Now then, you listening?"

I was listening.

The idea was to first read the romances, paying attention to their cookie-cutter formula, then write one. "You've got to be fast; you write two stories in six months; you'll make thirty-five to forty thousand dollars. In six months, Donna. That pays for the following six months and your real writing. Trust me, the writers I met were doing exactly that. Sure, all it takes is keeping your butt in the seat. I know what you've crawled out of, Donna. Most people would've taken to the bottle. But you've got guts, luv, you've got pluck. I think you can do it."

I shoved the books into my bag. I couldn't wait to get started. I gave Elly the widest grin and we high-fived. Then we lit a last smoke and admired what was left of the dahlias, still luscious and pink in their dying moments. I left her there with a book by Carl Jung, *Seven Sermons to the Dead*, and trotted off, racking my brain for a plot. I was so deep in thought that I smacked into a parking meter, busting open my bottom lip.

On I went. As I walked through the streets, I thought about Elly and her luxurious house, her travels. I thought about what she'd told me of her past. Her illegitimate and premature birth. How she'd been abandoned by her mother and raised by her granny. Wrapped in towels and kept in a basket on the oven door. How had she risen to such wealth?

When I got home the phone was ringing. Mae.

Just the week before I'd sent her a framed five-by-seven copy of the photograph I'd taken the day I left. The one where she was standing in the doorway, squinting against the sun.

"This is you, Donna?" she asked, her voice so faint that I strained to hear it.

"Yes, yes, Mae, how are you—ohh, how are you?"

"Well," she said, "I couldn't understand why you'd send me this picture of an old woman."

"Oh, you got it?"

"I—yes, but I kept looking at it, I couldn't figure *who it was*. I kept going to your letter and then back to the picture. I knew there had to be a *reason* why you'd send it to me. And by and by I recognized it—the collar of my dirty old blouse. My, Donna, it's awful—that's not me, is it?"

I was wordless. I heard a soft sob.

"Mae, ohh, don't be silly—Mae! It's beautiful. I have a copy, too. It's hanging right here by the phone. I see you every day."

"Oh, my, take it down, take it down."

I closed my eyes, trying to remember whether there was a mirror in her house. How long? How long, Mae, since you looked at yourself? I was struck by a memory of having once caught myself unawares in a mirror I hadn't known was there. For just that second I didn't recognize my face, and saw myself as others did. As Mae was seeing herself, a face ravaged by a lifetime.

She was saying something. "Mae, what? What did you say?"

Her voice grew fainter still, as though she were fading from being. I spoke louder to bring her back—something about the cat, she was talking about the old tom. ". . . got him. My, Donna, I got him. I heard him at the door, my dear. I looked through the window because it was dark and I was scared. And there he was, crouched in the easterly winds and rain, and his eyes were yellow, staring up at me. The misery in them. Like he was saying *I've had enough. Let me in, Mae, I've had enough.*"

"Ohh, Mae."

"Well, I've been combing his fur now for days, cutting out the burrs. I sits in the rocking chair, rocking him. He's dying, my dear. That's why he's letting me hold him in my lap and brush his fur. He's too weak to do anything about it. I won't take him to the vet. No, my dear, I won't do that to him. I'll just let him be. I better go, Donna, he's trying to make sounds, I better go now, my dear."

I hung up the phone after we'd said goodbye and then sat, absorbed by Mae. Her voice. Finally I got up, walked over to the kitchen table, and started writing. I wrote about Mae. I wrote about her rescuing that old cat who'd rejected the community around him just as Mae had. And how, when she sat in her rocker, rocking that tom into eternity, she was rocking herself further and further from the definition of who she used to be and deeper and deeper into the feral bed the old tom had just left.

Davey and Bridgette returned from their summer months with their father. Davey fixed me up with a computer, gave me several demonstrations on how to use it—complete with explicit instructions for the on/off switch—and then was off to university in Antigonish. Bridgette hugged into the new flat with its wooden floors and working fireplace and high ceilings and big bay window that gave us a lovely place to sit. Slouched in our rocking wingbacks, we'd prop our feet against the window and watch the huge oak tree outside showering rain through its bared limbs and then the first snows of winter.

Three months into it and Bridgette had still never really noted that she had the one bedroom while I slept on the futon in the living room. Then one day she came home after being with her upper-middle-class friends just down the street.

"Mom, are we poor?" she demanded.

"Noooo. We're choosing to live this way."

"Mom, Lily's room is bigger than this flat."

"Nice. Does she have an oak tree in her living room too?"

"Mom, listen—"

"Shhh. Tell your friends your mother's writing *historical fiction* and that she needs the company of trees. Then ask them what *their* mothers do for a living."

She skulked to her room, throwing *very* unpleasant looks my way. I pushed aside the guilt, sat before my computer on the straight-back wooden chair that creaked and groaned louder than I did after two or three hours of sitting on it, and went back to writing the story of Mae and her cats.

DIFFERENT DIRT

I TURNED OFF THE LIGHTS in the flat and sat in the bay window facing the street. It was warmish for May. It had been eight months now since I'd sat in the gardens with Elly. I pushed open the window looking out into the dark, pressed my forehead against the wet screen, and wept.

Three months earlier my mother's cancer had come back. And since then the vision I'd had—of all my siblings living here in Halifax—had, miraculously, come to pass. The whole family had been able to uproot themselves and were living in the city. Our parents lived with Wanda now. Mother was taking her chemo treatments at the Victoria General Hospital. Counting siblings and spouses and youngsters plus one brother-in-law with his twins, there were twenty-three of us sitting at the supper table every other day. All of us wanting to be with our mother through this wretched time. And to be nearer our father, and each other.

I pressed my face harder against the cool mesh screen and wiped away the tears that kept coming. Overwhelmed still by the secret I carried—the secret passed on to me by Mother's doctor three months before, in Hampden. She was a woman in her sixties, sturdy in body with a hard German accent and dark sober eyes. On that day, soon after Mother's second mastectomy, she slowly read out the oncologist's report as Mother and I sat quietly, listening. Seven months of follow-up chemotherapy would be required, she told us, along with radiation.

As I followed my mother out of the office, the doctor tugged on my arm, pulling me back. Then she closed the door, staring intently into my eyes.

"Your mother has spots on her liver," she said urgently, "and throughout her body. She has less than two years. Perhaps one, providing she does the chemo. It is your choice to tell her this, but I recommend that you don't." She gripped my arm, her fingers strong. "My husband was given nine months to live five years ago. He counted down the months, then the weeks, then the days. He was comparatively healthy; he might have lived another year had he not believed in his death sentence. Do you hear me? It is a hard thing to know the day you will die. I would not tell her; this is my personal advice to you." She released my arm and I turned from her, stumbling out to the waiting room on weakened legs.

My mother stood with her back to me, putting on her jacket and speaking with an elder, seemingly unaware of my delay. But when we got into the car she turned to me, her mouth a steady firm line. "I won't do those treatments if I've only got a couple of years."

She knew. Her instincts had already told her what the doctor had needed a scan to find out.

"Nobody knows anything about time," I replied and started the car, burdened with a truth whose pathway I couldn't change but whose lie could affect how we walked it. And the moment I spoke that lie to my mother, the rationale behind it held such conviction in my heart that it became its own truth. I drove us home on the snowy road, talking fast and hard to keep myself from falling onto her shoulder and sobbing like a youngster. I told her we'd fix it so that her treatments would be in Halifax, making it easy for the family to visit. She gave a quiet nod. I dropped her off in front of the house; Glenn was there, having driven down from Toronto on wintered highways for this second mastectomy.

Then I turned the car around and drove to the beach. I parked and got out. A young family with kids, bundled in heavy coats and scarves, was scavenging the shoreline. I ran towards a rotting footbridge that crossed a river running into the sea. Then I veered upriver, plowing a path through the snow. When I was far enough off, when I could no longer hear the kids singing out, when my ears were filled with the river water rustling over its ice-coated rocks, I dropped to my knees and screamed.

I shifted my forehead now against the window screen. A soft rain pattered against it, cool droplets touching my forehead. There was a stirring in the dark outside. I wiped my face with a soaked tissue and held my breath.

A male voice said quietly, "Tell me it's just a man you're crying over."

I recognized the voice. I gave a short laugh that sounded more like an involuntary sob. Then I leaned forward, looking down— he was a darker shape against the dark. Jeff lived in the flat next to mine. At night, when all was quiet and he lay sleeping, his bed along our shared wall, I could hear his snores through the mortar and board. I'd sometimes hear him pacing his floors, cursing into his phone. Once I heard him cry.

I wiped my nose and spoke hoarsely. "My mother has cancer."

He was quiet for a moment, then, "I beat cancer. I avoided the chemo and beat it with hope and prayers."

"I am glad for you."

He struck a match and it flared, caving his eyes and burnishing his high forehead. He lit his smoke then tossed the match aside, flickering like a firefly to the ground. "That's all, honey. I just wanted you to know there's power in hope and prayers. Hey, and you know the drill, right? Knock three times?"

Jeff vanished into the dark, and after a minute or two I wasn't sure if he'd even been there—perhaps he'd been an angel conjured by grief. I walked into the kitchen, switched on the light, picked up the letter I'd received that day, and read it again. And again.

Months earlier I'd revised that short story I'd read to Elly— the one about my first period (minus Durkheim)—by turning it into a script. Then, on the advice of an acquaintance at the Atlantic International Film Festival, I'd entered it into a competition it hosted. And as I'd learned that day, I'd won. Elly had been ecstatic when I called her. "It's all coming to be," she'd exclaimed, "just like I said."

I lay the letter back down, grateful for the little light it would give my mother as she struggled through this cancer cross-cutting her path. Then I glanced at my laptop on the kitchen table, the story of Mae unfolding on its screen. It was past the midway point of becoming a novel.

Mother was coming for the night; she'd be at the door any time now. I picked up the letter and read it once more and for the hundredth time searched through the past for that moment when the writing seed might have implanted itself. I could see no further back than Miss Tucker passing me *The Cat in the Hat*; how

I opened its glossy covers, how its words rooted me to its pages. And after that how my first picture show swooped me up with its gargantuan branches and flung me into the clouds and I landed on different dirt. I landed beside that brook running through the dark stretch where Grandmother's devil hid and where I spent hours and hours alone, digging tributaries into rivers that ran through lonely homesteads and making up stories about a masked lawman and a brown crippled horse saving drowning people from flooding rivers. They passed me over to Steinbeck on his *Travels with Charley* and a whole avenue of lights lit up with Huck and Pip and Scarlett and Jane and Siddhartha and an army of others that kept on coming, and I stood tiny and blinded in the glare of their floodlights and within the flattery of Elly's words, *You can write, you have a voice, you can write.*

It had all felt so feeble at first—the humbling view from a one-bedroom flat as I attempted to fashion a story of Mae. She kept refusing to be shaped, her past presenting characters I had no interest in knowing—an old woman with a shotgun and a mentally challenged daughter and a cat called Pirate and a girl called Kit. When I finally tired of editing them out, I gave the pen its rein and a young fellow appeared and his name was Sid and *he used to say he loved me but back then I didn't know what love was, I was just a girl running down a gully . . .*

I lay down the congratulatory letter, startled by the sudden ringing of the phone. It was Elly's number. I didn't answer.

I felt I'd failed her with the romances. I'd worked hard—eight to ten hours a day for a couple of months, creating layered characters and a plot within the confines of the Harlequin guidelines. I wrote the most lavish scenes and scenarios and was astonished at how the story kept growing—from nothing, seemingly. Then, when it was finished, at exactly sixty thousand words, I was flabbergasted: I'd written a book! Elly and I celebrated with wine. I mailed off the manuscript, and we waited. Three to four weeks later a rejection letter arrived, advising, *Do not rewrite, do not resend.*

I'd looked at Elly, dumbfounded. This, neither of us had expected.

"Let me read your story, dear," she said. I nodded, wondering why we hadn't thought of a possible rejection before.

She read it and groaned. "Donna, what kind of heroine is this? Good lord, she near rapes her man, then slaps him. You can't have your woman slapping her man around in Harlequins. And look— he's French? Sure, what're you doing, luv. Enough with the Italians and the French and Greek gods. This is 1997. Be fresh, original."

She took it, changed my male character from French to Indigenous, changed my location from France to Antigonish, and with each new change I eagerly agreed, yes, yes, this was *sooo* much better. We sent it off. A couple of weeks later, after not hearing back, I sat gloomily in a café, smoking. Elly sat before me, tapping her fingers, smoking.

"Well, common sense says I should give this writing thing up," I said.

"I tell you what, Donna. You must ask God, luv. You must ask God straight out when you go to bed tonight. Put it in your prayers. Ask God if you should write another romance. Then we'll decipher your dreams."

It was a long shot. But I made it good. I shoved aside the wine bottle that night, not wanting it to interfere with sleep, then smoked my last cigarette and got on my knees. "Dear God, should I write another romance? If the answer is yes, I'll never stop writing, ever. If the answer is no, I'll never write again. Amen."

I got into bed, lay back, and stared at the moon, searching through the barren winter branches of the oak tree outside my window. I went to sleep. I dreamt of a buxom, red-headed maiden sweeping dirt out the door of her little hut. Before her, staring at her through a massive wall of glass in a huge castle-like house, stood a handsome baron, his face dark with anger as he glowered at the maiden. His view of the ocean had been blocked by her hut.

The wind rattling the windows woke me up before dawn. When the dream flashed before me I nearly fell to my knees in gratitude. Thank you, Jesus, thank you, Lord. I had it. I had a story. The angry baron's father had died, leaving the hut to his dear friend's daughter, the buxom redhead. Conflict. It's what the other story had lacked.

I was at the computer before the sun cast a shadow. Elly was elated. "What did I tell you, luv? It's faith, girl. Faith! Common sense flies out the window when faith walks in the door."

Two months later the manuscript was finished. Couple weeks after that the rejection letter came. *Do not rewrite, do not resend.*

Thanks be to small blessings: by that time Mae's story had already taken hold. I turned my back on romance novels. But Elly didn't.

"It was God-given, luv. I think you should rewrite, then think of another story. Look how fast you wrote that second one. I know the publishing industry. It'll take years to make money—you'll need the romances for that."

I shook my head. No, I was done with it. I think it was my certainty that caused the slight look of disapproval on Elly's face. She liked making the decisions, I noted.

But there hadn't been time to dwell on her disapproval. The news of my mother's cancer returning had turned everything upside down. Everything, including Elly, was put aside as my brothers and sisters arrived from all over the country, bringing their belongings, settling into Halifax to be with our mother. Elly. I felt a twinge of guilt. I'll call her tomorrow, I thought.

❧

The doorbell rang: my mother. I hurried to let her in. It was Tuesday evening, the night before her fourth chemo treatment at the hospital, a ten-minute walk down the street. Tuesday nights were mine and Mom's. To take her mind off the treatment we'd watch movies, eat smoked hickory sticks, drink hot brandy. But first, Mother would always read whatever I'd written since the Tuesday before.

"Another two thousand words," I said proudly when she walked in, waving a fistful of printed copy at her. "But first, look at this." I gave her the letter about the script-writing competition.

While she read I grabbed a sweater and dashed outside where Father was bringing in Mother's overnight bag from Glenn's truck. The streetlight lent a sheen to his yellow hair. Sixty-three and not a grey hair on his head. *Got three on my chest, though*, he kept saying.

He set down Mother's bag on the stoop. "Have a nice night, lovie," he said in a quiet voice. Then, without looking at me, he started back to the truck.

"Wait, hey." I held on to his arm. "Just this once, stay. Come to the hospital with us in the morning."

He yanked his arm away, threatening me with a look fiercer than a winter's storm, and kept on walking. The closest he came to letting in Mother's cancer was this—dropping her off at my place the night before her treatment. Nor would he be home when we returned from the hospital. He was never home during the day. Running. Luckily for him he was able to spend time with Glenn and Tommy as they worked long hours, laying carpet or installing hardwood floors. Not so lucky for them, though.

"Geez, you got the best of it," said Glenn, hunched over the steering wheel, giving me a wink as Dad got into the truck. "You got Mom. I got to deal with this contrary old fucker."

"You thinks now I thinks you're joking?" muttered Father, fumbling with his seatbelt. "I rather be sitting on a rock in the middle of the bay than be here in this gawd-damn place."

"I rather you was too," said Glenn.

"When this is over now, cocky," Father grunted, "and your mother's ready to go home, I'll be having my last piss in *Ha-leeee-fax.*"

"Oh my gawd, Dad."

"Won't see me on the gawd-damn pavement no more."

Glenn started the truck, sticking his head out the window so Father wouldn't hear. "He got me drove nuts. He got me drove fawkin' nuts. He sits in the truck, paging me ten times an hour, *Whaddaya doin', Glennie, whaddaya doin'.* I'm halfways up twenty flights of stairs lugging a roll of carpet on me back and he's calling, *Whaddaya doin' Glennie, whaddaya doin'?*"

"Take the pager from him."

"Holliieee Lard Jeezes, you wants to see a tantrum? You try dealing with him in the mornings. He's like the dog, the surly dog."

"Ye thinks now I can't hear ye?"

"I wants you to," snapped Glenn, hauling his head back inside the truck. He gave Father a punch in the shoulder. "How ya doin', old dawg, how ya doin'?

"Haha, see ya, Sis," he called out, swinging his arm around Dad's shoulders, his laugh sounding over the roar of the truck as he drove off.

Shivering from the cold, I darted back inside. Mother was sitting at the kitchen table, her coat still on, reading the new pages. She was as curious as I was about this writing process and examined every word I wrote as though the grand dame of literature, George Eliot herself, had dropped by and wrote them explicitly for her.

I sat, watching her read, noting the calm look on her face. The same look was there the day Wanda and I had arrived at her home from Halifax and packed her bags. It was there the entire drive back, then all through her first round of chemo, and the following three. As though she'd made peace with God and would accept whatever was coming her way. Except for time. She'd made it clear twice now that she wanted to know nothing of time. So I burrowed inside that dissension and held tight to the pact I'd made with the doctor. Except for my sisters and brothers—I'd told them the secret. It made it easier with all five of us sharing the role of Mother's timekeeper.

Our father asked no questions, staying close to the boys as they worked ten to twelve hours a day, establishing themselves in this new and competitive flooring market in this new city. The boys tended to his needs just as we girls tended to our mother's. Glenn and Tom would sometimes groan from the onslaught of Father's demands, his attempts to keep step with them through their labour-intensive days, no matter his weakening heart. They'd sit with him in his favourite bar and smoke and play cards with him till hunger drove them home.

Evenings and weekends we all sprawled together in Wanda's living room, chewing on the dried squid Dad had brought with him from Hampden, drinking beer and rum and whisky and wine and humming along with Karen as she played guitar and sang our favourite songs. We'd laugh and argue and fight and bicker. We all knew each other's Achilles heel; we were each armed with quivers of arrows and we were all master shots, evidenced by the daily dancing competitions taking place whenever two or three of us found ourselves standing on the same tile in the kitchen and else-where. There were times, though, when we were just too exhausted and would limp off into the solace of silence.

"You know, Donna," said Mother as she finished reading the Mae pages, laid them aside, and then picked up the letter, "I always knew you could do something like this."

"You knew more than me, then."

"I used to." She smiled, a flush of pride tinting her cheeks as she put down the letter. I gave a silent thank-you to whoever had chosen my script as the winning submission.

I helped her take off her coat—she'd fallen three weeks before and broken a bone in her right shoulder, and her arm was in a sling now to help support it. But the slightest movement caused her pain.

After she'd slipped off her shoes and gone into Bridgette's room to say goodnight, we began our Tuesday night routine.

I'd pull out the futon and make up our bed while she put on her pyjamas in the washroom. Then, while she plugged in the kettle and poured two tall glasses of hot brandy, I'd pull the TV to the foot of our bed, prop up cushions, skim into my own pyjamas, then dig the movies out of my knapsack along with a box of Turtles and a bag of smoked hickory sticks. She'd set down our brandies as I pulled down the covers. Then she'd sit quietly at her bedside, facing away from me, whispering her prayers, just as she'd been doing since I was a child. And while she whispered hers I'd turn and whisper mine through the sprawling skeletal branches of the oak outside the window. We'd slide beneath the blankets, bicker over the movies I'd selected, bicker over which one to play first, then finally settle on one. I'd push the start button and turn off the lights. Moonlight would dapple through the oak tree onto our bed. Colours from the TV screen would flicker across my mother's face and glint off her glasses as we'd snuggle back, shoulders touching, and start crunching on the salty hickory sticks, savouring mouthfuls of chocolatey-nutty Turtles, sipping hot brandy. We'd watch two movies and then start drifting off during the third, awakening and drifting.

On our walk to the hospital the next morning we'd fill each other in on those parts of the third movie we missed. Then, once we'd reconstructed it, we'd begin our critiques. That took us inside the hospital and into the waiting room. Finally, with Mother sitting in a big comfy armchair along with six or seven other women all hooked up to their chemo bags, and with me on a small stool near Mother's knees, the both of us exhausted from talk, I would lean my head against her lap and she would twirl her fingers through my hair just as Wanda had done when we were girls and slept together. Mother and I would close our eyes then, allowing ourselves to be quiet.

Afterwards we'd gather our things and make our post-treatment trek to the mall. Nothing—not cancer, not an empty wallet, not a balding head, not nausea—*nothing* could dampen Mother's enthusiasm for shopping at the mall.

＊—▷

Father wasn't without his trials. He'd developed a serious gum infection, had his teeth pulled, and received dentures. They were lovely, though. Pearly white, perfectly fitting, and natural-looking, adding greater charm to his already Robert Redford–handsome face.

One evening at Wanda's I noted Mother's silence as she sat alone in the easy-back chair, watching Father's self-conscious smiles as we cheered and whistled, getting him to smile more. Her eyes darkened as she looked down, picking at her fingernails, and I felt, in that moment, her jealousy of Dad's health, of his good looks becoming enhanced as hers were diminished, with her hacked-up body and thinning hair and purpling fingernails.

Later I stood beside her in the bathroom as she washed her face, not looking in the mirror. I complimented the smooth curve of her cheekbones and her unlined skin.

She shook her head. "I can't look at myself."

"My, Mom, you're sixty-two and looks fifty-two. What's wrong with that?"

She pushed past me and went to bed, curling into the hard pain of her imperfect mirror.

I called Elly. No matter the lateness of the hour and the blustery wind, she offered to meet me for a coffee at the Bar 'n' Grill on Argyle. I got there before her and sat in a dimly lit corner, ordered a red wine, and waited with anticipation.

I'd lamented the loss of our daily visits since my family had arrived. Elly had met them all several times, and had even once received the full meal deal: a Sunday family dinner. All twenty-three of us swarming through the house, serving, arguing, nosing into each other's business, separating squabbling kids. Elly had smiled and nodded her way through the talk, understanding little of it as we lapsed into the comfort of our Newfoundland dialect. I noted her cringe when the big bottles of Coke hit the table, shoving aside the glass pitcher of water with its picturesque arrangement of lemon wedges around its rim. Yet what could be nicer than a glass of rum 'n' Coke to wash down a scoff of moose meat 'n' gravy and pease pudding and bread pudding and a pot full of root vegetables boiled up with a hunk of salt beef?

No doubt there were moments that could have been considered bedlam—even after supper, when the spuds and gravy and puddings weighed everyone down and we crawled from the table, looking for a place to stretch out, everyone fighting for a coveted spot on the sofa, the wingback chairs, the loveseat, with the losers sprawling onto the thick-carpeted floor, wrestling over pillows. For sure, Glenn and Tommy hammed it up as they always did, wrestling with the toddlers. The teens—Davey and Bridgette and Nikki and Michael—were quiet, flopped on the floor, their backs against the wall, heads drooping like wilting sunflowers from their post–Saturday night hangovers. But everyone perked up and quietened down when Karen picked up the guitar and sang Dad's favourite songs as he hugged into Mom, sitting together on their reserved loveseat. Not even the squealing toddlers could outdo us, the fam, as we accompanied Karen with our off-key harmonies. I kept a continual check on Elly, but she appeared to be fitting in, sitting near the table with the spouses and the added brother-in-law with his little-girl twins. And she liked the puddings, steaming and plump from the pot, just fine, she said.

"Too much for you?" I'd asked in the silence driving her home.

She looked at me, her eyes so crowded with thought from the gathering that it would probably take her a week to figure it all out.

"It's how we all grew up," I tried to explain. "Newfoundlanders are known for their big families and lax boundaries."

"But you're not growing up now, dear."

I left her thought hanging there. How to explain to a partly orphaned only child, one who'd never had babies of her own, how, when we're all together for Sunday dinner or any other form of gathering, we naturally fall into our old ways of being? Like an overflowing lake we were, seeking its ancient riverbed, no matter that it's been buried for years. And how reassuring it was to be revelling in patterns of familiarity in this time of great pain and confusion. And while it might be bedlam to her, it was a place of rest and regrouping for us. A refuelling of our courage from the love of one another.

A draft of cold swept across me now as Elly came in through the heavy doors of the Bar 'n' Grill. She stood over the table, unwrapping her scarves and shedding her coat.

"How are you, luv?" she said as she sat down and drew her shawl more tightly around her narrow shoulders. "It's bloody freezing out there; sure, I couldn't catch my breath for the wind."

I started talking right away. Despite our fewer visits we spoke frequently on the phone and she was always keen to hear about my family's challenges, especially my mother's ongoing battle with cancer. But this, my mother's sensitivities around her femininity, her struggle to find comfort in her battle-hewn woman's skin—I felt inept as I tried to put it into words. Just as when I'd stood in that hospital room, fumbling with her toiletries and feeling hugely discomfited with Mother standing behind me in her underwear as she changed into her hospital gown.

Noting my struggle, Elly touched a gentle hand to mine. "It calls for tenderness, Donna. And delicacy. She's your mother. It's hard to stop being a daughter and stand woman to woman with your mother."

"Ohh, I can't do it. I don't want to."

"Well, you have to, luv. Your mother needs you. She's alone here, no women friends. Your father's become barren to her, and if she lets her femininity perish, she'll become barren too. It's her virility," she said to my questioning look. "Our femininity is our virility. Sure, it's what motors us. Perhaps I should talk to her."

"Oh, no, she'd shoot me for talking about her like this."

"Like what? You think I'm going to welcome her in then dish up talk about her femininity? Get your head straight, Donna. It's through the Bible I'll connect with your mother. She thinks of me as a pastor of sorts: that'll do it. From there we'll move on. I've been counselling inside the Church for thirty years," she added, her face taking on a deep look of empathy. "You think I don't know how to talk to your mother?"

"I don't even know what religion you are," I said with mild curiosity. "Or what it is exactly that you do with the Church."

"Used to," she corrected. "I'm half retired, except for a few things. But you name it, I did it. From counselling to changing diapers to travelling internationally and working with missionaries." She lit up a smoke.

"Are you Catholic? You know we're Anglicans, right?"

She blew out a mouthful of smoke as though she were choking and mock-rolled her eyes towards heaven. "Is this what you give me?" she asked, raising her hands beseechingly. "After all those years on my knees, is this what you give me?"

"I'm just saying, it's important to Mom. She loves her church. Not that I've ever raced to any church myself."

She laughed. "Ahh, Donna, luv, I've missed you." She leaned forward. "And you've no need to race anywhere; you've already won the biggest of all races—"

"What race? Aside from that screenplay competition—which is the most amazing thing *ever*—I've never won a thing in my life."

"The night your father spent himself inside your mother he unleashed a billion sperm cells inside of her."

"Oh, Jeezes, Elly—"

"That's the population of India, luv—all swimming for that one egg. And you outswam them all. There, what does that tell you—you won there, didn't you?"

"I—never quite thought of it that way."

She took a last drag off her smoke, jabbed it out, and held my eyes without falter. "Now, then, let's talk about getting your mother over to my house for tea."

There were a hundred questions I wanted to ask Elly about her past, about who she was, really. But her past was the one thing she veered from. I gave her that. There were parts of my history I'd never share; parts of my thinking I'd never seek counsel over, no matter how illogical I knew them to be. Some parts of us are so enmeshed within the truth we hold ourselves to be that they can't be touched by reason or logic.

If only I'd given the same consideration to my mother's truth.

I brought her to meet with Elly. Mother sat in the car, looking at the red-bricked front of Elly's heritage home, complete with two little gargoyles looking down from each corner of her double front doors. She shook her head, hesitant. "I've nothing to speak to her about," she said.

In my own enthusiasm about the meeting, I continued to persuade her. "She's a spiritualist, Mom. You can talk to her about . . . you know, those things you can't talk to us about."

"Why would I talk to a stranger about them?"

"The same reason we talk to God, therapists, ministers."

"She's a God now?"

I should've caught it then, my mother's reservations. She got out of the car and I walked beside her up the flagstone path. Her shoulders were thin beneath her winter coat; she'd lost weight. Her hair had started to fall out from the chemo, and she wore it clipped back behind her ears, baring the pallor of her face.

When she pushed the doorbell she looked so uncomfortable that I started regretting the whole thing. Then Elly was standing there, so welcoming, smiling so gregariously, that I gently nudged Mother over her stoop.

To ensure their privacy, I went for a walk. My step lagged. The look of discomfort on my mother's face wouldn't leave me. It wouldn't last, I told myself. The minute she was alone with Elly her reluctance would vanish and she'd settle into Elly's comfort and knowledge, just as I had.

I was wrong.

My mother was unusually quiet on the drive home.

"You didn't get much from that, did you?" I ventured.

She gave a little shrug. I grasped for something more to say, found nothing.

It was Wanda who slapped me down for my misjudgment. It was after supper Sunday evening, and the two of us were standing at the sink, fitting dishes into the dishwasher.

"Don't talk Mom into seeing Elly anymore," she said in hushed tones verging on anger. "I think she's jealous. All you talks about is *Elly, Elly*."

"*Jealous?*"

"Yes, *jealous*. She lives in that rich house and with all that education—you think Mom's not measuring herself against all that?"

"Oh, gawd, no—"

"Oh, gawd, *yes*, Don. Plus, Elly said something about you *feeling like her daughter*—I don't think Mom liked that, either." She shut the dishwasher door and leaned against the sink. "I don't know how she's doing it," she half whispered. "She don't say a word, and she's so sick." I reached over, caressing my sister's shoulder. Wiping tears from her eyes, she shoved away from the sink, flung her long dark hair over her shoulder, and vanished into the hubbub of the living room.

➤—▷

Mother and I were both quiet come Tuesday evening, watching Dad and Glenn drive off from dropping her at my doorstep. We watched just two of the three movies, and after eating the last hickory stick and finishing off our brandies, we each turned aside on our darkened pillows. I gazed through the window at the rounded face of a yellow moon through the clawed branches of the oak, feeling tortured, unable to stop thinking of Wanda's words. I went to sleep berating myself for all the wrongful things I'd ever done, and not done, in my life. Then, throughout our morning ritual and during our walk to the hospital, I continued to brood.

It was in the hospital waiting room that I was shown how self-involved such brooding can be. Sitting next to Mother was a young woman, the picture of health with her bright eyes and tinted cheekbones despite her shaved head. It was her stance that held me—shoulders erect, chin slightly tilted—as though her shorn head and the shorn right side of her chest were in defiance of what fate had given her. She kept glancing at Mother's chest, fully shorn. And at Mother's thinning hair, her right arm held in a sling, the pallor of her skin. I knew what the young woman was doing. She was measuring herself against Mother. Against what she might become.

None of this was lost on Mom. Perhaps because she herself had just fallen victim to the measuring game. She bent her head, leaned sideways towards the woman, and spoke softly. I couldn't hear what she said. But I saw the flush on the woman's cheeks, as though her deepest fear had just been exposed. Then, a quick smile. Perhaps of relief.

"What did you say to her, Mom?" I asked after we were settled in the treatment room.

"I told her my cancer was in both my breasts before they caught it."

She'd lied, in other words. She'd made up the lie on the spot just to give that young woman some hope and comfort.

I lowered my eyes so she couldn't see them. Where was *your* compassion, Elly, with your thirty years of counselling and religious studies and therapy, that you missed my mother measuring herself against you? That you made a dying mother feel more vulnerable by professing maternal feelings towards the daughter she'd soon be leaving behind?

I couldn't look at my mother. Easy enough to take a kick at Elly. It was my own self-centered brooding that needed the kick. Humility is a thing felt, not known. It is a lamp whose glow touches softly on small things, transforming them into great things. It is fuelled by vulnerability and the courage to bare that vulnerability to two strange women in a hospital room and to a frightened girl waiting her turn for the chemotherapy needle. And all the while, carrying the weight of a daughter searching for comfort upon her mother's mangled breasts. Oh, mother. Never as there been so much of you!

A MOMENT OF HUMILITY

MOTHER'S CANCER WAS ITS own paradox, its ravaging of her body invoking new growth within her and within us, her family, as together we moved through it. None more poignant than the courage she took from that proud, defiant young woman sitting beside her in the hospital waiting room.

"Call Karen," she said, partway through her chemo treatment as I sat there at her knees. "Tell her to find her clippers. Time to get rid of this." She motioned towards her thinning hair, brushing a few strands of fallout off her shoulders. Then, when we were back in the car, she vetoed our regular post-chemo trip to the mall and asked that we drive straight to Wanda's.

"Did you pick up the wig?" Wanda asked, meeting me at the door. Mother had already gone inside.

"What wig?"

Wanda stared at me. "Her wig. She's shaving her head; she needs a wig. They give them out at the cancer ward in the hospital."

"Oh, I never thought of it."

"We can go back after," Mother called from the kitchen. "It'll fit better with a bald head."

"What's everybody waiting for?" Karen bawled from the second floor of the split-level. She walked out onto the landing, her slight frame in jeans and a T-shirt, holding up scissors and electric clippers, mock cutting the air. "Snip snip, who's first?"

Mother sat duly in the chair Karen had set in the middle of Wanda's bedroom. Karen wrapped a towel around Mom's shoulders as Wanda and I perched on the bed, fidgeting. Hair. It is everything. It is a woman's cloak. It is her broach, her favourite colour, her hope for a better tomorrow once the perm has set and the rollers are out. It is her armour.

Snip snip.

A piece of Mother fell to the floor.

Snip snip.

Another piece of her fell. Karen's fingers trembled and a lock of hair she'd lifted slipped from her fingers. She lifted it again, awkwardly holding the scissors for a better angle. *Snip snip.*

I felt faint and lay across the bed. Wanda, holding a multi-coloured silk scarf in her hands for Mom to wear afterwards, quivered as though frightened with each snip of the scissors. *Snip snip.* Mother's face was pinched now, as though she'd sucked on something sharp, and I turned away, looking through the window at a bird fluttering onto the windowsill, *snip snip snip.*

"Oh, Mom." Karen ran her hand tenderly over our mother's scalp. "Here, feel it. It's right smooth and warm. Looks just like Sinéad O'Connor."

"Who the hell's that?" said Mother. Her grumpy tone belied the softening of her mouth as she brushed hair off her shoulders and a snippet fell onto her foot. She nudged it off as though it were dirt and Wanda half sobbed and Karen spoke hard through trembling lips.

"She's the most beautiful woman in the world, that's who she is. That's not good enough for you?"

"Yes, mind now," said Mom, and I knew she needed anger just then. She needed it as a crutch as she rose from her chair and started towards the mirror on the wall. Her eyes were sooty dark against the pallor of her skin and the white of her scalp. *Please don't look*, I pleaded silently, *please don't look and see the brick and mortar of your worn-down house, don't see blood and skin over bone but hear instead the beating of your heart with its primal rhythm, heralding your entry into time and waiting now to herald your return home. Your bald head and crippled arm and shorn chest are nothing compared to your humble true self, the self that will forever resonate through the hearts of those who love you.*

She stopped before the mirror, emitted a small gasp, and stepped back as though the sight were too much. Then she turned towards us, uncertainty clouding her eyes.

"Well. I'm still the same old bird, I suppose. Just lost a few feathers."

Karen laughed. I laughed. Wanda gave another half sob and Mom pulled the scarf from her hands.

"Give me that; I covers it. It's fierce. Donna, go get the car."

⋙—▷

Back at the hospital, Mother and I were met by a social worker who led us to a sunny room with comfortably cushioned chairs and coffee tables—and a large box holding perhaps two dozen wigs carefully packaged in plastic bags. The social worker left us to pick through them. At one end of the room was another box with what looked to be discards. Hanging a bit over its side was a blond, big-haired wig with long dangly curls. It looked like a cross between Dolly Parton's flaxen locks and Dee Snider's in his Twisted Sister days.

"Here." I threw it at Mother. "Try it on."

She adjusted it on her head, the curls falling over her shoulders. "I always wanted hair like my sister Shirley's," she remarked, a whimsical look on her face as she admired herself in the mirror.

"I don't think so, Mom," I said with a laugh.

"Why not? If I'm going to wear a wig, might as well get what I always wanted." She cocked an eye towards me and I grinned back.

My mother left the room that day with Dolly Parton on her head and a more suitable dark brown bob in her purse. I called Wanda from the foyer of the hospital, Mother standing beside me.

"Now listen," I whispered. "Mom—well, she's having a moment or something. She picked out a wig and—oh my gawd, Wanda— it's *blond!* It's *awful.*"

"So what? If she wants it, get her ten."

"No, you don't know—I mean it's—oh, it's *bad.*"

"Jeezes, Don, what odds? If she wants it, get it. If she don't care, I don't care."

"You remember those words, okay? We're on our way."

At Wanda's door I hung back as Mom walked in, Dolly Parton curls spilling over her shoulders. Sisters-in-law Diana and Fronie, who'd been lounging on the couch, looked up and jolted to their feet.

Wanda appeared on the landing, looking down.

What did I tell you, I mouthed up to her as she slowly started shaking her head.

"No. No," she said hesitantly, and then with conviction. "No, Mom. You're not wearing that."

"I'll wear what I wants," said Mom, and walked into the kitchen, flicking a few curls over her shoulder.

Wanda ran down the stairs but I grabbed her by the sweater as she went by, hauling her back.

"Just leave her alone for a while," I whispered urgently.

"No." She brushed past me, wagging a finger at Mom. "No, you're not wearing that."

"Yes I am then," said Mom.

"No, you're not." Wanda was shaking her head. Her eyes filled with tears.

"Just leave it for now," I said quietly.

"No!" The tears started streaming down her face. "No, you're not wearing it!" she yelled. "No mother of mine is walking around looking like—like a *whore*." She bolted back up the stairs as Karen came in through the back door.

"What's going on?" she asked, staring after Wanda and hearing her room door slam.

"She don't like your mother's wig," Fronie called out from the living room.

"Don't think I do either," added Diana, starting to giggle. "Oh my gawd."

Karen peeked into the kitchen then drew back at the sight of Mom sitting there, poised and sombre, fingering a curl.

"Oh, Mom," she said with half a laugh. She walked over to her, touching the hair gently, just as she'd touched Mom's scalp an hour before. Then she shook her head. "Oh, Mom, I wouldn't have chosen it for you. But if it's what you want."

Mom, upset by a shriek coming from Wanda's room, threw off the curls and pulled the bob from her purse. Karen busted out laughing, helped her fix it on, and then followed Mother as she went up the stairs and into Wanda's room.

I stayed behind, giggling, as I heard Wanda's fit shift into self-righteous wails. *It's not funny. You're worse than Dad. None of it's funny!*

>>——▷

That evening I drove home and wrote the first draft of what would become the prologue to my first novel, *Kit's Law*, a story that had started off as Mae's but was now about a girl named Kit. I wrote about a grey, weather-worn house, its windows open to the sea and its walls slanted back as if beaten into the hillside by the easterly winds gusting off the Atlantic and whistling up the gully.

"And if you were a bird and were to hop onto a windowsill and look inside that house you would see three women: the eldest sits in a rocker by a fire-blistering wood stove, her iron-grey hair hanging down around her fat-padded shoulders and a pinched look on her wrinkled old face as she sucks on something sharp. Standing behind her, drawing a comb through the grey tresses, is another, younger woman with flaming red hair, a furrow deepening her brow and her tongue nipped betwixt her teeth as she clumsily attempts to gather the old woman's hair into a bun and fit it into a hairnet that she dangles from one finger. Sprawled across the daybed and watching the two is me, the

youngest, with fine yellow hair falling away from my forehead and a
smile, I imagine, rounding the curve of my cheek as I watch."

After I'd written it I sat back, pondering that process of entwining real life into fiction. How experiences tumble around inside our heads like balls in a bingo machine, shooting themselves onto the page in the shapes of fictitious characters and stories, the player with so little ability to manipulate the outcome that it renders everything a gamble. And yet, when a work of fiction is completed, it has followed a somewhat orderly procedure; most questions are answered and those that aren't are given a likely reason as to why. Life is a much bigger gamble, with its flux of ever-changing variables; it's consistent only in its random spates of disorder and often poses questions that can never be answered or traced back to a likely source. Yet walking that long, arduous, twisting, tumultuous, spirited journey through life with my mother, I found truth and meaning at every turn. Which is why, perhaps, I stumbled so hard over Elly.

>——▷

It was June, the weather warming now after a wet spring. I called Elly. I'd been spending so much time with my mother that even our phone conversations had grown infrequent. We'd barely spoken about the project she was doing for the Church, the survey she'd asked me to help her with. Meanwhile I'd nearly exhausted the money from the sale of my house back in St. John's. Now I was wanting to work out timelines. That way I could budget accordingly.

Elly met me at an outdoor café on the waterfront. The wind

was cool but already the heat from the sun warmed our faces. Tightening our scarves, we wrapped our hands around our coffee mugs and leaned into each other.

"I don't know, Donna girl," Elly said when I pressed her for possible dates. "I'm thinking I'm too old for this stuff. Sure, why do I want to be taking on more work?"

"Hey, let me help with the planning. I've been thinking up questions for the survey." I paused. Elly was peering at me as though I were suddenly speaking a different language.

"What about your social work, luv? You were so focused when you first moved here," she said, her tone slightly scolding, "passing out résumés, introducing yourself. How come you gave it all up?" She tutted, shaking her head; I stared at her. Wordless. Like a dog whose nose was being rubbed in its own piss by the same beloved master who'd forgotten to put him outside.

Her eyes brightened as though with a sudden thought. "Oh, by the way, I have that book we talked about." That had been some time ago. She creaked around in her chair, searching through her bag sitting on the ground beside her. "Here it is." She put the book on the table: George Eliot's *Adam Bede*. "The best of the batch, Donna, for understanding the different hero archetypes."

My face muscles were stiff; I forced them to smile. Feigned interest as she flitted her finger over the cover, talking about the tragedy of the sad young heroine within, who had committed infanticide and was wandering the countryside in a state of shock and disgrace.

I had never felt poor. Waltzing across the country as a teenager with nothing more than pennies in my pocket and no bed for the night, I never felt poor. Standing alongside my mother during that horrible winter of the stolen cheque, eating leftovers after the younger ones had been fed, I never felt poor. Nor when I was a single parent going through university on student loans and creeping through that big cold house for five winters straight, living on canned tomato soup and grilled cheese sandwiches. Or when I drove a car with one door that opened and was secured shut with the end of a scarf tied around its door-handle and the other end levered around my neck. But in that moment, sitting before Elly, I felt poor. It took my voice.

"Archetypes, Donna, luv. Patterns of behaviours found across all time," she added with a flourish, her cheeks tinting like a girl's as she warmed into her talk. "Think of the fella counting his rubles and sorting his bills and checking over his house, seeing what's got to be done before winter comes. Now think about your tribal chief in some jungle, a thousand years ago, checking out his thatched roof, his store of roots and nuts, seeing what's got to be done before the monsoons come. What do you think, Donna? That's your ruler archetype, girl. Everybody has something of the ruler in them; it's a law of personality. What is it, luv? Is it your mother—is your mother all right?"

I nodded. "She's fine," I said, my voice hollow as a reed. "Are there other laws?"

"*Hah*, are there other laws? Are there sequins in Liberace's closet? *Hah* . . ." And off she went on another of her rich, humorous talks, and despite the swamp hole in my belly I fought hard to listen, to be drawn back into her words and feel comforted again by the same old Elly sitting before me, wisps of hair from her

messy topknot dancing around her face as she gestured and giggled and hammed up her yarns, illustrating some point. But all
the while I could focus only on the way, the shockingly dirty way,
she had just extricated herself from my future welfare.

Anger stirred my step as I walked home. Not at Elly, but at
myself for not challenging her word, not reminding her of our
plan. Of my *turning down a fucking job* so that I could work with
her. *Never show your hand*, she'd said during our first meeting
back in Antigonish. Hah, hadn't I done just that? Turned down a
good-paying job for a project that was more fantasy than reality?
Hadn't I done just that?

Pride. Perhaps it was pride that had kept me from saying anything. Or cowardice? Perhaps cowardice. Definitely cowardice. If
it was the former, then God bless it. Pride trumps beggary, and to
have mentioned our arrangement would have felt like begging.
And given the number of times I'd beggared myself before God
these past number of years, I'd paid a healthy price for that little
bit of pride.

By the time I got home I'd given up trying to understand *why*.
But the truth of it was clear. Betrayal. It was a hard light to stare
into. I wasn't ready. Throughout the recurrence of my mother's
cancer, in those deepening moments of vulnerability and grief, I'd
clung to the hope Elly had offered through what she'd taught me
of the philosophical, mythical, and spiritual worlds. And I've no
doubt that I would have overcome my hurt and disappointment.
Except for another incident, one that followed a week or so later.

An unexpected turn in a phone call with Elly ended with my
inviting her to another family dinner. It would be smaller, just

sixteen or seventeen of us, and this time I'd keep the rum and Coke bottles *off* the table.

As before, Elly devoured the steamed puddings and wild meat, just as we all did. What undid her began with our customary pre-dessert pandemonium.

First came our typical hammed-up fight over forks (there were never enough) for the partridgeberry pies. As usual Glenn had two stashed in his back pocket, and it was while I was wrestling him to the floor and Wanda had hauled his pants partway down his butt in her winning battle for the forks that I caught Elly shaking her head at me in shocked disapproval. Then, after we'd polished off the pies, Karen started playing her guitar and singing Dad's favourite songs as he hugged into Mother on the settee. We siblings and spouses sprawled around each other on the carpeted floor, giggling at Glenn's off-key harmonizing and Tommy's sombre face as he orchestrated with two spoons, the youngsters crawling all over us, looking to be tickled and roughed around. And again I found Elly looking at me, shaking her head.

Later that evening, over coffee at the Argyle: "Isn't it confusing for the children," she began, "seeing everyone lying around like that? And not just the children," she added as I stared at her in silence. "Tommy's wife. I saw her face, Donna. When you had your head on her husband's lap."

I stared at her so hard that her face broke into pixels. "Her *husband* is my baby *brother*."

Elly frowned like a mother disappointed in an obstinate child, then assumed a look of concern as I stiffened towards her. She reached forward, patting my hand comfortingly. But it was too late. The spell had been broken.

"That you can think such a thing—about my brother—" I lapsed into silence as she adamantly shook her head, fluttering her hands about her.

"I don't know how to take your family, luv. But I know how tough it is with your mother so sick. I remember when my granny passed away, I wanted to crawl into the coffin with her." She leaned in, her voice softening. "How're you nourishing your soul, Donna?"

"By being with my family."

She drew back, nodded. "Fair. That's fair. We all have our ways. After Granny passed I went to the church every day before eleven o'clock mass. And I prayed. I still do it to this day. I tell you, luv, everything falls from me there. Except the rawness of what's real. You should come with me."

"How do you keep out thoughts of priests molesting boys?" I asked, the sting meant for her, not the priests.

I thought she'd rap my knuckles, so shocked was the look on her face. She rapped the table instead. "When I bow at that altar, it's between me and His Self, up there. That priest and his sins don't contaminate my place of worship."

"Then I ask that you not judge or contaminate my place of worship with my family."

"Your mother wasn't comfortable either, Donna. I was watching her face. She didn't know what to make of what you were doing either."

What was left of my fascination with Elly popped like a bubble.

≫—▷

But that was nothing like the jolt awaiting me just a few months down the road. I'd been missing her hugely—her knowledge, her wisdom, the comforts I'd found at her spiritual bosom. I loved her—she was the fairy godmother with her basket of sparkles, casting hope and wonder across the grimmest of days. And as my mother's end grew closer my days were growing increasingly sombre. Small wonder, then, that my heart leapt when I thought I'd spotted her through the window of the café where we always sat. I went inside, but then drew back tentatively as I approached her from behind—her reddish, typically messy hair was neatly coiffed, her pert little shoulders more exposed in an elegant wool suit, as opposed to her usual swirl of scarves. Then she looked up—and I stared with surprise into a pair of flat blue eyes, a too-wide face, and a mouth so cockled it looked as though she was biting back bile.

"Sorry," I said. "I mistook you for someone else."

"Happens all the time," she replied, with the tinge of an Irish accent.

It was too much of a coincidence. I kept staring. "You—you're so much like her—Elly. My friend Elly."

"Let me guess: she lives alone in the south end, has no family, and Elly is short for Evelyn. 'Course, she would never divulge that much about her name."

I sat down across from her without being asked.

"I'm Andrea, her sister."

"Sister?"

A waitress floated past and I ordered a coffee. It felt as though I were sitting on the edge of a crevasse with my eyes closed, and that when I opened them a whole different world would be blazing back at me.

She spoke directly, without her sister's flourish. Her words were clipped, with a resigned sort of anger, as she looked at her watch and laid out the money for her coffee. "Evelyn's an educated, talented widow who's seldom left the province," she said. "She's never flown, and never held a professional job. You can deduce the rest from that."

She was gathering her gloves and purse now, preparing to leave, but she couldn't help being curious, I could see. And so I began besieging her with questions.

My eyes bugged with incredulity as I learned the extent of Elly's lies: that she'd never travelled internationally for the Church, had never been to Zurich, had never undergone Jungian analysis or studied dream therapy. She didn't have a PhD in world religions, or a PhD in anything. She'd never been a Harlequin editor, and neither was there a dear old granny. She had inherited her wealth from her deceased husband. I thought back to that time when I'd first arrived at her house alongside the mailman, how quickly she'd ushered me inside and closed the door. Had she been trying to prevent me from overhearing something, like the mailman calling her by her proper name, *Mrs.* Evelyn O'Rourke?

I sat there in a state of shock, reeling back over the past couple of years like an unwary wife after learning her husband has been having an affair. I was trying to determine what was real.

"But *why*? Is she mad?" I asked.

"Nope. Just a pathological liar." The sister gave me a sympathetic smile. "If it's any consolation, she's spoken of you several times. She seldom does that." She rose to go.

I held out my hands, imploring her to stay; I had just one more question. "Please, just . . . Elly told me I had entered her through the sister archetype."

Andrea gave a cryptic laugh. "She always wanted a sister who would believe her lies. It was . . . Well, nice meeting you, I guess."

Then she was gone—a lipstick-dabbed napkin lying on the table the only proof she'd actually been there, that she wasn't the product of some kind of passing psychotic break.

I walked for days. Weeks. Prowling back over our hundreds of hours spent talking, sharing. I tried to unravel what had been lies, what hadn't. I figured Elly really did work with a church. She'd once shown me a mockup of a survey she'd written. Then again, she'd also shown me a picture of her granny.

Her sister must have forewarned her of our chat. Five or six months later, after my mother's passing, I glanced out the window and saw her on my doorstep, the wind tugging her hair and bil-lowing out her scarves as she rang the bell. My heart thudded. I flew to let her in, already accepting her apologies and explana-tions—as long as we own those parts of our damaged selves, right?

Elly walked slowly behind me into the kitchen, an air of solem-nity about her. She thanked me for inviting her in, sat down at the table, and looked at my copy of a book by Robert Johnson, an American Jungian analyst and author. It was a brand-new release.

"It's wonderful," I said, nudging it towards her, thinking to ease our way into the "big talk." "I've just finished—"

She interrupted me, shaking her head knowingly. "I read this years ago in Zurich," she said, "in one of his classes."

There is a gravity that seems to act solely on our bodily fluids, drawing them down around our ankles in times of moral upset while we remain standing, feeling the crushing void of nothing-ness in our hearts. I drew out a chair and sat at the table, half-turned away, unable to look at her.

Elly didn't look at me either, but played at flipping through the book as she offered her prayers about my mother. She tried explaining why she hadn't gotten in touch—something to do with allowing me time to heal from the trauma. Then she spoke of "a very angry sister" she'd never told me about—something about deeply suppressed issues—and I nodded, unwilling to hear her words, tongue leaden in my mouth, unable, or too cowardly, to confront her with her own shadow.

Without my saying anything, she knew the jig was up.

She is one of my greatest losses. I gain comfort from the sage words of the big man himself, Carl Gustav Jung. The only per-sonality type he would never work with, he once said, was the pathological liar—because liars reinvent themselves at every turn. Looking back, I was amazed at how, despite my street smarts, I'd been so utterly taken in.

One thing that *was* real, though, was Elly's knowledge—and, I like to think, her intuition in believing me to be a writer. Her pushing me to find my voice. For that I am eternally grateful. And in those times when I find myself missing her, and then becom-ing angry all over again, I remember her words: *Donna, you're the most innocent person I've ever met, and at your age that's not a com-pliment, luv.*

Fair. Fool me once . . .

CHARADES

MOTHER'S HEALTH WAS WORSENING. We were nearing late August now; it had been nearly two years since I'd moved to Halifax, and four months since Mother had begun the chemo treatments. After her eighth session, two weeks earlier, she'd been so weakened that her oncologist delayed further treatments until she could regain some strength.

During this time Mother and I continued spending Tuesday nights together, although we kept putting aside the movies in favour of writing. The story of Kit was nearly finished, and both Mother and I were eager for the ending. I wrote and wrote with Mom just lying there, watching. From time to time I'd turn to her, in need of relevant details.

"Mom, after you plucked the feathers from the turrs then dipped them in scalding hot water so's to buff them, how was it you held them so easy-like?"

"So's not to break the skin and sap the oil from the meat."

I wrote her words.

"Mom, what's the best thing you like about starfish?"

"It grows back its lost limb. Wish I could grow my arm back."

I wrote her words.

"Mom, that old yarn ye all told on the Beaches about the worm leaving the partridgeberry and carrying the seed for next year's planting—?"

"That's not a yarn."

"Oh, gawd, Mom, you know it's a yarn."

"Ask them who picked their patches too early. Nothing growed back for years. I seen that too many times."

"Mom! Worms don't crawl out of berries with seeds in their mouths and plant them."

"That's what they do, then. We were never allowed to pick the berries too early, and we had our patch all while we were growing up. And them that picked too early were always scrounging around and looking for ours, their own patches bare."

I wrote her words. Then I read out what I'd written and she nodded her approval.

On this Tuesday evening, before Mother's treatments started up again in the morning, our bed was made, movies rented, and brandies poured. But Mother again elected that I continue writing. She lay on our futon bed, sipping her brandy and holding her broken arm in its sling as though it were a baby.

She'd broken several bones in her wrist this past month. One snapped as she was struggling with a button on her shirt. Just snapped like a pretzel. The cancer had moved into her bones. She claimed that her arm was merely weakening from the broken bone in her shoulder and the sling. How much of it she allowed herself to believe, I don't know. Or perhaps I did. For just a second, after we'd returned from her X-ray at the hospital and Dad asked her about it, I caught a look on her face. It was hard to read. Perhaps it was resignation. Then she perked up, cherry-picked some of the doctor's words with some of her own, and offered them nicely to Father: *Her arm was weak from all the chemo and non-use. She'd need to get physio after the sling was removed.*

"When? When is the sling coming off?" Father demanded.

"Oh, now—not like it's the doctor's doing," she said sharply.

"All right, all right, lovie. He knows what he's doing, I suppose."

Charades. It was all a game of charades that everyone played and knew they were playing. But it was a game Mother directed and, in those moments when she took control, it was more than a simple denial of the truth. It was a respite she felt she was offering us. And a respite for herself as well, from having to contain us while we contained her. Besides, it wasn't as if facing the truth would change anything. Perhaps, in times such as those, denial was a necessary thing.

On this night before her chemo treatment, with me writing and her lying there, she was restless. She got up, went to the washroom, came back with a second hot brandy for each of us. Then she stood over my shoulder, reading as I edited.

"Mom, I can't write with you watching."

"You got *these* instead of *those*. Right there." She pointed to the screen.

"I never know how to use them."

"*These* brandies are here in my hands, *those* not yet poured are over there in the bottle." She set my brandy down beside me and lay back on her cushions.

"I got myself in a jam with the ending," I told her, and recounted the plot.

"Don't give it the happy ending. Keep it real," she said.

"What's wrong with happy endings?"

"There's things more important than being *happy*," she said with a thread of bitterness. "*Happy* is for babies."

"What's better than happy?"

"Having a strong heart, is what. Crippled up with arthritis like I was, I always felt strong in here," she said, patting her chest. "And I still feels strong in there."

I paused. "How? With so much going on?"

"Because that's where I keeps all of ye. And that's the one thing I gets to take with me."

The game was over. I closed my eyes, struggling with how to pick up on her words. She rose again and went to the washroom. I engraved her words on my heart. I engraved them on the final page of the manuscript: *There's more than happy . . . there's peace. And pride. And those things measure good.*

The book was done. It was past midnight. Mother was still awake. We sat in awe of it. A book. We'd written a book.

The morning sun poked through the old oak, tickling across my face and resting on Mother's. She squinted, so tired she could scarcely lift her hand to shade her eyes.

"Perhaps we should cancel," I said, but she shook her head.

Instead of the ten-minute walk to the hospital, I drove us. I parked near the emergency entrance and went inside, for the first time bringing back a wheelchair. She stared at it for a moment, then sat in it. And later, as we walked to the car after the treatment, she took my arm. By that point I thought we'd drive straight home, but no.

"I have to buy socks for your father."

"Mom, you can hardly walk you're so tired."

"What else we gonna do, Donna? Lie down and die?"

I was silenced. She looked ghastly as we walked the short distance from the handicap parking spot to the vast reaches of Sears bargain basement. Where the best socks were, according to Mother.

I looked around, Mother leaning on my arm. It was cold in there with the air conditioning, and the harsh fluorescent lights sucked what colour there was from our faces and turned our lips blue. Ten steps in from the entrance doors, Mother faltered.

"Mom?"

She pointed to a row of sofas; I led her towards one. She sat, holding herself forward, her elbows on her knees. I perched on the arm of the sofa, my thigh resting against her shoulder; I'd never seen her so weak. We were facing a white wall, bare except for water stains near the top, and a row of carts near the door where we'd come in, the floors muddied beneath them. I shivered.

"Mom, let's go home."

"I have to get socks for your father."

"Screw the socks. You're not feeling well."

She shook her head. "Something come over me. Be better in a minute."

"Can you stand up?"

She tried to move but sagged deeper into herself.

"*Okay*, just sit right there, all right? I'll be right back."

I charged to a checkout about sixty feet down the way. "Wheelchair," I demanded. "My mother needs a wheelchair. Do you have one?"

They did. For their elderly customers, they said pleasantly.

I pushed it towards Mom, who was still sitting forward on the couch, her back to me. A wheelchair. A house of cold silver. I positioned it next to her, saying cheerily, "Don't know why we never thought of this before. Sure, everybody uses wheelchairs in the mall if they have bad knees or something."

I bent down, busying myself with the brake to keep her from seeing the anguish burning in my eyes. She got up; she was silent. Then, after a little quarter-turn, she sank down into the chair, graceful as a queen.

Settling her purse onto her lap, she pointed to a rack of cards off in the distance. "It's Shirley's birthday next week."

⋙—▷

In the face of Mother's growing weakness, her oncologist again delayed her final treatment for yet another two weeks. During that time I researched publishers and agents at the library, ending up with seven addresses along with instructions for how to write a letter of introduction to an editor. Plus seven sets of the first thirty pages of *Kit*. I'd read that writers should send in just those first pages of their manuscript; otherwise, the package would be too daunting for an editor taking home work on a weekend.

Sitting around Wanda's dining room table one rainy summer morning, Mother looked much better, and she was cheerful. We packaged up the seven bundles and started addressing envelopes. Five Canadian publishers and one agent, Beverley Slopen, in Toronto. Only one package left to address, the seventh. And one publisher left, Penguin. My all-time favourite classics came from there, and I smiled fondly.

"They only publish dead people," I said to Mother.

"Then put my name on it," she said.

We both looked up as Father shadowed the doorway, his face grimacing at Mother's words. The boys must have dropped him off early; neither one of us had heard him come in. Then he vanished and Mother bit her lip, looking away.

"Go," she said to me. "See where he's at."

He was sitting on his haunches outside the back door, leaning back out of the rain, the eaves an umbrella above him.

"She's not going nowhere yet," I said, trying for a jocular tone.

He turned his face aside, just as Mother had done. I crouched beside him. It was barely noon and already he smelled of booze. His opium for everything these days. The only world he controlled, until he didn't.

I muscled back my resentment. "You got to stop running from her, Dad. Going off with the boys all the time. Drinking. Why don't you stay home more? Be with her?"

When he looked at me I saw his eyes darkened with despair. It wasn't my mother he was running from; it was himself. For he saw the future coming, and he possessed no hope of changing it.

"We got to accept it, Dad."

"Go on in, lovie."

"Tomorrow's Sunday. Mom wants to go to the harbourfront. Come with us. Please come with us, you'll be glad you did. After."

He turned his face aside again. I squeezed his shoulder and left him there.

Inside, Mother was addressing the last package to Penguin. For good luck, she said. She came with me as I drove to the post office, mailing them off. Then, at her request, we drove again to Sears bargain basement: she'd noticed the bedroom suites on sale the last time we were there, and she wanted to have a look. Her mattress, she said, was old.

⊁—▷

No doubt we were all inept at learning how to live alongside our mother as we watched her learning how to die. None more so than our father. We were readying for our walk around the harbourfront the following morning when he came downstairs wearing a clean pair of jeans and his plaid cotton shirt—the one he wore on Sundays. Mother sniffed at him like a suspicious dog over an unexpected piece of beef appearing on its plate. He nearly growled back, daring her to say one critical word about his clothes, his hair, the smell of beer on his breath.

I got us out the door, drove to the harbour, and parked. It was warm and sunny—and with the cry of the gulls and the smell of seaweed and salt water, it was feeling like home. I pulled the wheelchair out from the back of the van as Dad opened Mom's door. He turned to me, staring at the wheelchair as it clunked onto the pavement. Only then did I realize that he hadn't seen it before.

"Here, unfold it. I helps Mom out."

He shook his head. "She's not getting in that."

"Why, what's wrong with *that*?" Mother asked, already out of the van. She walked over and sat herself into it, looking up at him defiantly. "I got to push it, too?"

He kept staring at the chair as though it had taken something from him.

I began pushing the chair and Mother; she kept her eyes straight ahead, wearing the same begrudging expression she'd worn back when Father, newly dentured, was showing off his charming smile. I felt her loss—unable now to walk by her husband's side on this breezy day, the sun frolicking through the trees over the boardwalk, enjoying the familiar salty smells of the sea. I pushed the chair faster, struggling for something to say to bridge the distance between us, but I was as shuttered from her broken woman's heart as my father was.

The waterfront was relatively quiet, the tourist season slowing down for the fall. Dad veered off, heading towards an ice cream kiosk just ahead.

"What's he doing?" asked Mom, with more wonder in her voice than curiosity. For unless his body was on fire and he needed a bucket of water to douse himself with, Father never approached strangers with his baywop accent. Mother tutted. I smiled. We both recognized the grandeur of his gesture. His words were often awkward, futile. They became tools, weapons she'd fling back at him. So this braving of talk to a mainlander, this spending of money we knew he'd rather devote to smokes and beer and gas, was a huge expression of the depth of his emotion.

I stopped next to a picnic table as Father stood before the kiosk, fumbling in his pockets.

"Go with him," Mother said.

"He can order an ice cream, I suppose, Mom."

"You'd think."

I locked the wheels of her chair and walked over to Dad.

"Plain," he was saying to the girl behind the wicket. "Plain," he repeated as she kept looking at him, puzzled. "*Plain. Plain.*"

He jabbed a finger towards the cardboard cutout on the counter depicting a scoop of vanilla ice cream atop a waffle cone.

"Ohh, vanilla?" she asked.

"Three," said Father.

"Three cones, sir? Or three scoops?"

"Cones," I answered for him. "My, this is nice, Dad."

He muttered something, taking a five-dollar bill from his wallet. Reconsidered, and took out another five. The girl placed three waffle cones with a scoop each of vanilla ice cream before him. "That'll be eighteen dollars and thirty-two cents, sir."

He went bug-eyed. "How much?"

"Eighteen dollars and thirty-two cents."

Pulling a ten-dollar bill from his wallet, he smacked it on the counter alongside the two fives, his eyes fierce. "Get the gawd-damn change," he muttered to me, shoving his wallet back in his pocket. Then he snatched the tray of cones off the counter.

"Keep your mouth shut and say nothing to Mom," I muttered back. After smiling and tipping the serving girl, I hurried over to where he was handing Mother her cone.

"Get every gawd-damn lick," he ordered. "That just cost me three pension cheques."

"You don't mind buying beer and cigarettes," Mother chided him.

"Cheaper than this gawd-damn stuff."

"It's the cones, Dad. You ordered the expensive cones."

"I told her *plain*. Three *plain* ice creams."

"You pointed to the waffle cones."

"I pointed to the gawd-damn ice cream."

"In waffle cones."

"That's the only ones they had on the poster."

"Good choice. They're really good, hey Mom?"

"*Plain*," mimicked Mother. "What's *plain*?

"White, gawd-dammit, white."

"White is *vanilla*. That's a *flavour*, not a colour."

"How come snow don't taste like vanilla, then."

"Ohh, frig, all right, everybody eat!" I yelled. "It's all freakin' melting."

Father took his cone over to the wooden bollard by the edge of the wharf and crouched beside it, looking out to sea. I chatted to Mother as we licked our ice cream, keeping her attention away from Father as he lit up a smoke, his scoop of white ice cream and waffle cone floating on the water.

≫——▷

It was evening of the same day. Once Mother was resting, I ventured into Wanda's garage where Glenn and Tommy had been helping our nephew Michael fix his motorcycle. They were all sitting around, the overhead light bright and glinting off Tommy's red truck, its bonnet up. The air was so thick with everyone smoking I scarcely saw Father sitting on a plastic chair beside a stack of tires. A tinny tape deck had been perched on a cluttered shelf above his head, Hank Williams singing about some mansion on a hill.

"You done pretty good today," I said, taking the chair beside him.

He slowly shook his head, his face crinkling up like a youngster's verging on tears. "Let's go home, lovie," he pleaded. "Let's take her home."

"She got one treatment left, Dad. Then we'll see."

He gave me a fierce look. "You think that one treatment's going to make her better? Home. Home," he repeated. "She'd be better off home."

"Who's going home?" asked Wanda, coming into the garage, lighting a smoke.

"Home? Who's going home?" asked Glenn.

"Nobody's going home," I said loudly.

"*Home, home,*" mimicked Tommy. "Everybody's always talking about *home.* Ain't nobody going *home* while Mom's doing her treatments."

"One more. She got one more left, gawd-dammit. What difference do it make?"

"Might make a lot to her," said Tommy.

"I wants to take her home," said Dad, his eyes blooming with tears.

Wanda marched over to him, jabbing her finger. "You don't go bawling and talking about our mother while you're drinking. She deserves more than that—and that goes for all of ye," she added, looking at the boys.

"Get outta the garage and leave him alone," grunted Glenn.

"*You* get outta the garage and go be with Mom," Wanda shouted, red in the face now, giving in to her day's angst. "All of ye get outta the garage and be with Mom. Holed up out here, drinking and smoking like teenagers. Ye don't do nothing but drink and smoke."

"And work twelve hours a day," Glenn added.

"*Fourteen,*" said Tommy.

"And what's me, Don, and Karen doing then, playing patty cake?" asked Wanda.

"Sir, what's ye all arguing about?" Karen yelled, coming in through the garage door. "Mom can hear ye."

"Close the gawd-damn door then," Glenn snapped.

"Close your gawd-damn mouth," Karen snapped back.

"Come sing me a song, lovie," croaked Father to Karen, knuckling the tears off his face.

"I'll sing you your death song you don't smarten up," said Karen.

"You'll all be dead before me ye keeps it up," said Mother, appearing behind Karen in the doorway.

"Lovie, come sit beside me, come sit," begged Father.

"You come sit beside *me*," said Mother, then vanished back inside the house.

The place erupted, everybody yelling at everybody else, then fell to a low spate of mumblings when Mother reappeared with a cushion. As she made her way across the cluttered garage I got up, giving her my seat next to Dad. Tommy wrapped a blanket around her shoulders and Wanda fired up a joint and Michael brought Karen her guitar and she pretended to whack Father in the head with it.

Sitting on a spare tire, she started humming and playing along with Hank and soon we were all harmonizing, *I'm sooo lonesome I could cry,* and Father muffled his face into Mother's shoulder and wept.

ROCKING HER BABIES

WITHIN SIX WEEKS AFTER SENDING off the *Kit* packages, we received a rejection letter from Penguin. It was the most astonishing thing. They *did* publish living people. And they wrote the loveliest note, saying the manuscript wasn't for them, *but they liked the voice.*

I read the letter out to Mother, and several other letters that came in requesting the full manuscript. Mother was so pleased. She smiled a lot but had grown much quieter. Her body was breaking down fast. She'd snapped another bone in her wrist. Then another. Her bones were riddled with cancer now. It became more and more of an effort for her to simply stand, and yet she did. She persisted in hovering before the sink, leaning against it for balance as she loaded the dishwasher with her good hand and wiped down the sink. She even complained about having to keep her broken arm in the sling. *I'll lose the use of it*, she worried.

The oncologist had cancelled her final treatment and sent her for radiation instead to relieve the pain in her arm. While Mother was undergoing the radiation he sat with my sisters and me and told us that, based on her most recent CT scan, our mother had approximately two weeks left to live. The cancer had taken her liver.

Two weeks.

Afterwards, when we'd all gotten back into the car, Mother saw it in our eyes: the days were slipping from her calendar. She turned from us.

"Can we go back to the jeweller's, Donna? I want to buy that silver watch with the big numbers on the face. Can't see this anymore," she said, squinting at the little gold-plated watch on her wrist.

I drove us to the store. I no longer knew what courage was or what denial wasn't or where avoidance slipped in. It was all a mixed bag of rules and emotions directing us to the one ending. And given how the endgame was Mother's alone, I steered where she directed. Perhaps, like the rest of us, she let in as much as she could bear during each moment.

We went inside the little shop and Mother bought the silver watch. "Here, you wear it for me," she said, handing it over. "My wrist is too tender."

I spent the night at Wanda's. Everyone was there. Words were carefully whispered through the room: we had two weeks. When our father started sobbing in the corner Karen went to him, put her fist to his mouth, and said, "Not one more fuckin' croak. She don't need to hear you bawlin'." Then she got her guitar and sat with her back to us. She was silent for some time until finally she turned to Dad, and in a voice as soft as summer rain, she sang his favourite songs. We huddled among ourselves for comfort and listened. Glenn and Tom stared into their beers. Mom came from her room and sat next to Dad on the loveseat. She rested her head on his shoulder and Karen sang and sang . . .

Everyone reluctantly left the house for work before seven the following morning. Wanda had a doctor's appointment, she said, but I knew she needed to be by herself. For a while, then, I was alone with Mom.

I approached her as she stood before the bathroom mirror, fixing her wig in place. "Mom. I think we should go home now. To Newfoundland."

She gazed at me, then slowly nodded. She understood. To go home meant her time was up.

She walked into the living room, and there, in the middle of the morning and for the first time I could remember, she stretched out on the sofa and pulled a blanket over herself. She had laid her hammer down.

And I went down with it. Bizarrely, after telling her we must go home, I'd somehow expected her to make things right again. To play the charade and allow me to play it along with her. But standing there, staring at her covered back as she turned from it all, I realized how it had always been Mother leading me, leading all of us. And that we'd duped ourselves into believing that we were leading her.

I kept looking at her helplessly, until I was saved by the phone ringing. It was Bridgette, telling me that Purolator had left a note on our door. "It says there's an envelope at their depot from McClelland and Stewart. Is that a publishing house?"

After the call Mother turned onto her side, looking at me.

I told her about the courier's note. "It's from that publishing house," I told her. "The one that called last week. Mac and Stewart or something. The ones that said they'd make a decision this week."

She nodded with certainty. "They've accepted it."

I shrugged. "It doesn't matter. You want some tea?"

"Go get that envelope," she urged. "They wouldn't send a rejection letter by Purolator."

"I don't care, Mom."

"I do. Go get it."

"When Wanda comes back."

"Go get it now."

I heard something in her voice. A sense of aloneness that I couldn't breach. I fled to the car, needing aloneness at that moment as much as she did. I cried long and hard. I cried during the fifteen-minute drive to the depot, even turning on the wipers once, thinking I would see better. After I got there I spent another ten minutes composing myself before going inside.

Back in the car, I stared at the white cardboard envelope. Mother was right: surely they wouldn't send a rejection letter by courier. I ripped open the envelope and drew out the smaller one inside.

They were sorry. They wanted to believe in Kit, but—but—times were tough—*blah blah*. I dropped my head onto the steering wheel, wishing for the energy to scream out to God, *What the fuck is it with You? It was for her, you Jerk. It was for her!*

I'll lie. It came to me like a bolt. I'll just fuckin' lie. I'll tell Mom they want the book. She's got two weeks left. I'll deal with the fall-out after. What the hell, right?

Then I thought of Elly. This was before I'd met her sister, but I'd distanced myself since our last conversation and struggled with the prospect of calling her. Still, I remembered her saying once, *Nourish your soul with just a drop of water, and it'll net you a river in return.* And I needed a drop of nourishment. My river had gone dry.

I went back inside the Purolator office, asking to use their phone. The kindly clerk, seeming to sense my distress, guided me behind the counter and into his office. I called Elly's number from memory. She answered, her voice a little cool but accepting.

So I blurted it all out: my mother having two weeks left to live; that I was taking her home tomorrow; how much my manuscript meant to her. "I'm the only one not married and she worries about that," I told her. "She don't say, but I knows she wants this book published so's I can have something after she's gone." So I'm going to lie to her, I went on. And say that a publisher has accepted the manuscript. Besides, it was just for two weeks. I'd alert the family to the lie and we'd keep it to ourselves.

Elly listened. Then, before I was quite finished, she cut in with a rush of impatience. "Let me get this straight, Donna. The last thing you're going to tell your dying mother is a lie?"

I cringed at the sound of those words.

"It's not just you playing this game, luv. You can only play the cards you've been dealt."

I closed my eyes, resigning myself to the truth. I heard Elly's breathing, then her words softly spoken: "You've got pluck, girl. You've shown that. You'll do what it takes."

When I got back Mother was where I'd left her, lying on the sofa, covered up. Her eyes were vacant, as though she'd already left herself, and when she stirred it was as though she were returning from a long way off.

"A rejection letter," I said, my voice coming out singsongy. I tossed it on the side table. "I don't care anyway. Can I get you some tea? Gawd, I'm thirsty."

She looked at the letter. "Let me see," she said as she struggled to sit up.

"It don't matter, Mom. It's a nice rejection, but there's other places to send it to. At least we know it's getting some consideration."

She was half sitting now, reaching out her hand, insisting. She read the letter as I stood there, waiting. For what, I didn't know. For her to make it better?

She sniffed. Wrinkled the letter with her one good hand and cast it aside. "Thought they were a smart crowd, them publishing people."

Mother got up then. She faltered, her legs stiff, but they were fully straightened by the time she reached her room. I trailed in behind her. She walked over to her closet, took out the dark blue dress she always wore to church, and passed it to me. "Bury me in this," she said. Then, standing before my shocked face, she removed the diamond earrings that Wanda had given her some years ago and placed them in my hand. "Give them to Amy," she said—the only daughter of Glenn, her eldest living son.

"Mom, my gawd."

"Get the suitcases. And no foolishness. I spent my time with ye. Now I'm going to see my other babies, them I never got a chance to rock. And that's what I wants you to see when I'm gone," she said, her voice softening. "Me, sitting up there, rocking my babies."

Sunday, August 27, 1998. Four p.m. Mother slumbered into her deepest sleep. We sat beside her till we heard those rockers creaking. And then we left her in peace. Our father couldn't be there at the hospital for her last hours. It would have been too hard. The boys were nurturing him at home as we girls were nurturing our mother through to the beyond.

That night I lay on the sofa in my father's house, pulling the blankets over me and sipping hot brandy. Feeling it burn in my chest, I put it aside, unfinished, so that it wouldn't interfere with my dreams—for I knew there'd be one.

And it came. I was back inside the hospital room with my sisters and our mother during her final moments. We were sitting just as we'd been in real time: Wanda and I on one side of her bed, Karen on the other. All of us holding her hands, our bodies pressed up against hers. And just as it had been in real time, so it was in the dream—her breathing becoming more and more erratic as she struggled through death's curtain. And then she let out a huge, calming, and most peaceful of sighs as she broke through.

At that moment, in my dream, I was suddenly outside my body and watching. I watched us as we wept. I saw a soft bluish light emanating around each of us sisters, and around our mother as she lay there. As though it were coming from inside of us. The same bluish light emanated from each individual object in the room—the phone, the chair, the side table—everything. And the word *holy* permeated the room. *Holy. Holy. Holy.* Just as the word *forgiveness* had permeated the room during that moment with Ford at Doctor Burns's house.

It was still dark when I woke up. I closed my eyes, trying to bring back the dream, pondering it. Such a simple lesson: everything is holy. It filled my heart. There were no feelings of peace or anything remotely resembling those dreams I'd had of Ford. There was simply a knowing in my heart and a deep hurting wrapped around it.

I listened to the quiet of the house. The boys were sleeping in the room with Dad. Wanda slept at the foot of the sofa beside me. Karen was curled on the settee. The babies and youngsters and all the others were sleeping in the bedrooms. I heard their stirrings, their breathing through the hush.

I sat up, feeling comforted by their sounds. I sipped the brandy, gone cold now but burning hot in my belly. I curled into its comfort. I curled into the comfort of grief.

Grief hurts. It hurts because our mother had taken a piece of us with her, because Ford had taken a piece of us with him. Everyone we've loved and lost has taken a piece of us and so no wonder we suffer; we're only half of ourselves left here, trying to function as if we were still complete. In that moment of grieving my mother I felt my diminishment hard, and yet that too was a comfort. For I knew that the missing part of me was with her. And that a part of her lived within the hurt of my wounding. My suffering was my validation of her, and of myself. If we had not loved so, we could not hurt so. And as I awakened more fully and hurt deepened through me, so too did love deepen within me. It wrapped itself around each tear slipping down my face just as that bluish light had wrapped itself around each blessed thing in that hospital room. Perhaps, if love were a colour, it would be blue. And the blue light emanating from every soul and object in that hospital room in my dream was love. For love is God. Everything is God. God is the light and the dark. I would trade not one moment of what I've lived. I would trade them all had I not lived with love. Surely no moment could bring a deeper knowing?

My sisters whimpered in their sleep. My brothers murmured over our fretting father. As it is in heaven, so it is here. We rock our babies.

EPILOGUE

MY MOTHER DIED AT FOUR O'CLOCK on a Sunday. Monday morning, the phone rang. It was Beverley Slopen, the one literary agent I'd sent my manuscript to. She'd read *Kit's Law* and had forwarded it to Penguin, where it was read for a second time by a different editor, Cynthia Good. It had been accepted for publication that very morning.

I hadn't looked to be a writer; it was a side road I'd happened upon and then never left. *Kit's Law* became a national bestseller. It sold nearly two hundred thousand copies worldwide, won awards in Canada, the U.S., and the U.K., and underwent several translations. Five more bestselling and award-winning novels followed, with a seventh novel underway.

"Fiction," Albert Camus wrote, "is the lie through which we tell the truth." True. But first we need to confront the lie. Writing nonfiction forces that confrontation, often resulting in a drama most fiction writers can only dream about.

I did not go looking for the mystic. It presented itself to me in tiny pieces till I was able to fit together a composite that helped shine a light onto some of the darkness shrouding my path.

I did not go looking for God, the Keeper of the light and the Giver of gifts. I found God through tragedy, horror, and grief, and within the gifts of grace, of joy, and of love.

I *did* go looking for those SSRIs—driven as I was by two major things that happened, both of them wonderful and yet terrifying. First, the story about pads and Durkheim, the one I'd read to Elly, was made into a thirty-minute CBC film and then nominated for two Geminis. My fear of public speaking was such that even at awards ceremonies I had to ask someone else to accept my prize. I desperately wanted to leap to my feet shouting, "*It's me, I wrote it!*" but instead I cowered, despising my fear, despising myself for being so afraid. Then came the success of *Kit's Law*, the story inspired by Mae and written with my mother at my side, and my publisher's request that I travel to promote it. I went to the doctor and got a prescription.

Then sat up half the night with one of the little white pills in my hand, afraid to take it. I was scared it wouldn't work, thereby taking away my last vestige of hope, should the anxiety someday become even worse. Equally as frightening was the thought that it might work against me, distorting and breaking the thin hold on sanity I felt I had.

Thankfully, I'd been warned that the first night would be tough, that the pill would heighten my anxiety levels. It did. I rocked myself through the hours, whispering prayers into the dark. Come morning I still felt the fear, but it was blunted. By the next day the fear was gone. And to this day, twenty years later, the fear has not come back. Yes, there are moments when anxiety breaks through, and yes, the knowing that such fear exists always lends itself to a certain wariness. But I know the way back now. There is always help if we shove fear aside and reach for it. SSRIs gave me back my life. They declawed the vulture that hovers always just out of sight so that even on overcast days I can look up into clear blue skies.

Well, most days. Unlike fiction, real life seldom has a tidy ending. We were to bear another tragedy in our family. On August 31, 2010, our brother Glenn and his wife Diana lost their precious daughter Amy in an awful car accident. She was nineteen—the same age as our brother Ford had been when he was taken. And Glenn was the same age as our father had been when Ford was taken from him.

We don't look for meaning in the coincidence. We can't think beyond the fact that she's gone. Just as with Ford, the forces that determine such things are outside our knowing.

At least for now.

AUTHOR'S NOTE

This is a work of nonfiction, a real-life account of my past that relies mostly on my memories of people and places. Occasionally, these recollections may not fit with others' perceptions. I have tried to be as accurate as I can, checking details with family and friends. I have used the real names of my family members, friends, and acquaintances. In some passages, I have disguised the identity of a person, changing the name and biographical details in order to protect that person's privacy. But the events I describe are wholly true and recounted in good faith.

ACKNOWLEDGMENTS

For living this story with me, for sharing my grief, joys, and love, even when your own hearts were breaking, I thank my two beautiful kids, David and Bridgette; my brothers, Tommy and Glenn; and sisters, Wanda and Karen. *I could not live if I were not loved by you.*

For allowing me to share their parts in my story, I thank my dear friends Karen Pottle, Aunt Marina (Tucker) Osmond, Ruby (from Down Below) Osmond, our beloved Joan Rideout, Dear Aunt Shirley Dyke, and, for all that we were, Lance (Dave) Morrissey.

For her relentless support, belief, and guidance, I thank my most patient editor, Diane Turbide. Thank you to copyeditor Karen Alliston for her incredible eye for detail, and the rest of the Penguin Canada team members for their impeccable work.

And thank you to my raucous and amazing agent, Beverley Slopen, for keeping those doors open.